# Biomedical Scientists and Public Policy

# Biomedical Scientists and Public Policy

Edited by

## H. Hugh Fudenberg

*Medical University of South Carolina*
*Charleston, South Carolina*

and

## Vijaya L. Melnick

*University of the District of Columbia*
*Washington, D.C.*

PLENUM PRESS • NEW YORK AND LONDON

Library of Congress Cataloging in Publication Data

Main entry under title:

Biomedical scientists and public policy.

Includes index.
1. Medical research – United States. 2. Medical policy – United States. 3. Medical
scientists – United States. I. Fudenberg, H. Hugh. II. Melnick, Vijaya L. [DNLM: 1.
Research – U.S. 2. Public policy – U.S. W20.5 B618]
R854.U5B53                          610'.7'2073                          78-15052
ISBN 0-306-40085-5

© 1978 Plenum Press, New York
A Division of Plenum Publishing Corporation
227 West 17th Street, New York, N.Y. 10011

Printed in the United States of America

# Contributors

**Julius H. Comroe, Jr.** • Department of Physiology, Director of the Pulmonary Research Center, Cardiovascular Research Institute, University of California, San Francisco, California

**Theodore Cooper** • Office of the Assistant Secretary for Health, Department of Health, Education and Welfare, Washington, D.C.

**Robert D. Dripps** • Late Professor of Anesthesia and Vice-President for Health Affairs, University of Pennsylvania, Philadelphia, Pennsylvania.

**H. Hugh Fudenberg** • Professor and Chairman, Department of Basic and Clinical Immunology and Microbiology, Medical University of South Carolina, Charleston, South Carolina

**Jane Fullarton** • Office of the Assistant Secretary for Health, Department of Health, Education and Welfare, Washington, D.C.

**Philip Handler** • Chairman, Governing Board of the National Research Council, and President, National Academy of Sciences, Washington, D.C.

**Hon. Ernest F. Hollings** • United States Senator from South Carolina, Washington, D.C.

**Daniel C. Maldonado** • Assistant Director (Legislative and Governmental Affairs), ACTION, Washington, D.C.

**Robert Q. Marston** • President, University of Florida, Gainesville, Florida

**Daniel Melnick** • Government Division, Congressional Research Service, Library of Congress, Washington, D.C.

**Vijaya L. Melnick** • Department of Biology, University of the District of Columbia, Washington, D.C.

**Robert J. Schlegel** • Department of Pediatrics, Charles R. Drew Postgraduate Medical School, and Los Angeles County Martin Luther King, Jr., General Hospital, Los Angeles, California

**Donald W. Seldin** • Department of Internal Medicine, University of Texas Southwestern Medical School, Dallas, Texas

**Louis W. Sullivan** • School of Medicine at Morehouse College, Atlanta, Georgia

**Waclaw Szybalski** • McArdle Laboratory for Cancer Research, University of Wisconsin, Madison, Wisconsin

**Lewis Thomas** • President, Memorial Sloan-Kettering Cancer Center, New York, New York

**LeRoy Walters** • Center for Bioethics, Kennedy Institute, Georgetown University, Washington, D.C.

**Nina B. Woodside** • Northern Virginia Mental Health Institute, Falls Church, Virginia

# Acknowledgment

This volume was made possible by the diligence and cooperation of those who contributed its chapters, as well as by the many concerned scientists, legislators, and others with whom we have spent uncounted hours of fruitful discussion. We are indebted to Dr. D. E. Koshland, Jr., Dr. Lewis Thomas, Dr. David Baltimore, Dr. Robert Austrian, and Sen. Charles Mathias for allowing us to excerpt portions of previously published articles, and to Mr. Charles Smith for his valuable editorial assistance.

H.H.F.
V.L.M.

# Foreword

This volume brings together the views of authors involved in many aspects of biomedicine—from research on basic biology to clinical investigation of the causes and treatment of human disease to hospital administration to health care planning on the state and Federal levels to Congressional legislation covering biomedical research, medical education, the development of medical technology, and the delivery of health care. The purpose is not to present a "party line" representing a consensus of these often divergent viewpoints, and we do not suggest that we have found solutions to the many problems encountered in the interaction of scientists, administrators, legislators, and the recipients of health care. These articles are intended primarily to communicate to both biomedical scientists and intelligent laymen the processes, social and political as well as scientific, whereby biomedical science advances, and the need for biomedical scientists to take an interest and initiative not only in scientific research but also in research on health care delivery and in related public issues before the legislative and administrative branches of government.

The problem facing those of us involved in biological and medical research was described recently by Dr. Dan Koshland, addressing a special session of the Public Policy Committee of the American Society of Biological Chemists:

> Once upon a time scientists lived in a world of scholarly bliss, requiring only inexpensive equipment made of pins and sealing wax, investigating knowledge for its own sake, and being funded by benevolent unquestioning wealthy patrons. At least that is the mythical kingdom to which some scientists would like to return from an era of progress reports, congressional hearings and inflationary costs. For better or worse, science today has millions of patrons, it is supported by billions of dollars, and the concept of knowledge for the sake of knowledge is under fire.
>
> Some of the patrons are saying we are going too fast, creating changes in society and in the environment which are irreversible and dangerous. Some of the patrons are saying we are proceeding too slowly; we should be less concerned with knowledge for its own sake, and more concerned with "curing diseases." Some say we are organized too tightly; peer review is the buddy system to exclude the nonestablishment. Others say we are organized too loosely; we should be much quicker to cut off nonproductive research. Many patrons mean many voices and many scientists mean many answers.
>
> In the midst of this multifaceted chaos, how is the public policy determined? The answer is by an unusually amorphous, but rather effective system. Various individuals—the directors of the National Institutes of Health

and the National Science Foundation, advisory boards of scientists, legislators, learned societies, individual letter writers, and even Dear Abby—
contribute to a potpourri of ideas which eventually chart the governmental
course. There is no high priesthood for science and no single instrument in
government. If the organization is untidy, it still provides a vehicle for multiple
inputs, and that is an essential where the output is a new frontier, not a
predictable past. The administrators must hear from the scientist at the bench,
and the scientist cannot ignore the voice of the patrons unless he is willing to
have his funds run out. In such a system the interchange of views is essential.[1]

Indeed, in this era of increasing public awareness and involvement,
perhaps most dramatically illustrated by the still-growing consumer
movement, and at a time when the mandatory participation of laymen in
biomedical research involving human subjects has been legislated by
Congress, it has become the duty of the scientific community to make
itself understood. Research is becoming more complex and more interdisciplinary and as a result more difficult to explain to the taxpayers and their
elected representatives, and therefore a greater effort will be required by
bioscientists in seeking greater public understanding.

The urgent need for an effort to build a public constituency for
biomedical research is clearly illustrated by the recent history of Federal
research funding. The National Science Board last year reported that
support for basic research, in terms of constant dollars, declined by 13%
from 1968 to 1974, and that the level of support per individual scientist
decreased by 30% over the same period. And this problem is further
compounded by the increasingly cumbersome and restrictive control of
research by legislation and regulation. New and rigid rules governing the
actual conduct of federally supported research programs have produced a
dramatic escalation of research costs and, in addition, have come danger-
ously close to eliminating the flexibility and opportunity for serendipity
on which original scientific discovery depends. To counter these disturbing trends will require the active cooperation of bioscientists, concerned
legislators, and an informed public.

In this context, then, it is of particular concern that public and legislative demands for increased "relevance" of basic research and for the
application of scientific endeavor in biomedical fields to such immediate
needs as health care delivery and clinical trials of newly developed drugs
and techniques are accompanied by an apparent feeling of apprehension
and even mistrust toward science, and biomedical science in particular,
on the part of the general public. This is largely the result of our failure as
scientists to communicate clearly to the lay public the nature of scientific
investigation. The problem has been analyzed by Dr. Lewis Thomas as
follows:

The codeword for criticism of science and scientists these days is *hubris*. Once you've said that word, you've said it all; it sums up, in a word, all of today's apprehensions and misgivings in the public mind—not just about what is perceived as the insufferable attitude of the scientists themselves, but, enclosed in the same word, what science and technology are perceived to be doing to make this century, this near to its ending, turn out so wrong.

The biomedical sciences are now caught up with physical science and technology in the same kind of critical judgment, with the same pejorative word. Hubris is responsible, it is said, for the whole biologic revolution. It is hubris that has given us the prospects of behavior control, psychosurgery, fetal research, heart transplants, the cloning of prominent politicians from bits of their own eminent tissue, iatrogenic disease, overpopulation and recombinant DNA. This last, the new technology that permits the stitching of one creature's genes into the DNA of another, to make hybrids, is currently cited as the ultimate example of hubris. It is hubris for man to manufacture a hybrid, on his own.

To be charged with hubris is . . . an extremely serious matter, and not to be dealt with by murmuring things about anti-science and anti-intellectualism, which is what many of us engaged in science tend to do these days. The doubts about our enterprise have their origin in the most profound kind of human anxiety. If we are right, and the critics are wrong, then it has to be that the word *hubris* is being mistakenly employed, that this is not what we are up to, that there is, for the time being anyway, a fundamental misunderstanding of science.

It is hard to predict how science is going to turn out, and if it is really good science it is impossible to predict. This is in the nature of the enterprise. If the things to be found are actually new, they are by definition unknown in advance, and there is no way of foretelling in advance where a really new line of inquiry will lead. We cannot make choices in this matter, selecting things we think we're going to like and shutting off the lines that make for discomfort. Either we have science, or we don't, and if we have it we are obliged to accept the surprising and disturbing pieces of information, even the overwhelming and upheaving ones, along with the neat and promptly useful bits. It is like that.[2]

What can be done to bring this message, so eloquently stated by Dr. Thomas, to those who ultimately direct the nation's science policy? Obviously, there must be better communication with the public, legislators, and federal administration at all levels. To quote from a recent address by Dr. David Baltimore, speaking on the subject of scientists' involvement in recombinant DNA legislation:

The new biology has become the new politics in a very concrete manner: Biologists are spending their time in the halls of Congress trying to prevent the establishment of the first commission to be appointed to control basic research. I believe that our success or failure will determine whether America continues to have a tradition of free inquiry into matters of science or falls under the fist of orthodoxy.[3]

We believe that the approaches outlined in this volume, although they do not provide final solutions, are a beginning. They reflect a growing awareness on the part of those involved in biomedical science and health care at all levels that the problems of communicating with intelligent and persuasive members of the nation's lawmaking bodies, and of building an informed constituency among the general public, will not solve themselves. The future of biomedical research may well depend on the willingness of bioscientists to become actively engaged in such "unscientific" issues.

The foundation for this effort exists already not only among concerned laymen but also in the Congress, as demonstrated by the recent call for increased funding for basic research, issued by Sen. Charles Mathias of Maryland:

> The United States is not making the commitment to scientific research that our resources and our responsibilities demand. Last year Congress finally managed to reverse an eight-year trend of declining support for basic research, but by that time funding had declined so drastically in terms of real dollars that we were barely spending at the 1965 level.
>
> While the federal budget increased almost 100% over the past decade, spending on research dropped from 1.5 cents in every federal dollar to 1.2 cents. Most of that money is earmarked for specific projects. The amount available for unfettered research is negligible.
>
> Some believe that the United States is suffering a "technology gap"; that our reduced research effort has made our exports less attractive and our industry less competitive. The jury is still out on that question. But what is clear is that basic research, so vital to the growth and well-being of our society, has been short-changed.
>
> Basic research—the pure search for knowledge—does not press for immediate, predictable results, but it is central to scientific and economic progress. An investment in basic research admittedly is an act of faith—a gamble, but it is a gamble that has paid off for us over and over again.
>
> The frontiers of knowledge have advanced so far that new discoveries can be made only at great cost. It is unrealistic to expect private enterprise to underwrite such costs when the returns, however sure, are generally neither direct enough nor immediate enough to justify the investment. Industry should be encouraged to stimulate basic research wherever possible, but it is government that must shoulder most of the burden.
>
> We cannot hope to meet . . . future problems by buying knowledge on a crisis-by-crisis basis. We cannot expect to push a button and have science supply answers instantaneously. We must lay broad foundations now, to have a scientific structure adequate to tomorrow's needs.[4]

## REFERENCES AND NOTES

1. Koshland, D. E., Jr., 1976, The future of biomedical sciences, *Fed. Proc.* **35**:2535.
2. Thomas, L., 1977, The hazards of science, *N. Engl. J. Med.* **296**:324.
3. Baltimore, D., 1977, Center for Cancer Research, M.I.T., *The new biology becomes the new politics,* speech delivered at the University of Missouri.
4. Mathias, C. McC., Jr., 1977, Wanted: More support for basic research, *Chem. Eng. News* **55**:2.

# Contents

*Chapter 8*

**The Place of Biomedical Science in National Health Policy**

*Chapter 9*

**Beyond the Warring Elements: A Search for Balance in Health Funding**

*Chapter 10*

**The Formulation of Health Policy**

*Chapter 11*

**Specialization as Scientific Advancement and Overspecialization as Social Distortion**

*Chapter 12*

**The Education of Black Health Professionals**

*Chapter 13*

**Women in Health Care Decision Making**

*Chapter 14*

**Technology Assessment and Genetics**

# Introduction

# The New Health Constituency: Consumerism, Professionalism, and National Health Care Policy

## HON. ERNEST F. HOLLINGS

To know the story of the development of medical science and education is to know one of the great wonders of human development. What medicine can do for people—what it can do right now—is mind-boggling. The technological and human advances, the breakthroughs that have come as the result of the diligence, brilliance, and dedication of biomedical scientists and their supporting institutions are breathtaking. The lives that can now be saved that once were doomed to be lost, the pains that can now be stilled, the diseases that can now be prevented—all this is vindication of the perseverance, courage, and hope of biomedical investigators. Medical research has given us vaccines, antibiotics, and miracle drugs. Medicine has controlled and in many cases practically wiped out such dread diseases as poliomyelitis, diphtheria, pneumonia, mumps, and measles. The life-span of the average American has been extended by a decade. Yet, just as American medicine reaches its flood, the doctor is barred from practice by malpractice suits. The young graduate cannot enter the operating room because of the prohibitive cost of malpractice insurance. In some parts of the country (for example, New York) "pool plans" have been introduced for underwriting malpractice insurance. In other areas, doctors have resorted to the solution of arbitration. Perhaps we in the Congress could best treat this as a national problem and provide some kind of no-fault insurance to doctors. But malpractice can be seen as just one of many aspects of the larger movement of consumerism.

American medicine may be able to build a better mousetrap, but there will be no support for building unless medicine accepts the partner-

HON. ERNEST F. HOLLINGS · United States Senator from South Carolina.

ship that consumerism has forced upon it. When I write a law brief, the last thing I want is to have my client looking over my shoulder; and perhaps the medical scientists who program and conduct research want to be free from the interference of the average layman or potential patient. But the times have changed. The *Reader's Digest* publishes millions of copies monthly, and as a result, millions of Americans become "experts" on a certain disease each month. The TV beams in "Medical Center" and "Marcus Welby, M.D.," and millions of families play medical crisis each week. The wars have made us health-wise, the feeding programs have made us nutrition-wise. Medicare and Medicaid have developed a health purchasing power.

This awareness and these dollars have developed a new health constituency in this country vastly different from the older one that health professionals represented almost alone for so many years. They—doctors of medicine and biomedical scientists—were concerned about the art and science of medicine. This new constituency is concerned almost solely about the delivery of health care and the cost of that delivery. With the passage of the major social legislation of the 1960s, millions of Americans began to regard health care as one of their rights. This has happened concurrently with the development of the most pervasive consumer participation movement in the history of this country, and as a result, at a time when millions of Americans are seeking greater participation in all kinds of institutions and systems, they also want greater participation in assuring that they receive quality health care.

Today, around the country, there are thousands of community boards relating to thousands of health care institutions, both public and private. The community boards very often have research committees. Through these boards and committees, people are beginning to exert influence in areas where laymen never before ventured. One of these previously uninvaded areas is biomedical science. The tragic, but understandable, thing is that many of these committees have just one song to sing: "Stop doing research, just deliver the health care." For this to occur is tragic enough. But to fail to understand it and to fail to make good-faith efforts to grapple with it increase vastly the potential harm.

We are trying to understand it in the Congress. To us it appears in the form of such questions as "How can I get a doctor?" and "How can I afford a doctor?" This is not simply a problem of maldistribution of available health care. It is first the problem of educating more doctors. During the Ford administration, we were in confrontation with the Secretary of

Health, Education and Welfare, who promulgated the theory that we have more than enough doctors. How such a statement could be made during an era when we were importing 10,000 doctors a year from abroad was beyond me. The secretary seemed to be unaware of a report by his own department. Earlier in the same year, the Department of Health, Education and Welfare, citing an 1100-page study by the National Institutes of Health, reported that the current shortage of doctors was estimated at 30,000, with a conservative estimate of a shortage of 27,000 family care physicians. The National Institutes of Health concluded that it will be at least a dozen years before a balance is struck between the nation's demand for and supply of physicians.

Without the use of foreign medical graduates, who now account for more than 60,000 of the 350,000 doctors in America, we would be in more desperate shape than we are. On the other hand, while we import each year as many doctors as we graduate from all of our 116 medical schools, we turn down two out of every three young students who apply to enter American medical schools each year. According to the NIH studies, at least one-half of the students rejected by American medical schools are considered qualified to become good doctors. I would not recommend lowering standards, and surely I do not oppose foreign doctors. What makes me angry is that while thousands of these doctors are needed in their home countries, they come here to fill a shortage that should not exist. In Korea, large sections of the country have no medical services at all; yet Korea has exported 2000 medical graduates to the United States. Thailand, with only 4000 doctors, has exported 1000 to this country. There are more graduates from the medical schools in Thailand now serving the people of New York than are serving the rural population of 28 million in Thailand.

In addition to this shortage, we have the problem of maldistribution. For example, while New York has 195 doctors for every 100,000 residents, South Carolina has only 95. And there are 300 counties in the United States without a physician. On a per capita basis, there are more physicians in the East and West than there are in the Midwest and South, and in all parts of the country the number of physicians in inner city and rural areas continues to decline dramatically.

I believe we can rectify these two problems with one solution. Most medical schools in the country would gladly train more doctors—but they're broke. We all know that the tuition paid by medical students covers only a small portion of the educational expenses assumed by the medical schools. I believe, therefore, that we ought to institute a scholarship program; not a mandatory one, but one that would make available a means to pay the student's tuition of about $7500 per year (the estimated cost is about twice that). The program would be geared to about 80% of the schools' enrollment; the remaining 20%, whose families can afford this tuition, would be admitted in the customary fashion. Whether or not $7500 is appropriate can easily be worked out. The important point is that the school then be able to raise its tuition to the realistic level it needs. Instead of the desperate year-to-year battle for an adequate federal capitation fee per student, a realistic and guaranteed source of federal funds would be available for the first time. More importantly, it would allow low- and middle-income students to cross the financial barrier and enter medical school on merit alone. Too many bright young Americans are being denied a medical education, and as a result, medicine is becoming a rich man's profession. This is intolerable.

How do we justify the required level of investment? First of all, the student who availed himself of a National Health Service Corps scholarship would be required to serve a minimum of two years in an underserved area after graduation. He could do this as a member of the corps, or he could exercise the option of private practice with a federal guarantee of at least the minimum corps salary (approximately $30,000). If he agreed to stay in the underserved area beyond the minimum two-year obligation, he would be given reenlistment incentives depending on the length of his stay beyond the minimum two years.

As for costs, the medical profession must help government devise an equitable health care financing system. True, the majority of those in the profession feel that this is not their problem, but no longer can either physicians or biomedical researchers ignore the direct relationship between the provision of health care and the methods by which that care is financed. All proposals before the Congress run into billions. All plans are skewed toward inpatient care, the most expensive kind, and loaded against outpatient clinic care. At the same time, the yearly overdrafts from Medicaid and Medicare are burgeoning. Somehow, we must rethink and replan how to make quality health care accessible to all Americans, and how we intend to foot the bill.

We in the Congress will continue to contest and contend, on this and other issues involving health care and biomedical science. We will continue to follow the leadership of foward-looking scientists; but we need their input, and especially hard facts on which judgments can be based.

Decisions made without scientific input will be decisions against science. And in the face of increasing numbers of health care programs, rapidly increasing costs, and the growing demands of newly involved consumer groups, dollars for the federal support of biomedical education and research will inevitably be contracted, in the absence of scientific advice or consent, if there is no involvement on the part of physicians and researchers. If there is to be a balance between the need for more doctors and a better distribution, then an accommodation based on information will be required. Otherwise, the public will not go along. The angry, sometimes strident voices of the new constituency will prevail over the others. And we will all be the losers.

And yet, medical research can have no greater potential ally and friend than an informed constituency. Biomedical scientists must meet the challenge of the new health constituency and work with it. The potentials for success and failure of research must be explained, and the relationship between research and health care must be made clear.

Twenty years ago, the federal government was still operating under the assumption that a constitutional barrier limited its role in promoting the health of the people. Any proposal under which the federal government would provide direct care or finance medical care for segments of the citizenry other than society's specialized wards was attacked as socialized medicine. But with the passage of Medicare and Medicaid in 1965, the barrier was broken. The watchword is ever-increasing involvement. We have moved from construction grants to research to changing the manner whereby doctors practice (under Health Maintenance Organizations) to ensuring the quality of that practice (under Professional Standards Review Organizations). Since 1971, the Congress has accepted the philosophy that medical schools constitute a national resource. Medical schools *are* a national resource, and they are entitled to national tax support. The next step is making sure that the right doctors with the right specialties are provided in the right places.

This must become a major concern of academic medicine. It must consistently forge ahead on the research front, but it must also expand its vital mission of community service. It must take the science of biomedical research and similarly apply it to the practical art of community health care, especially in the areas of outpatient care, early detection of disease, and genetic screening for predisposition to potential disease, rather than focusing only on severe illnesses at a stage that requires hospitalization. In its daily operations, it must work closely with all levels of government and all segments of the community. In this way, a new partnership can be turned into unprecedented progress. And this should also be the federal government's approach to medicine.

Back in the 1960s we enacted a federal program with the hopeful title, "The Partnership for Health." The program never achieved the promise of its name, but its title remains a challenge. The struggle against disease requires a full-fledged national effort. It depends on research, expanded programs for biomedical education and training, and an improved health care delivery system. It also depends upon those of us in government. But its ultimate support rests on the willingness and enthusiasm of the people. They can become a constituency in support of biomedicine and biomedical research as surely as they are my constituency in government. The success of all our endeavors rests ultimately with them.

# Biomedical Scientists
# and Public Policy

# 1

# The Silent Elite: Biologists and the Shaping of Science Policy

VIJAYA L. MELNICK and DANIEL MELNICK

If basic research is to be properly regarded, it must be better understood. I ask you to reflect on this problem and on the means by which, in the years to come, our society can assure continuing backing to fundamental research in the life sciences. . . . Together, the scientific community, the government, industry, and education must work out the way to nourish American science in all its power and vitality.

President John Fitzgerald Kennedy
Address to the National Academy of Sciences

In recent years the number of issues addressed by Congress which involve biological science has been growing almost as rapidly as the participation of the federal government in the support of biomedical research. However, the professional congressional staff includes few, if any, individuals with biomedical research backgrounds (although some physicians are included). Iglehart[1] recently wrote, "Only six years ago, the number of professional staff members on the four House and Senate authorizing committees and two appropriations subcommittees that write virtually all federal health legislation could be counted on one hand. Now, these staff number 26 professionals and still are growing." He also pointed out, "Ironically, many of the new staff members have come from the Department of Health, Education and Welfare (HEW), where their activist instincts have been turned off by the go-slow policies of the Nixon and Ford Administrations."

Clearly, biologists who understand how public policies are formulated can make an invaluable contribution to national debates on health, environment, nutrition, drug safety, and their related areas by working for policy decisions that are consonant with the current state of scientific

VIJAYA L. MELNICK • Department of Biology, University of the District of Columbia, Mount Vernon Campus, Washington, D.C. 20005. DANIEL MELNICK • Government Division, Congressional Research Service, Library of Congress, Washington, D.C. 20540. This article was written in 1975 while D.M. was at the Department of Politics, University of Maryland, College Park, and in no way reflects an opinion of the Congressional Research Service or the Library of Congress.

knowledge; yet, such biologists are unfortunately both rare and reticent. To date, activity by biologists (independently or through their societies) has with rare exception been limited to situations in which officials of the executive or legislative branch have requested help, or in which biologists have become aware of cuts in their own program budgets or regulations that would limit their research. Furthermore, almost all such "crisis-induced" activity has been uncoordinated and ineffective.[2]

## VIEWS OF THE ROLE OF BIOLOGY

The strength of our nation and the welfare of its people are widely viewed as being enhanced by the work of biologists.* Biologists constitute a potential element of the "guidance sector" of our society[3]—that is, they can be seen as belonging to a unit in the society, detached from narrow or vested interests, which can help the public to see where its broader interests lie and can anticipate the results of technological change and act as a force for the general public directing change to the greater benefit of all. Unfortunately, though, only a few biologists approach government decisions about biomedical policy from the broad perspective of the public welfare. Such a perspective includes active concern with the regulations that protect the safety of the public and the delivery of health care, with the controls placed on research, the use of new drugs, and other medical procedures, as well as with direct support of science. It encompasses the evaluation of a broad range of policies to assess their impact both on the advance of biological science and on human welfare.

We have found in the course of a series of discussions with research biologists that their attention is focused almost exclusively on issues that might affect the support of research. Thus the initiative is left in the hands of legislators and administrators, whose legal background has led them to a public orientation. Their attitude toward biologists, on the other hand, is epitomized by the comment of one administrator in Wash-

---

*It is true that some people[4] have warned about the dangers that increased control over the biosphere may hold. But the 1974 action of a National Academy of Science panel calling for a halt, even temporarily, to a line of research is a rare occurrence.[5] In general, attempts at regulating research have been motivated by concerns unrelated to its goals. Antiabortionists have tried to use the back door of control over fetal research to address the issues of a woman's right to have an abortion. Advocates of prison reform have sought to limit the kinds of research that can be done on human subjects.

ington: "Those guys come down the hall looking for money. All they care about is the support of their own laboratories." The irony is that in the face of an expanding role of government in health care delivery, environmental protection, and control over technological innovations, biologists as a group have relatively few vested interests in comparison with lobbying groups centered around strictly economic concerns.

The divergent views held by scientists, administrators and legislators emanate from their different views of the purpose of biological science. When we asked representatives of each group to characterize their views of the nature of biomedical research, we found that bench scientists have a deep sense of the internal logic of the scientific process and see this process as following a rhythm of its own, which produces unknown and unanticipated results. Real progress is measured by them in terms of increased understanding of life processes.[6] Administrators, in contrast, confront the need to justify and support their activities in terms of the "practical" results that can be obtained. They must not only answer to their scientific colleagues, who place science qua science at the apex of their values; they must also convince their publics that such activity will benefit society. They feel constantly faced with the need to ride herd over reluctant researchers, whose status among other researchers is enhanced more by the quality of science than by its applicability to the public domain. The administrators, of course, are judged by the applicability of the results.[7] Finally, legislators in general see science as a secondary concern. They live in a world in which the ability to articulate a position that will build a constituency is a key skill. The number of people who will be served by a given measure is an important element in their concern, since it determines the potential support that can be shifted to them at election time.

The stereotypes of the bench scientist (only concerned about getting enough money to perform "exotic and incomprehensible" experiments), the administrator (obsessed with "protecting his bailiwick"), and the legislator (more concerned with "votes and headlines" than scientific advance) form a growing motif in the views that scientists, administrators, and legislators have of each other. The origin of these different points of view can be traced to the institutions within which scientist, administrator, and politician must work. The remedy does not lie merely in making a better case for one position or another. The key to the process is to define the constituency of biological science to include the entire public.

## THE NEED FOR A NEW CONSTITUENCY

A good example of the effect of biologists' failure to take the lead in building a constituency for their work is illustrated by the 1971 National Cancer Act and its 1974 renewal.[8] Many biomedical scientists viewed the passage of the 1971 act as the revival of a trend to support research directed at understanding the basic mechanisms of disease. Practically every nonscientist who testified at those hearings called for increased basic research. However, the administrators, politicians, lobbyists, and clinicians who are for basic research are also for many other aspects of the program. Because of the structure of the institutions, they (not the laboratory scientists or academics) are the ones who have to face parents of children with leukemia. The mission of the National Cancer Institute places significant emphasis on cancer care because the political leaders who created the program must answer to the victims of disease.

In contrast, when the records of the hearings held in regard to the cancer program (or a host of other health research or delivery issues) are examined, it is difficult to find a single instance in which a research biologist makes a plea for increased delivery of health care. This is *not* to say that many biologists do not recognize the need; our discussions reveal that they do. They just do not define their area of interest as including issues of this kind. The present state of affairs apparently reflects a lack of interest in the issues rather than a lack of the background necessary to understand them. And yet they have immediate relevance to basic research. For example, Berger[5] has indicated that plans for a national health insurance scheme may well depend upon increased support for research. Thus, by increasing their area of responsibility to include the call for *all* measures that will improve health research, care, and delivery, research biologists will increase the size of the constituency that can be called upon to support their work.

## THE COMPLEXITY OF GOVERNMENTAL PROCESSES

As knowledge becomes more important, its complexity leads to the rise of technological and scientific elites.[9] Government procedures have also grown more complex. Both science and government have developed special realms of knowledge and expertise that govern the success of participants in shaping policy. We suffer from a condition in which many scientists who could contribute to the formulation of public policies, about which they have special competence, are hampered by the complexity of the policy-making process. Conversely, the politicians (legislators and administrators) are hampered by an absence of relevant advice. They need a mechanism for sorting out competing claims for resources and regulations. As scientists we must recognize our responsibility to bridge this gap.

If biologists are to be effective in influencing public policy, it is imperative that they realize the scope and complexity of the governmental process. Our observations reveal that this is very rarely the case. Not long ago, Congress was in the process of enacting the National Research Act. An analysis of scientists' views of that piece of legislation will illustrate the problems in this area.

First, many biologists were unaware that the act was being considered, although notable exceptions were found among executive committee members of professional societies (such as Developmental Biology, AAMC, FASEB, Biophysics, etc.).

Second, the exact content of the act was often misunderstood. The research act contains two titles. Title I provides for a new traineeship program, with provisions that require the recipients to perform relevant service to society after the end of their support period. Title II deals with the protection of human research subjects. Concerned with preventing the demise of the training programs of NIH, biological scientists largely ignored the provisions of the regulatory Title II, which has proved in many ways to be of greater significance for the work of biologists than the new training program. Further, few biologists realized the importance of the *payback* provisions of the act. The provisions established the principle that the aid received in a traineeship is a "loan" that must be repaid in service or appropriate employment, failing which the recipient must repay the government according to a formula included in the law. This provision is a victory for those who would equate research support for young Ph.D.'s and M.D.'s with scholarships to graduate and undergraduate students. Although the law seemed to settle this issue, its implementation in fact depended on the regulations promulgated by the Secretary of HEW.

Third, among scientists who were generally aware of the legislative enactments, most seemed to be unaware either of the distinction between the authorization and appropriation processes or of the nature of the regulatory process. According to the National Research Act, the Congress authorized more than $200 million for the training programs of the NIH and the Alcohol, Drug Abuse, and Mental Health Administration. Indeed, the scientists worked hard for this. It is then ironic that when it came to the appropriation of monies for the training programs, only about $41 million was made available to the NIH to initiate new training programs and fellowships under the new act. This amount was closer to the $30 million suggested under the original Weinberger program for postdoctoral fellowship awards! Apparently the appropriation process somehow escaped the attention of all those scientists who fought so long and hard for the increased authorization. As for the regulatory process, the law seemed to indicate strong congressional participation in directing the training program; in fact, viewed from the side of the beneficiaries of the distributive Title I, it made the HEW Secretary more powerful. These seemingly trivial but actually central aspects of the law were not addressed by the biomedical scientists who testified before the Kennedy and Rogers committees.

Even the criticism directed at the law after its passage[10] was directed not to these provisions but to the sections that provided for a determination by a National Academy of Sciences (NAS) panel of the areas of scientific need. Most biologists argued that it is just not possible to determine need since no one knows which path of scientific investigation will lead to important results. They missed the point that the question was not *whether* need would be determined but *who* would make the determination. By having the NAS panel do this, the Congress chose NAS over two other methods. One method, advocated by the administration, would have keyed the number of traineeships to the rate of funding of scientifically acceptable research grants by NIH. HEW used the fact that over half the approved grants were not funded as an argument for the position that *no* new authorization was needed for traineeships. Another method, advocated by some members of Congress and implied in the approach taken by Mrs. Albert Lasker as early as 1944, would have required the secretary of HEW to spend research and training money on the basis of the number of fatalities and disabilities attributable to a given disease, thus essentially eradicating direct support of non-disease-oriented biomedical research. By going the way of NAS, the scientific community in fact retained control over the method to be used in allocating traineeships. Yet, bogged down in an argument over whether science can be "planned," many biologists failed to appreciate their "victory."

This failure to appreciate the nature of legislative victory and defeat can be laid to differences in the definition of substantial issues. Biologists are trained to see issues in terms of their manifest content: "Should basic research be managed? Should fetal reserach be allowed?" In the political process these issues are often secondary to the issue of *who* will decide. The outcome of a given policy is often decided by the place in the system at which the authority to implement legislation is lodged.

## WHAT ARE THE FACTORS RESPONSIBLE FOR THE LOW LEVEL OF PUBLIC POLICY ACTIVITY AMONG BIOLOGISTS?[11]

Taken as a group, biologists have a very low level of concern with the political processes that govern the work they do and shape the limits of its applications. Compared to those who deliver health care—physicians, dentists, nurses, etc.—the researchers constitute a "silent elite." What are the reasons for, and implications of, such docility?

We suggest that the frequent disjunctions between researchers, health providers, and politicians result from a general process that limits the participation of scientists in health policy issues. This involves the following influences:

*Scientists Who Chose Research after Having Considered and Rejected the More Activist Route of Medicine.* Biologists in this group are primarily those who decided to devote themselves to research because they found scientific discovery more meaningful. They associate the formulation of health policy with the physician. Political processes involve the use of those communicative skills that are essential to the practice of medicine. Hence, physicians are forced to acquire the skills needed for the articulation of political positions. Policy processes are seen as an interruption to the scientist's routine, an interruption that physicians are thought to be more suited to handle.

*Education That Discourages Biomedical Graduate Students from Exploring the Policy Implications of Research.* In graduate training in the sciences the emphasis is on research, with little regard for teaching or student training. The ideal professional position is one in which the researcher (1) has his own laboratory, (2) has large resources and freedom to select problems, and (3) is relatively free from teaching or the responsibility of administration. In his world of research he operates autonomously and is dependent only upon a few respected colleagues for guidance and direction. When the government does not support the exponential expansion of the number of researchers, the research scientists find that their education has not prepared them for jobs that require a high degree of skill in interpersonal relationships. Such positions might include teaching, administration, government service, and work in private foundations.

*Professional Advancement Criteria That Do Not Credit Public Policy Activity.* Scientists feel that no amount of public policy activity will contribute anything to their professional status. They see such activity as strictly extracurricular and often to the detriment of their academic advancement. In the scientist's vocabulary, the term *real work* has only one meaning —work on the bench. Everything outside of that is peripheral. Many of the scientists felt that reports of their work in the public media would not only fail to enhance their status as scientists but would instead taint their position with a certain color of notoriety. Many biologists felt that science and politics (even the politics of science policy) are incompatible pursuits.

*A Widespread Belief That Policy Problems Are Handled by the "Over-the-Hill" Scientists.* When asked which scientists were knowledgeable with regard to policy issues, scientists tended to list older colleagues, who they suggested were past the prime of research productivity: They could no longer maintain the momentum of their research, and so they turned their attention to policy issues and became "scientific statesmen" (the implication being that they had entered semiretirement). In fact, records of the relevant Senate and House Committee hearings show numerous examples of productive research scientists who have taken an active interest in policy matters.

*Fears of Budgetary Cuts That Inhibit Outspokenness.* The views of many of the scientists are best summed up in a statement quoted in an article written by Homer, Habib, and Jacobson (all of the Center for Science in the Public Interest). A high official of the National Heart and Lung Institute, discussing the effect of diet and nutrition on Americans, said, "It is my opinion that the average American eats too much saturated fats and cholesterol . . . but because I am a scientist I cannot advocate a government position to that effect."[12]

*A Belief That the Pursuit of "Real" Science Does Not Require Justification.* The scientists were asked to list what they felt were the best arguments for "basic" research. In almost every case, they recited the well-known argument that scientific progress can be justified by the benefits produced. Many then confided that these arguments were for the consumption of the public. In fact, anyone who understood science (they meant, *really understood* it) would know that it needs no such justification. During congressional questions on NIH public accountability, Jeremy Stone, Director of the Federation of American Scientists (FAS), reportedly said, "We believe at FAS, that scientists engaged in basic research should not be told how to run their business. . . . We want our scientists at NIH left, as much as possible, alone to do their thing." Commenting on this, Barbara Culliton (of *Science*) rightly asked, "With $2 billion of public money?"[13]

These conditions are the result of scientists' reticence in the public policy field, the higher status society assigns to physicians, and the relatively small number of scientists among the general population. More importantly, while most physicians operate autonomously, scientists are part of large bureaucratic organizations—universities or national laboratories. Their bureaucratic loyalty may often inhibit their public activity. This is not to say that all scientists should try to directly participate in the formulation of public policy. Rather, scientists should be prepared to propose policies in the national interest.

## FACTORS THAT DETERMINE BIOLOGISTS' INFLUENCE IN THE FORMATION OF PUBLIC POLICY

When we asked biologists to identify the scientists in their laboratories who *they* thought were the most influential in science policy matters and asked them to describe the characteristics of influential scientists, by and large the biologists felt that political influence came along with scientific prominence. True, congressional aides told us that Nobel Prize winners would have a greater chance than ordinary scientists of getting their way with Congress, but in general, scientific eminence and political influence are by no means related in a straight-line fashion. There are at least five factors that govern a scientist's impact on policy. These factors do not exist in the realm of politics or the realm of science but rather at the boundary of the two.

1. Is the biologist an "authority" or is he merely an "expert?" An expert is a scientist who has achieved recognition among his colleagues and is regarded by them as having competence in a given field. An expert becomes an authority when his expertise is recognized outside the scientific community and he is called upon to give advice and counsel to the *public*. In this sense, a biologist becomes an authority because of a political process that calls his work to the attention of legislators.

2. Do other biologists think the person is influential in public policy issues? We found that the official status of an individual was widely regarded as a key to his influence. For example, chairmen of departments, deans, section heads, directors, group leaders, presidents of professional societies, or members of the NAS were regarded as "influential"

(although many may have been too long away from contact with average biomedical scientists to know their views).

3. Does the scientist define his work as serving a broader public than the scientific community? This depends not so much on the nature of the scientific work as on the biologist's interpretation of its implications. For example, a scientist doing work on ultraviolet irradiation might explain his work in terms of biophysical phenomena alone, whereas another scientist doing the same work might view it as part of an effort to understand the implications of changes in the ozone layer, which might lead to increased irradiation of living organisms. The second approach might lead him to make the connection between his "basic" research and "remote" public policy issues such as the advisability of building an SST or the continued widespread use of aerosol sprays.

4. Does the biologist wait to be called upon or does he come forward with new ideas about the way society can benefit from biological research? Only the most effective biologists are both interested in and able to recognize the possibilities for exploiting their own work for the benefit of society. And many of those are unaware of ways in which new ideas can be brought to the attention of policy-makers.

5. In which arenas does the scientist choose to state his point of view? The scientist who feels he has something to say that should be heard by policy-makers has a large number of alternatives for presenting his point of view: scientific journals, meetings, study group sections, advisory bodies, Congress, or the public media. The traditional hesitancy of scientists to expose themselves to a public forum does not negate the fact that the most effective biologists (unfortunately very few), we know, choose a multiplicity of arenas to get their point across. They do so to the benefit of all concerned.

Of the factors we have listed, the extent to which other scientists regard a colleague as being influential in public policy matters is one of the *least* predictive indicators of his actual impact. Although some of the most effective biologists are recognized as such by their colleagues, these scientists usually occupy top positions in the organizational hierarchies of their laboratories or universities. The impact of younger or more independent colleagues that results from their active orientation toward public policy often goes unrecognized within the scientific community. The influence of these men and women derives from their excellence at articulating their position in ways that broaden their constituency and are addressed to the general welfare.

## MAKING SCIENTISTS MORE EFFECTIVE IN THE REALM
## OF PUBLIC POLICY

We require new institutions to integrate biomedical scientists into the decision-making process. Professional societies (FASEB, Federation of American Scientists, public affairs committees of various professional organizations, congressional and public policy fellowships), citizen activist groups (Center for Science in the Public Interest, Health Research Group, Environment Fund, etc.), and many individual biologists have already begun efforts to establish the necessary links. The recently formed Biology Alliance for Public Affairs (BAPA) is an excellent case in point, and it is hoped it will bring together a large majority of professional life science societies in an effort to promote concern, communication, and coordination between such societies in the areas of public affairs and public policy, with the goal of achieving the greatest benefit to human welfare. It will seek to unite its efforts with physical, behavioral, and social sciences in a collaborative approach to bring maximum welfare to world society. Five lines of institution building can increase their effectiveness.

1. Work should begin for the mobilization of biomedical scientists in the public policy field. Professional societies should assume the responsibility of informing their members of the impact of government actions on their work. To be effective this information must be timely. The governmental watchdogs should recognize that seemingly unrelated legislation can have an impact on scientific research (for example, privacy legislation could place limits for epidemiological research).

2. Biomedical scientists should initiate legislation not only in the area of biomedical research support but also in adjacent issues that touch on national welfare. Examples include the impact of technology on the environment, the regulation of biomedical research, and perhaps even health care delivery practices. Biologists can acquire and evaluate information on various forms of such delivery now under practice and those new ones that will no doubt become widespread in the near future. Since biomedical scientists have only a tangentially vested interest in some of these topics and yet possess the requisite expertise, they may be able to speak more clearly and authoritatively in the public interest.

3. To ensure that the legislative branch of government is supplied with the most informed advice, biologists should work for the establishment of a Washington area liaison office. This office should work to keep scientists informed of congressional action and provide independent

sources of advice. Such an office should also conduct independent, non-partisan evaluations of government programs and proposed legislation. The office should *not* act as a lobby for scientists or for any one policy position on a scientific issue. It should merely provide a mechanism for biologists to initiate policy alternatives that might be considered by the public and their elected representatives. In other words, while the center would not take a position, its clientele would be encouraged to make their particular positions known. The National Academy of Sciences frequently performs some of these evaluative tasks, but it does so at the specific request of the executive or legislative branch of government. Being an elite semigovernmental organization, it is inhibited from conducting studies initiated by the scientific community. Thus the advice comes only *after* the need for such advice is recognized and actually requested by the government. The role of the NAS as the arbitrator of many scientific disputes should be preserved. Hence, a Washington area office disseminating information to biologists and to the public will in no way conflict with the prerogatives of the NAS.

4. Biologists should endeavor to create a format for frequent and regular informal meetings between themselves, selected members of appropriate congressional committees and their aides, and officials of the executive branch. These meetings should focus on specific areas of concern to the national interest and should not be used merely to encourage the respective political leaders to support research. Rather, their aim should be to engender an understanding of the complexity of the new biology so that officials who are in a position to make decisions would have the opportunity to interact with scientists in a forum that does not require anyone to adopt a public stance.

5. Biologists should take advantage of disciplines such as law, economics, sociology, and political science which are focused upon the analysis of the impact of science on society. A multidisciplinary perspective and collaborative approach will enhance the possibility of succeeding in efforts to build a broad constituency and to inform the public as to how basic biomedical science works.

## CONCLUSION

Examination of the place of biologists in national science policy indicates the importance of the institutions that shape the interaction between scientists and the public. Scientists must direct more of their efforts toward initiating policy innovations for the benefit of the public. They must take responsibility for bringing to the attention of the public and their representatives the tangible fiscal benefits that emanate from progress in biomedical research. They should beware of becoming bogged down in debates over the need for "basic" versus "applied" research. Rather, they will be more successful if they concentrate on mobilizing support for long-term and continuing efforts at unearthing knowledge that will benefit mankind. This can best be done by broadening the constituency of biology. The day is long gone when one congressional or administrative patron (such as a James Shannon, Emilio Dadario, Lister Hill, or John Fogarty) can look after the interests of scientists. Rather, the time has arrived when scientists must fully acknowledge that there is no essential distinction between their interests and the public interest.

## ACKNOWLEDGMENTS

The authors would like to acknowledge the cooperation of the numerous scientists, administrators, and Congressional aides who gave so freely of their time. Special thanks are due to Dr. Philip Siekevitz, Dr. Elizabeth Hay, and Dr. Thomas Malone for their many helpful comments.

## REFERENCES AND NOTES

1. Iglehart, J. K., 1975, Health report/Congress expands capacity to contest executive policy, *Nat. J.* **May 17**:730-739.
2. Melnick, V., Melnick, D., and Fudenberg, H. H., 1976, Participation of biologists in the formulation of national science policy, *Fed. Proc.* **35**:1957-62.
3. Etzioni, A., 1968, *The Active Society,* Free Press, New York.
4. Etzioni, A., 1972, *The Genetic Fix,* Macmillan, New York.
5. Berger, E., Jr., 1974, Health and health services in the United States, *Ann. Int. Med.* **80**:645-650.
6. The eloquent essays of Lewis Thomas speak clearly to this issue: Thomas, L., 1974, *The Lives of a Cell,* Viking Press, New York.
7. Weinberg, A., 1974, Institutions and strategies in the planning of research, *Minerva* **12**(1):January.
8. Sub-Committee on Public Health and Environment, Committee on Interstate and Foreign Commerce, U.S. House of Representatives, *Hearings on the National Cancer Act Amendments–1974* (Committee Print, 1974).
9. Price, D. K., 1965, *The Scientific Estate,* Harvard University Press, Cambridge.
10. Culliton, B., 1974, National Research Act: Restores training bans fetal research, *Science* **187**:47.
11. The information presented here was gathered from interviews with a group of biomedical scientists from various academic and research institutions. The procedures used included extended observation, focused interviews, and a questionnaire to explore the way scientists interact with the policy-making process. Included were questions designed (1) to identify the scientists' orientation to their own work, (2) to trace their

encounters with and perceptions of the way government distributes resources for scientific research, (3) to elicit their views of the way government uses its power to regulate scientific research, and (4) to evaluate the scientific advice government gets. Because no attempt was made to select a probability sample of respondents, statistical results are not presented. In any case, our aim was to identify patterns of interaction without measuring their frequency. Other researchers may wish to pursue a more quantitative approach to this problem in the future.

12. Homer *et al.*, *Washington Post,* 29 December, 1974.
13. Culliton, B., 1974, *Science* **185**:426.

# 2

# Scientific Basis for the Support of Biomedical Science

## JULIUS H. COMROE, JR., AND ROBERT D. DRIPPS

Our project had only one goal: to demonstrate that objective, scientific techniques—instead of the present anecdotal approach—can be used to design and justify a national biomedical research policy.

Our interest in this project began in 1966 when President Lyndon Johnson said, "Presidents . . . need to show more interest in what the specific results of research are—in their lifetime, and in their administration. A great deal of *basic* research has been done . . . but I think the time has come to zero in on the targets—by trying to get our knowledge fully applied. . . . *We must make sure that no lifesaving discovery is locked up in the laboratory* [italics ours]."

The position of the Johnson administration on basic research was bolstered by a preliminary report of a study. "Project Hindsight," commissioned by the Department of Defense and published in 1966.[1] A team of scientists and engineers analyzed retrospectively how 20 important military weapons came to be developed. Among these were weapons such as Polaris and Minuteman missiles, nuclear warheads, C-141 aircraft, the Mark 46 torpedo, and the M 102 Howitzer.

Some of the conclusions of that study were as follows (1) The contributions of university research were minimal. (2) Scientists contributed most effectively when their effort was mission-oriented. (3) The lag between initial discovery and final application was shortest when the scientist worked in areas targeted by his sponsor.

The president's words and the Department of Defense's report popularized a new set of terms such as research in the service of man, strategy for the cure of disease, targeted research, mission-oriented re-

Reprinted from *Science* **192**:105-111, 1976, with permission.

JULIUS H. COMROE, JR. • Department of Physiology, Director of the Pulmonary Research Center, Cardiovascular Research Institute, University of California, San Francisco, California 94143. ROBERT D. DRIPPS • Dr. Dripps died 30 October, 1973. He was professor of Anesthesia and Vice-President for Health Affairs at the University of Pennsylvania.

search, disease-oriented research, programmatic research, relevant research, commission-initiated research, contract-supported research, and payoff research. These phrases had a great impact on Congress and on the Office of Management and Budget and led to a sharp upsurge of contract research and commission-initiated research supported by the National Institutes of Health (NIH).

Medical and other scientists countered with carefully prepared case reports that illustrated the important contributions of basic, fundamental, undirected, nontargeted research to advances in medicine, social sciences, and physics.[2]

Since 1966 there has been a continuing debate whether the federal government would get more for its biomedical research dollars if they were used to support clinically oriented research or if they were used to support research that was not clinically oriented.

We believe that the Department of Defense's study suffered from two factors. (1) Only a preliminary report has been released (and that nine years ago) and even it is not yet widely available. (2) Some who have read it have transferred conclusions drawn from that study on development of military weapons directly to biomedical research. However, the reports of those who countered Project Hindsight also suffered from one or both of two problems. (1) Some presented single case reports and so were anecdotal or "for instance" arguments. (2) The cases were selected by those who did the study and so were subject to their bias.

It is easy to select examples in which basic, undirected, nonclinical research led to dramatic advance in clinical medicine and equally easy to give examples in which either clinically oriented research or development was all-important. A classic example of the great importance of research completely unrelated to clinical medicine or surgery was that of Wilhelm Roentgen. While studying a basic problem in the physics of rays emitted from a Crookes tube, he discovered X rays that immediately became vital for precise diagnosis of many diseases and later for the treatment of some. A classic example of the importance of mission-oriented research was that of Louis Pasteur. Pasteur, originally trained as a chemist, was employed by the French government as an industrial troubleshooter. Among the problems assigned to him were the practical ones of how to keep wine from turning to vinegar, how to cure ailing silkworms, and how to save sheep dying of anthrax and chickens dying of cholera. The solution of these practical problems led Pasteur to discover bacteria and become the founder of modern bacteriology and the father of the germ theory of disease. A classic example of the importance to medicine of development (as opposed to research) was the mass production of penicillin in the United States in the early 1940s when it was required immediately for England's war effort and later for our own.

The anecdotal or "let me give you an example" approach provides fascinating after-dinner conversation and even interesting testimony before congressional appropriations committees. However, we believe that the time has come for the nation's biomedical research policy to be based on something more substantial than a preliminary analysis of weapons development by the Department of Defense and informal let-me-give-you-an-example arguments by concerned scientists, and that Congress and the administration should require more than for-instances from proponents or opponents of any policy for the support of medical research. We believe that the design and the broad scope of our study avoid the weaknesses of previous studies and provide an example to show how long-term policies on support of biomedical research can be developed on an objective basis.

## SCOPE OF OUR STUDY

Because the heart of our thesis is that the support of research should not be based on selected examples or anecdotes, it was mandatory that we study all of a broad field. We selected the field of cardiovascular and pulmonary diseases because these are responsible for more than half of all deaths in the United States each year and because we have some competence in evaluating research on the heart, blood vessels, and lungs, or know where to go for advice. To ensure that our study was concerned directly with the health of the nation and not with esoteric scientific discoveries, we directed our attention only to clinical advances since the early 1940s that have been directly responsible for diagnosing, preventing, or curing cardiovascular or pulmonary disease; stopping its progression; decreasing suffering; or prolonging useful life.

To avoid our own bias, we asked 40 physicians to list the advances they considered to be the most important for their patients. We then divided their selections into a cardiovascular and a pulmonary list and sent the appropriate list to 40 to 50 specialists in each field, asking each to vote on the list and to add additional advances that they believed belonged on the list. Their votes selected the top ten advances (Table I). With these as a starting point, we worked retrospectively to learn why and how they occurred.

**Table I.** The Top Ten Clinical Advances in Cardiovascular and Pulmonary
Medicine and Surgery in the Last 30 Years

Cardiac surgery (including open-heart repair of congenital defects and replacement of
  diseased valves)
Vascular surgery (including repair or bypass of obstructions or other lesions in aorta,
  coronary, cerebral, renal, and limb arteries)
Drug treatment of hypertension
Medical treatment of coronary insufficiency (myocardial ischemia)
Cardiac resuscitation, defibrillation, "cardioversion" and pacing in patients with cardiac
  arrest, slow hearts, or serious arrhythmias
Oral diuretics (in treatment of patients with congestive heart failure or hypertension)
Intensive cardiovascular and respiratory care units (including those for postoperative care,
  coronary care, respiratory failure, and disorders of newborn)
Chemotherapy and antibiotics (including prevention of acute rheumatic fever and treatment
  of tuberculosis, pneumonias, and cardiovascular syphilis)
New diagnostic methods (for earlier and more accurate diagnosis of disease of
  cardiovascular and pulmonary-respiratory systems)
Prevention of poliomyelitis (especially of respiratory paralysis due to polio)

With the help of 140 consultants,[3] including 46 interviewed personally, we identified the essential bodies of knowledge that had to be developed before each of the ten clinical advances could reach its current
state of achievement. To make clear what we mean by this, let us consider
cardiac surgery.

When general anesthesia was first put to use in 1846, the practice of
surgery exploded in many directions, except for thoracic surgery. Cardiac
surgery did not take off until almost 100 years later, and John Gibbon did
not perform the first successful operation on an open heart with complete
cardiopulmonary bypass apparatus until 108 years after the first use of
ether anesthesia. What held back cardiac surgery? What had to be known
before a surgeon could predictably and successfully repair cardiac defects? First of all, the surgeon required precise preoperative diagnosis in
every patient whose heart needed repair. That required selective an-
giocardiography, which, in turn, required the earlier discovery of cardiac
catheterization, which required the still earlier discovery of X rays. But the
surgeon also needed an artificial heart-lung apparatus (pump-
oxygenator) to take over the function of the patient's heart and lungs
while he stopped the patient's heart in order to open and repair it. For
pumps, this required a design that would not damage blood; for

oxygenators, this required basic knowledge of the exchange of $O_2$ and $CO_2$ between gas and blood. However, even a perfect pump-oxygenator would be useless if the blood in it clotted. Thus the cardiac surgeon had to await the discovery and purification of a potent, nontoxic anticoagulant—heparin.

These are just a few examples; obviously Gibbon needed many more essential bodies of knowledge. Table II lists 25 that we believe he needed in 1954 before he could perform open-heart surgery with confidence in the result; we list all of these because some, such as antibiotics, are so commonplace in 1976 that we forget that even they once had to be discovered! For the ten advances, we identified 137 essential bodies of knowledge.

**Table II.** Essential Bodies of Knowledge Required for Successful Open-Heart Surgery

Preoperative diagnosis of cardiac defects
    Anatomic and clinical
    Physiologic: electrocardiography, other noninvasive tests
    Physiologic: cardiac catheterization
    Radiologic: selective angiocardiography
Preoperative care and preparation
    Blood groups and typing; blood preservation; blood banks
    Nutrition
    Assessment of cardiac, pulmonary, renal, hepatic, and brain function
    Management of heart failure
Intraoperative management
    Asepsis
    Monitoring ECG, blood pressure, heart rate, EEG, and blood $O_2$, $CO_2$, and pH
    Anesthesia and neuromuscular blocking agents
    Hypothermia and survival of ischemic organs
    Ventilation of open thorax
    Anticoagulants
    Pump-oxygenator
    Elective cardiac arrest; defibrillation
    Transfusions; fluid and electrolytes; acid-base balance
    Surgical instruments and materials
    Surgical techniques and operations
Postoperative care
    Relief of pain
    General principles of intensive care; recording and warning systems
    Management of infection
    Diagnosis and management of circulatory failure
    Diagnosis and management of other postoperative complications
    Wound healing

The knowledge essential for these advances has accumulated over decades or centuries from the lifetime work of many thousands of scientists. It was clearly impossible for us to read all of their publications to determine how and why the research of each was done. But, because we were determined to avoid the let-me-give-you-an-example approach, we did examine about 4000 published articles. Of these, we identified about 2500 specific scientific reports that were particularly important to the development of one or more of the 137 essential bodies of knowledge. We arranged these chronologically in 137 tables. From these, with the advice of consultants, we then selected more than 500 essential or key articles for careful study.

Why did we spend several years collecting and reading thousands of articles and arranging more than 2500 of these in 137 chronological tables before doing our final analysis? There were several reasons.

1. It was essential that we have tangible evidence that our selections came from painstaking, scholarly review and not from the imperfect memories of a group of scientists at a cocktail party.

2. The chronological lists facilitate analysis of lags between initial discovery and clinical application (to be reported elsewhere).

3. They emphasize to the reader that scientific advance requires far more work than that reported by the discoverer or by those who wrote key articles essential for his discovery. We believe that a major defect in education in science in high school and colleges is the perpetuation of the one person = one discovery myth (for example, Marconi = wireless; Edison = electric light) and that this is partly responsible for the anecdotal approach to national science policy. Without a long chronologic tabulation, such as the electrocardiography (ECG) list in Table III, some might consider that Einthoven in 1903 invented the ECG in its 1976 form, without help from those who preceded or followed him. Chronological tables provide specific evidence for policy-makers that scientists earlier and later than the discoverer have always been essential to each discovery and its full development. A defect in tables is that they can convey only a bit of the message, because even a long list includes only a small fraction of the good, original research that helped to move us away from complete ignorance toward full knowledge.

## DEFINITION OF A KEY ARTICLE

1. It had an important effect on the direction of subsequent research and development, which, in turn, proved to be important for clinical advance in one or more of the ten clinical advances under study.

**Table III.** Chronological Events in the Development of Electrocardiography

| Year of discovery | Scientist | Event and publication |
|---|---|---|
| B.C. | Ancients | Early manifestations of electricity: electric fish, rubbed amber, lodestone, terrestrial lightning |
| 1660 | von Guericke | First electricity machine (friction of glass and hand) [1672, *Experimenta Nova Magdeburgica*, book 4, p. 147, Jansson, Amsterdam] |
| 1745 | von Kleist | Charge from electricity machine stored in glass bottle and delivered as static electric shock [Letter to Dr. Lieberkühn, 4 November 1745; J. G. Krüger, 1746, *Geschichte der Erde*, Luderwaldischen, Halle] |
| 1745–1750 | Musschenbroek | Electricity stored in Leyden jar; shocks killed small animals [1762, *Introductio ad Philosophiam Naturalem*, pp. 477–1132, Luchtmans, Leyden] |
| 1752 | **Franklin**[a] | Kite and key used to charge Leyden jar from lightning; identity of lightning and electricity proved [1751–1752, *Philos. Trans. R. Soc. London* **47**:565] |
| 1756–1757 | Caldani | Nerve and muscle excited by discharge from Leyden jar [1786, *Institutiones Physiologicae*, Pezzana, Venice] |
| 1780 | Galvani | Stimulation of nerve by Leyden jar and "electricity machine" caused identical muscle contraction [1791, *Bononiensi Scientiarum et Artium Instituto Atque Academia Commentarii* **7**:363] |
| 1786 | **Galvani** | Concept of animal electricity [1791, *Bononiensi Scientiarum et Artium Instituto Atque Academia Commentarii* **7**:363] |
| 1791 | **Galvani** | Contraction of heart muscle produced by discharge from electric eel; contraction of muscle caused by injury current [1794, *Dell'uso e dell'attività dell'arco, conduttòre, nelle contrazioni dei muscoli*, Tommaso d'Aquino, Bologna] |

*(Continued)*

[a] The scientists' names that are printed in boldface type indicate key articles.

**Table III.** (*Continued*)

| Year of discovery | Scientist | Event and publication |
|---|---|---|
| 1800 | Volta | Electricity generated by dissimilar metals; voltaic pile or battery [1800, *Philos. Trans. R. Soc. London* Part 2 **90**:403] |
| 1839 | Purkinje | Purkinje's fibers in the cardiac ventricles [1839, *De Musculari Cordis Structura,* Friedlaender, Vratislava] |
| 1842 | **Matteucci** | Muscle contracts if its nerve is laid across another contracting muscle [see Dumas, 1842, *C. R. Acad. Sci.* **15**:797] |
| 1843 | DuBois-Reymond | Action current in nerve as well as muscle [1848-1849, *Untersuchungen über Thierische Elektricität,* Reimer, Berlin] |
| 1852 | Stannius | Ligatures demonstrating specific conduction paths in heart [1852, *Arch. Anat. Physiol. Wiss. Med.* p. 85] |
| 1856 | Kölliker and Müller | Frog muscle contraction used as indicator of cardiac currents [1856, *Verh. Phys.-Med. Ges. Würzberg* **6**:428] |
| 1875 | Lippmann | Use of capillary electrometer [1875, *Ann. Chim. Phys. Ser. 5* **5**:494] |
| 1876 | Marey | Refractory period in early cardiac systole [1876, *Physiol. Exp. Trav. Lab. Marey* **2**:63] |
| 1878 | Engelmann | Studied electrical excitation of isolated frog heart [1878, *Pflügers Arch.* **17**:68] |
| 1879-1880 | **Burdon-Sanderson and Page** | First ECG in intact animals (frogs) [1879-1880, *J. Physiol.* **2**:384] |
| 1883 | Gaskell | Sequence of contraction from sinus venosus to atria to ventricles [1883, *J. Physiol.* **4**:43] |
| 1887 | **Waller** | First human ECG using Lippmann's capillary electrometer [1887, *J. Physiol.* **8**:229] |
| 1887 | McWilliam | Noted fibrillary contractions of heart [1887, *J. Physiol.* **8**:296] |

|  |  |  |
|---|---|---|
| 1893 | His | Atrioventricular bundle [1893, *Arbeit. Med. Klin. Leipzig.* **14**:14] |
| 1893 | Kent | Atrioventricular bundle [1893, *J. Physiol.* **14**:233] |
| 1897 | Ader | Thread or string galvanometer [1897, *C. R. Acad. Sci.* **124**:1440] |
| 1903 | **Einthoven** | Sensitive string galvanometer for measuring human ECG; telemetry of ECG signals [1903, *Pflügers Arch.* **99**:472] |
| 1906 | Tawara | Atrioventricular node [1906, *Das Reizleitungssystem des Säugethierherzens*, Fischer, Jena] |
| 1907 | Keith and Flack | Sinoatrial node, mammals [1907, *J. Anat. Physiol.* **41**:172] |
| 1908 | Mackenzie | Polygraph, venous pulse and arrhythmias [1908, *Diseases of the Heart*, Frowde, London] |
| 1909–1920 | **Lewis** | ECG and arrhythmias in man (numerous articles in *Heart*, a magazine he founded) |
| 1913 | Einthoven, Fahr, de Waart | Equilateral triangle theory of ECG [1913, *Arch. Ges. Physiol.* **150**:275] |
| 1914 | Garrey | Mechanisms of flutter and fibrillation; "circus" movements [1914, *Am. J. Physiol.* **33**:397] |
| 1915 | Lewis and Rothschild | Excitation wave in dog heart [1915, *Philos. Trans. R. Soc. London Ser. B* **206**:181] |
| 1918 | Smith | ECG changes after ligating a branch of coronary artery in dogs [1918, *Arch. Int. Med.* **22**:8] |
| 1926 | Rothberger | Arrhythmias in man [1926, *in: Handbuch der Normalen und Pathologischen Physiologie*, vol. 7, Springer, Berlin] |
| 1927 | Wenckebach and Winterberg | Arrhythmias in man [1927, *Die Unregelmässige Herztätigkeit*, Engelmann, Leipzig] |
| 1930 | **Wilson** | Laws of distribution of potential differences in solid conductors; modern theory of ECG [1930, *Am. Heart J.* **5**:599] |
| 1939 | Hodgkin and Huxley | Transmembrane action potential recorded in giant axon of squid [1939, *Nature (London)* **144**:710] |
| 1946 1949 | Graham and Gerard Ling and Gerard | First measurement of transmembrane potential in skeletal muscle with intracellular microelectrodes [1946, *J. Cell. Comp. Physiol.* **28**:99; 1949, ibid. **34**:383] |

(Continued)

**Table III.** (*Continued*)

| Year of discovery | Scientist | Event and publication |
|---|---|---|
| 1949 | Coraboeuf and Weidmann | Intracellular electrode to record mammalian cardiac potentials [1949, *C. R. Séances Soc. Biol. Paris* **143**:1329] |
| 1951 | **Draper and Weidmann** | Intracellular electrode to record mammalian cardiac potentials [1949, *C. R. Séances Soc. Biol. Paris Physiol.* **115**:74] |
| 1958 | Alanís, González, López | Electrical activity of bundle of His [1958, *J. Physiol.* **142**:127] |
| 1960 | Giraud, Peuch, Latour | Electrical activity of bundle of His in man [1960, *Bull. Acad. Natl. Med. Paris* **144**:363] |
| 1967–1968 | **Scherlag** *et. al.* | Recording from bundle of His by cardiac catheter in man [1967, *J. Appl. Physiol.* **22**:584; 1968, ibid. **25**:425] |
| 1967 | Watson, Emslie-Smith, Lowe | Recording from bundle of His in patient undergoing cardiac catheterization [1967, *Am. Heart J.* **74**:66] |

2. It reported new data, new ways of looking at old data, a new concept or hypothesis, a new method, new drug, new apparatus, or a new technique that either was essential for full development of one or more of the clinical advances (or necessary bodies of knowledge) or greatly accelerated it. The key article might report basic laboratory investigation, clinical investigation, development of apparatus or essential components, synthesis of data and ideas of others, or wholly theoretical work.

3. A study is not a key study (even if it won the Nobel Prize for its author) if it has not yet served directly or indirectly as a step toward solving one of the ten clinical advances.

4. An article is a key article if it described the final step in the clinical advance, even though it was an inevitable step requiring no unusual imagination, creativity, or special competence (for example, first person to report on a new drug in humans even though basic work on animals had been done and results in humans were largely predictable).[4]

## SELECTION AND ANALYSIS OF KEY ARTICLES

Because these key articles formed the basis of our analysis, we devoted considerable thought to their selection. We realized that bias in selecting them could invalidate our study and that their careful review by consultants was essential. At the same time, experience with pilot studies showed us that scientists are rarely unanimous in voting that Jones's discovery is more important than Smith's. Sometimes this is because of justified differences in judgment; sometimes it is because there is no one article that can be singled out from many in a steady advance with many equal contributors. We solved this problem for the purposes of this study (though not for election of individual scientists to a "Hall of Fame") by first selecting key articles in 42 of our tables and then sending the same tables (with no clue to our choices) to reviewers for their independent selection. We then analyzed the articles that we had selected to determine the goal of the investigators and repeated the same process for the articles selected by our reviewers. Although there was not complete agreement on the selection of individual key articles, there was almost exact agreement on the type of articles selected. Thus the percentage of key articles reporting research that was not clinically oriented was almost identical in their selections and in ours (Table IV). Because our interest was in determining the type of research reported in key articles (for example, clinically oriented research or that which was not clinically oriented) rather than in identifying specific scientists and their reports, we believe that the agreement on type, based on a sample of more than 50% of our key articles, justifies our extending it to the whole group.[5]

Once the key articles were selected, we reread and analyzed each article to determine the answers to the following questions: (1) How many key studies were clinically oriented? How many were not directed toward the solution of a clinical problem? (2) How many key articles reported basic research? Other kinds of research? Development or engineering?


## WAS THE KEY RESEARCH CLINICALLY ORIENTED?

To eliminate uncertainty about our definitions, in this section we avoid classifying research as clinical investigation, basic research, fundamental studies, directed or undirected research, or targeted or nontargeted research. Instead, we use only two terms: (1) clinically oriented research and (2) research that was not clinically oriented.

We define research as clinically oriented, even if it was performed entirely on animals, tissues, cells, or subcellular particles, if the author mentions even briefly an interest in diagnosis, treatment or prevention of a clinical disorder or in explaining the basic mechanisms of a sign or symptom of the disease itself. Thus the Nobel Prize-winning research of Enders, Weller, and Robbins on extraneural culture of poliovirus in vitro was classified as clinically oriented because the team expressed an interest in multiplication of poliovirus outside the nervous system (for example, in the patient's gastrointestinal tract).

We define research as not clinically oriented if the authors neither state nor suggest any direct or indirect bearing that their research might have on a clinical disorder of humans, even though their work later helped to clarify some aspect of it. An article can be classified as not clinically oriented even if the research is done on a human (for example, Oliver's administration of an adrenal extract, later known as epinephrine, to his son in 1895 to see whether it would narrow the diameter of his radial artery).

Each article was classified as one or the other without consideration of earlier or later work of the same investigator and without being influenced by later stories (written or verbal) of "Why I did my research." The results of classifying 529 key articles into these two categories are shown in Table V.

These data strongly support our contention that those concerned

**Table IV.** Goal of Authors of Key Articles as Selected by Reviewers and by Us from the Same 42 Tables

| Key articles selected by | Number of articles | Goal was not clinically oriented | Goal was clinically oriented | Percent of total not clinically oriented |
|---|---|---|---|---|
| Reviewers | 494[a] | 189[a] | 305[a] | 38.3 |
| Us | 267 | 101 | 166 | 37.8 |

[a] Total number of key articles selected by reviewers is higher than number selected by us because (1) the reviewers on the average selected 8.4 key articles per table and we selected on the average only 6.7 for these 42 tables, and (2) we sent some tables to more than one reviewer.

with preserving or changing national biomedical science policy should disregard anecdotal "evidence" no matter how convincingly the case is presented. Table V shows that someone looking for evidence to defend any position on the support of research can get it by choosing the right clinical advance as his example or his for-instance. If one picks vascular surgery or antibiotics or poliomyelitis, one can "prove" that clinically oriented research deserves major support; if one selects hypertension or oral diuretics or new diagnostic tests, one can "prove" that research that is not clinically oriented deserves major support.

The most important figure in Table V is that, for cardiovascular and pulmonary advances as a whole, 41% of all work judged to be essential or crucial for later clinical advances was not clinically oriented at the time of the research; 41% of the investigators, when they did their work, expressed no interest in a clinical problem—their goal was knowledge for the sake of knowledge. These data indicate clearly that planning for future clinical advances must include generous support for innovative and imaginative research that bears no discernible relation to a clinical problem at the time of peer review. Because of many unknown factors (for example, ratio of clinical as compared to nonclinical scientists who do not produce key articles to those who do; relative costs of supporting one type of scientist versus the other), we cannot translate "generous support" into a percentage of NIH's budget for extramural programs. Nor can we transfer conclusions from a study of cardiovascular and pulmonary research to other research fields, such as cancer research. But the conclusion seems inescapable that programs to identify and then to provide long-term support for creative individuals or groups (judged more likely than others to produce key research) should be expanded.

**Table V.**  Goal of Authors of 529 Key Articles That Later Were Judged to Be Essential for a Clinical Advance

| Clinical advance | Clinically oriented | Not clinically oriented | Total | Percent of total not clinically oriented |
|---|---|---|---|---|
| Cardiac surgery | 53 | 35 | 88 | 39.8 |
| Vascular surgery | 40 | 8 | 48 | 16.7 |
| Hypertension | 35 | 44 | 79 | 55.7 |
| Coronary insufficiency | 44 | 21 | 65 | 32.3 |
| Cardiac resuscitation | 24 | 16 | 40 | 40.0 |
| Oral diuretics | 19 | 24 | 43 | 55.8 |
| Intensive care[a] | — | — | — | — |
| Antibiotics | 40 | 13 | 53 | 24.5 |
| New diagnostic methods | 41 | 53 | 94 | 56.4 |
| Poliomyelitis | 16 | 3 | 19 | 15.8 |
| Total | 312 | 217 | 529 | 41.0 |

[a] A key article is assigned to only one advance even though it may have been essential to more than one. Because practically every key article in intensive care was also essential to other advances, these articles were assigned elsewhere (for example, to cardiac or vascular surgery, coronary insufficiency, resuscitation, or antibiotics.)

## WAS THE KEY RESEARCH BASIC OR NOT?

Earlier, we avoided using the term *basic research*. We must now use it and define what we mean by it. We classify research as basic when the investigator, in addition to observing, describing, or measuring, attempts to determine the mechanisms responsible for the observed effects; with our definition, basic research can be on healthy or sick people, on animals, tissues, cells, or subcellular components. Our definition differs from the layman's (and some scientists') concept that research is more and more basic when the unit investigated is smaller and smaller; further, it allows that work on small units, such as cells, need not be basic if it is purely descriptive. It steers clear of whether the research was initiated by the investigator or by a commission, whether it was undirected or directed, whether supported by grant or by contract, because who initiated, directed, or supported the research has nothing to do with whether it is basic.

We analyzed each key article to determine how each investigator carried out his research and put each article in one or more of six categories.

1. Basic research unrelated to the solution of a clinical problem.

2. Basic research related to the solution of a clinical problem.

The clinical relationship was obvious when the investigator studied basic mechanisms of disease in patients; when it was not obvious, we depended on the investigator's statement, no matter how brief, that he initiated his research to gain further insights to the diagnosis, treatment, or prevention of human disease.

Two examples will clarify the difference between categories 1 and 2. When Landsteiner discovered human blood groups in 1900 he was investigating a basic problem in immunology and had no thought of the importance of his discovery to the transfusion of blood; this was clearly basic research unrelated at the time to the solution of a clinical problem (category 1). When Landsteiner, in 1909, found that a nonbacterial material (a virus) caused poliomyelitis in monkeys, this again was basic research but, since it was clearly related to a clinical problem, it fits category 2.

3. Studies not concerned with basic biological, chemical, or physical mechanisms.

These include purely descriptive studies (for example, description of a new disease, such as Stokes-Adams disease, without an investigation of the mechanism); an important observation that initially required no research (inhalation of ether causes anesthesia); a new procedure that required no research (cardiac catheterization); a new operation on humans that first required only perfecting surgical techniques in animals; and clinical tests of a new diuretic, antibiotic, or antihypertensive drug in humans without measurements designed to determine its mechanism of action.

4. Review and critical analysis of published work and synthesis of new concepts (without new experimental data).

5. Developmental work or engineering to create, improve, or perfect apparatus or a technique for research use.

6. Developmental work or engineering to create, improve, or perfect apparatus or a technique for use in diagnosis or care of patients.

The difference between categories 5 and 6 can be clarified by an example. Bayliss and Müller developed a roller-pump in 1929 to solve a problem in basic cardiac physiology; we classify this under category 5 even though later, as the DeBakey pump, it had widespread clinical use.

The Drinker respirator (iron lung), developed for clinical use, we classify under category 6.

The results of classifying 529 key articles into these six categories are shown in Table VI. Note that of 567 entries, 209 are in category 1 and 141 in category 2; the total of studies in basic research, either unrelated or related to a clinical problem, was 350, or 61.7% of the total number of entries. Other types of clinically oriented studies (some inevitable once the basic research was done)[4] accounted for 21.2% of the total; development and engineering (much of it inevitable once the basic research was done)[4] accounted for 15.3%; synthesis accounted for less than 2%. Basic research therefore was responsible for almost three times as many key articles as other types of research and almost twice as many as nonbasic research and development combined.

## OBJECTIVITY OF OUR STUDY

Research on the process of discovery is unusually difficult in that the data come from judgments and decisions and not from physical measurements. Further, no matter how many consultants participate in the judgments and no matter how distinguished each is, to be a consultant each must be an expert in his field of knowledge (we cannot ask clergy, lawyers, or ethicists to determine which were the key advances leading to the prevention of poliomyelitis), and as such, each is likely to have some bias.

In the case of our study, its objectivity is strengthened by the fact that, although the data and conclusions emphasize the importance of nonclinically oriented research and of basic research for clinical advance, only 26% of our consultants and only 24% of advisers on key articles were basic scientists.[3,5]

In the long run, data and conclusions from any single study should stand, fall, or be modified not by anecdotes or gut reactions but by confirmation or refutation by better studies with improved design and more objective methods. We believe that a $2-billion industry might well put more of its annual budget into research on improving its main product, which in this case is discovery and its application.

## SUMMARY AND CONCLUSIONS

There has been much expert testimony before congressional committees and much national debate on the relative value of targeted in contrast to nontargeted and of applied in contrast to basic biomedical research.

**Table VI.** Types of Research Reported in 529 Key Articles

| Type | Basic: not clinically oriented | Basic: clinically oriented | Not basic | Review and synthesis | Develop- ment: research | Develop- ment: clinical | Total |
|---|---|---|---|---|---|---|---|
| Cardiac surgery | 34 | 23 | 19 | 0 | 3 | 11 | 90 |
| Vascular surgery | 9 | 7 | 14 | 3 | 0 | 21 | 54 |
| Hypertension | 42 | 16 | 21 | 2 | 0 | 0 | 81 |
| Coronary insufficiency | 21 | 20 | 22 | 1 | 1 | 3 | 68 |
| Cardiac resuscitation | 16 | 11 | 9 | 0 | 0 | 6 | 42 |
| Oral diuretics | 23 | 13 | 6 | 1 | 0 | 0 | 43 |
| Intensive care[a] | — | — | — | — | — | — | — |
| Antibiotics | 12 | 18 | 21 | 1 | 0 | 2 | 54 |
| New diagnostic methods | 49 | 21 | 5 | 2 | 17 | 22 | 116 |
| Poliomyelitis | 3 | 12 | 3 | 0 | 1 | 0 | 19 |
| Total | 209 | 141 | 120 | 10 | 22 | 65 | 567[b] |
| Percent of total | 36.8 | 24.9 | 21.2 | 1.8 | 3.9 | 11.4 | |

[a] Because practically every key article in intensive care was also essential to other advances, these articles were assigned elsewhere (for example, to cardiac or vascular surgery, coronary insufficiency, resuscitation, or antibiotics).
[b] The total number of entries in the six categories (567) exceeds the total in Table V (529) by 38 entries. This is because some key articles fit into more than one category here, particularly when articles reporting development of new apparatus also reported research using it; no article in Table V was classified more than once.

Most of it has been based on anecdotal evidence and little or none on an objective analysis of research in broad fields of medicine and surgery. This is understandable because for-instances are easy to come by, whereas research on research is unusually difficult and time-consuming. Because we believe that national biomedical science policy should be based on research on the nature of discovery and its application, we have devoted several years to analyzing how and why lifesaving advances have come about in cardiovascular and pulmonary diseases. The advances that we studied were open-heart surgery, blood vessel surgery, treatment of hypertension, management of coronary artery disease, prevention of poliomyelitis, chemotherapy of tuberculosis and acute rheumatic fever, cardiac resuscitation and cardiac pacemakers, oral diuretics (for treatment of high blood pressure or of congestive heart failure), intensive care units, and new diagnostic methods. We screened more than 4000 scientific articles published in these fields, selected 2500 of these for further consideration, and then analyzed 529 of those that we (and 140 consultants) considered to be essential for the clinical advances.

Our analysis showed the following: (1) Of 529 key articles, 41% of all work judged to be essential for later clinical advance was not clinically oriented at the time it was done; the scientists responsible for these key articles sought knowledge for the sake of knowledge. (2) Of the 529 articles, 61.7% described basic research (defined as research to determine mechanisms by which living organisms—including humans—function, or mechanisms by which drugs act); 21.2% reported other types of research; 15.3% were concerned with development of new apparatus, techniques, operations, or procedures; and 1.8% were review articles or reported synthesis of the data of others. Our data show that clinical advance requires different types of research and development and not one to the exclusion of another. Thus the problem is not either/or but a question of how much support to one type and how much to another. Our data compel us to conclude (1) that a generous portion of the nation's biomedical research dollars should be used to identify and then to provide long-term support for creative scientists whose main goal is to learn how living organisms function, without regard to the immediate relation of their research to specific human diseases, and (2) that basic research, as we have defined it, pays off in terms of key discoveries almost twice as handsomely as other types of research and development combined.

We believe that much more research needs to be done on the nature of research and its application so that data from objective studies can be applied to all aspects of biomedical research. Because the very nature of research on research, particularly if it is prospective rather than retrospective, requires long periods of time, we recommend that an independent, highly competent group be established with ample, long-term support to conduct and support retrospective and prospective research on the nature of scientific discovery, to analyze the causes of long and short lags between discovery and clinical application and to suggest and test means of decreasing long lags, and to evaluate present and proposed mechanisms for the support of biomedical research and development.

## ACKNOWLEDGMENTS

Work reported in this paper was supported by contract 1-HO-1-2327 from the National Heart and Lung Institute and grants from the Commonwealth Fund and The Burroughs Wellcome Fund. The final report on this project, *Top Ten Clinical Advances in Cardiovascular-Pulmonary Medicine and Surgery between 1945 and 1975,* is available from Public Inquiries and Reports Branch, NIH, Building 31, Room 5A03, Bethesda, MD 20014.

## REFERENCES AND NOTES

1. Sherwin, C. W., and Isenson, R. S., *First Interim Report on Project Hindsight* (Office of Director of Defense Research and Engineering, Washington, D.C., June 30, 1966, revised October 13, 1966).
2. Shannon, J. A., 1967, in: *Research in the Service of Man: Biomedical Knowledge, Development and Use,* pp. 72-85 (Document 55, U.S. Senate, 90th Congress, 1st session); Visscher, M. B., 1967, in: *Applied Science and Technological Progress,* pp. 185-206 (National Academy of Sciences Report, Washington, D.C.); *Technology in Retrospect and Critical Events in Science* (National Science Foundation, Washington, D.C., 1968), prepared by Illinois Institute of Technology; Deutsch, K. W., Platt, J., Senghass, D., 1971, *Science* **171**:450; Holton, G., 1973, *Grad. J.* **9**:397; *Interactions of Science and Technology in the Innovative Process: Some Case Studies* (National Science Foundation Report NSF C667, Washington, D.C., 1973), prepared by Battelle Laboratories; Kone, E. H., and Jordan, H. J., eds., 1974, *The Greatest Adventure: Basic Research That Shapes Our Lives,* Rockefeller University Press, New York.
3. Of these, 70 were clinicians, 37 were basic medical scientists, and 33 were engineers, science administrators (in industry, government, or universities), or science writers.
4. Some consultants did not designate such contributions as key articles. We did, however, because we knew of a number of instances in which the final step was "inevitable" but no one seemed willing to take it (for example, vascular surgery was inevitable by 1910 but was not applied until 1939).
5. Bias could also enter into our selection of reviewers of tables. Thirty-two reviewers were physicians, surgeons, or medical or surgical specialists; ten were basic medical scientists. All were highly knowledgeable in the field that they reviewed.

# 3

# Informing the Public: Fiscal Returns of Biomedical Research

## H. HUGH FUDENBERG

## SUMMARY

The total annual health bill for the United States is in the neighborhood of $160 billion; yet, the total funding for research and specialized health care delivery is only approximately 2% of that amount. This seems fiscally irresponsible. Any corporate manager running a $160 billion-a-year enterprise would, I suggest, devote at least 5% of his total budget to fundamental research. This figure (5% of health costs) would be a reasonable one for NIH research, since the benefits to be derived will touch many if not all present and future citizens.

Efforts must be made to prevent the "roller-coaster" effect of rapid changes in federal funding. Some sort of continuity for long-range funding, so that adequate plans can be made and research teams not be disrupted only to begin rebuilding several years later, is obviously highly desirable if not mandatory for continued progress.

At present, the percentage of approved grants funded varies considerably from one NIH institute to another. Some consideration must be given to reducing the discrepancies between the percentages of grants funded by different institutes—for example, so that 35 to 50% of all grants with sufficient scientific merit to warrant approval would be funded.

NIH funds allocated for health care delivery, so that newer methods of health care can be made available to a greater percentage of the population, must be distinguished as separate from NIH research funding, since the average citizen apparently regards the NIH budget as totally devoted to biomedical research. Research in health care delivery, which is indeed necessary for upgrading of health care, must be continued or expanded (and improved in quality), but the cost thereof should not be balanced against biomedical research and biomedical training costs. Indeed, each

H. HUGH FUDENBERG • Professor and Chairman, Department of Basic and Clinical Immunology and Microbiology, Medical University of South Carolina, Charleston, South Carolina 29401.

should perhaps be balanced against other forms of government-sponsored research (e.g., the SST).

It would appear that the budgets for the NIH proposed in recent years do not reflect sound fiscal policy, as shown by the benefit-cost analysis presented here. Congress has been more diligent and has increased budgets or restored cutbacks; perhaps the current Congress will arrive at a budget that will be more realistic in meeting current and future biomedical research needs and thus, eventually, in reducing the costs of health care delivery in our country.


## INTRODUCTION

The goal of this article is to provide some fiscal data on the dollar savings that result from biomedical research—an analysis made possible through the nationwide Committee on the Impact of Biomedical Research, representing such diverse areas of biomedicine as photobiology and neurochemistry on the one extreme and allergy and dermatology on the other. It is hoped this information will be sufficient for readers to reach their own conclusions as to the net dollar savings resulting from basic biomedical research. (Our own estimate is that taxpayers are currently saving $20 to $30 for each dollar spent five to ten years ago, and that with proper funding and proper division of funds, this trend will continue and perhaps increase.) I shall concentrate on the savings from areas of basic research in the past which eventually led to improvement in health care; i.e., new, better, and less costly methods for diagnosis, treatment, prophylaxis, or eradication of disease. My reason for arguing in support of basic research funds is that without the past advances from "basic sciences," there would be far fewer clinical tools available for the aforementioned goals.

Most of the data presented here relate to research in immunology and infectious diseases, for two reasons. As a clinical immunologist, this is the area which I have analyzed in the greatest detail in my own studies[1,2] of fiscal benefits; also, it is the area which appears to have provided the greatest "bang for the buck," to use the words of a previous Secretary of Defense.

It is estimated that 15% of all hospitalized patients suffer from one or another immunologic deficiency or aberration. In addition, it is estimated that there are over 30 million Americans with significant allergies, more than 8 million of whom are asthmatics. In this era of increasing demands on the federal budget, however, justification of biomedical research in terms of improvements in quality of life or indeed of lives saved no longer seems sufficient to convince the general public and their elected representatives in Congress that such expenditures deserve high priority. Rather, it appears that expenditures for biomedical research must be shown to be justified in view of taxpayer dollars saved, if such research is to be supported by the general public.

It is quite clear to biomedical scientists, though rarely to laymen, that the achievement of a new therapeutic modality is almost never a "breakthrough." The new advances, when examined in historic perspective, are clearly dependent on observations that preceded the final triumph by 5 to 20 years. (Indeed, some clearly date back over the centuries.) Understanding of this point is essential if we expect an informed willingness to support studies that appear at a given time to have no relevance to major health problems today, although certain data already accumulated do have immediate relevance.

Dr. Lewis Thomas has divided biomedical research into two types: One asks "what if" and the other "how to." *What if* and *how to* are terms which I believe are preferable to the common designations of "basic" versus "applied" (or "targeted") research.

In any event, if dollar benefits are to be a major criterion of expenditures for "what if" research, several guidelines can be used: (1) past performance in terms of dollar savings, (2) probable dollar savings in the near future as a result of recent research advances now ready for clinical applications, and (3) the magnitude of the problems still existing in terms of (a) mortality, (b) morbidity, (c) loss of earnings, (d) prolonged or lifelong institutionalization, and (e) effect on the quality of life.

A good example is the current budget and past benefits of the National Institute of Allergy and Infectious Diseases. For this institute, the FY 1977 appropriation was $140.8 million. In FY 1978 the Institute's own estimate of adequate funding for worthwhile research was approximately $180 million. The proposed allocations of the President's budget constituted $153.4 million, in spite of the toll taken by inflation.[3] The amount finally awarded by Congress was $162 million. For FY 1979, the President's request is $166 million (Table I). Only about 5% of the total NIH budget is devoted to this institute, which supports research in virologic diseases, bacteriologic diseases, parasitic diseases, fungal diseases, allergy, and autoimmune diseases, plus almost all of the basic research in immunology, currently the most rapidly exploding of the various biologic disciplines.

**Table I.**  National Institutes of Health Proposed and Approved Budget Figures for 1977, 1978, and 1979 (Millions of Dollars)

| Institute | FY 1977 amount | FY 1978[a] amount | FY 1979 request |
|---|---|---|---|
| Cancer | 814.2 | 872.3 | 878.8 |
| Heart, lung, blood | 396.4 | 447.9 | 454.3 |
| Dental | 55.5 | 61.7 | 62.0 |
| Arthritis, metabolism, digestive diseases | 219.4 | 260.2 | 267.2 |
| Neurological communicative | 155.3 | 178.4 | 180.9 |
| Allergy, infectious diseases | 140.8 | 162.3 | 166.8 |
| General medical sciences | 204.9 | 230.7 | 234.4 |
| Child health | 145.4 | 166.4 | 198.9 |
| Aging | 29.9 | 37.3 | 37.9 |
| Eye | 63.9 | 85.4 | 86.4 |
| Environmental health sciences | 51.0 | 64.2 | 69.2 |
| Research resources | 137.5 | 145.1 | 149.0 |
| Fogarty center | 8.0 | 8.5 | 8.5 |
| Library | 35.1 | 37.5 | 39.8 |
| Building and facilities | 67.4 | 65.7 | 31.0 |
| Director's office | 16.9 | 18.9 | 19.4 |
| Total NIH | 2541.7 | 2842.5 | 2884.7 |

[a] Includes proposed supplement for pay costs ($19.7 million).

## WHAT HAVE BEEN THE FISCAL SAVINGS IN PAST YEARS?

Research in areas supported by NIAID has resulted in the following: (1) Polio has been eradicated, with dollar savings of approximately $2 billion yearly (Table II). (2) A measles vaccine has been developed, resulting in prevention of congenital deformations, which occur in children of pregnant mothers who contract the disease, and which often require lifelong institutionalization of such infants. Savings are estimated at about $180 million yearly. (3) Basic immunologic studies designed to learn the mechanism of antibody feedback control have resulted in data which were applied to the eradication of Rh hemolytic diseases in newborns (by the administration of small amounts of anti-Rh antibody to Rh-negative mothers) and thus have eliminated this serious illness, which in the past resulted in significant fetal and neonatal mortality and furthermore caused mental impairment of sufficient degree to necessitate lifelong institutionalization for a significant percentage of its victims. Estimated savings from eradication of this disease are about $60 million yearly in the United States, and at least tenfold that throughout the world. (4) By immunologic means, the antigen associated with transfusion hepatitis has been identified, so that symptom-free donors who are silent carriers of this virus can now be screened and their blood not used for transfusion purposes. Such protection is eliminating sufficient cases of chronic hepatitis so that dollar savings now total approximately $100 million yearly. Furthermore, detection of antibodies to this antigen in certain human sera has led to isolation of the antibodies and production of a vaccine which can now be used to prevent additional cases. Recent evidence suggests that another form of hepatitis due to a different

**Table II.** Estimated Losses Avoided in the United States through the Prevention of Paralytic Poliomyelitis during the Period 1955-1961, and Estimated Cost of Avoidance[a]

| Estimate | Millions of dollars |
|---|---|
| Losses avoided | |
| Medical care costs | 326.8 |
| Gross lifetime income lost | 6389.7 |
| Total | 6716.5 |
| Cost of avoidance | |
| Vaccine purchase | 129.8 |
| Physicians' vaccination fees | 468.6 |
| Vaccine administration | 13.3 |
| Government-funded research and field trials | 41.3 |
| Total | 653.0 |
| Net gain | 6063.5 |

[a] Production of polio vaccine was made possible by the observation that viruses could be grown in cultured monkey cells. This finding was made by Dr. J. F. Enders, who was doing basic research into virus propagation. Subsequently, after the Salk vaccine had been developed and introduced, basic research into the immunology of the gastrointestinal tract produced the finding that an orally administered vaccine is preferable to one administered intramuscularly or subcutaneously because it leads to better protection, even though the serum antibody levels induced are the same. The greater protection conferred by oral vaccine results from the induction of higher levels of "secretory immunoglobulins" (a form of antibody localized to the intestinal tract), preventing penetration of the gastrointestinal tract by the polio virus. (Basic studies by a number of groups have shown that secretory immunoglobulin A plays an important role in preventing reinfection of viruses that enter and multiply in the respiratory and enteric tracts.) For this reason, the Sabin oral vaccine is much more effective than the Salk vaccine.

hepatitis agent, so-called hepatitis A, has now also been made amenable to eradication by a vaccine due to isolation of the virus by immunologic means from stools of patients with the disease. Production of a vaccine thereto is currently in progress. (5) In the field of transplantation immunology, as a result of research on genetically determined antigens on immunologic cells, and as a result of fundamental research on the effects of antitumor drugs on the immune response in mice, subsequent scientific developments have delineated the genetic differences responsible for rejection of kidney transplants, using a technique called "mixed leukocyte culture," which originally was thought to represent the test tube equivalent of graft-host reactions. Through close matching of donors and recipients by these newly developed immunologic techniques, and through administration of immunosuppressive drugs in correct amounts, transplantation is replacing dialysis. Estimated savings are approximately $100 million yearly.

All these immunologic advances, saving the country hundreds of millions of dollars a year, have been supported by one arm, representing perhaps one-sixth of the total activity, of one institute of the NIH—that is, the National Institute of Allergy and Infectious Diseases. In summary, the amount of the NIAID budget directed to immunology is about $33 million per year, and cost savings from past research total about $3.3 billion per year, for a dollar benefit-cost ratio of 100 to 1.

## WHAT ARE THE PROSPECTS FOR FISCAL SAVINGS IN THE NEAR FUTURE?

In the past ten years, studies of the immunology of the sugar molecules present in the cell walls of certain bacteria have led to the isolation of the different sugar components that form the capsules of such bacteria as meningococcus, pneumococcus, and *Hemophilus influenzae*. Infections with the latter two organisms during the first three years of life account for 90% of deafness in infants. During the first six years of life, the average child has three attacks of middle ear infection (otitis media), about 75% of which are due to pneumococcus or *Hemophilus*. Total cost for routine treatment is about $40 per attack, or $120—that is, $300 million yearly. Further, 5 to 10% of these infants (those severely affected) develop hearing disability; others, because of the hearing defects, have a learning disability.[4] (In certain population groups the incidence of learning disability is much higher. Among Navajo Indians it appears to be 30 to 35%).

Estimated loss to this country in terms of institutionalization of the mentally deficient and loss of earnings of the slow learners, often not recognized as to cause, is approximately $700 million yearly. Vaccines for the *Hemophilus influenzae* polysaccharide have been developed and are currently being tested in adults.[5] Preliminary results appear very promising. In the case of pneumococcus, which accounts for 50% of the cases of otitis media in infants, vaccines for thirteen pneumococcal serotypes (specific sugars) have been developed. These have been extremely effective for preventing pneumonia in adults and have prevented several epidemics, most notably in Brazil. But funding restrictions may eliminate the studies in infants planned for upcoming years.

Meningococcal polysaccharide vaccines have already been applied with great success in preventing epidemics of meningitis in our military. Tests in infants have been scheduled, and based on what theoretical background we have, these pure polysaccharides, whose isolation entailed a great deal of labor by many investigators, should eventually prove successful. They should also prove very useful in preventing meningitis epidemics in this country; such epidemics have recently swept countries with ecologies as diverse as Brazil, Finland, and Denmark.

In the United States there are 15,000 cases of acute meningitis yearly. One-third of those are due to meningococcus and pneumococcus and two-thirds to *Hemophilus*. About half the children affected develop behavioral disorders, seizures, etc. Thus meningitis is a leading cause of acquired mental retardation in this country. In addition to the long-term dollar losses that result from institutionalization of the most severely affected patients and from the decreased earning capacities of the less severely affected individuals, acute cases require hospitalization for an average of approximately 15 days. Assuming $100 a day (a very conservative estimate) for hospitalization costs (without physicians' fees and other costs), the total cost for hospitalization alone is $25 million yearly; yet the NIH budget for development of vaccines is no more than $250,000 per year. In light of the large dollar savings that were made possible by the eradication of polio (a disease that left 12 to 20 thousand children per year with severe residual muscular defects), advances in the eradication of meningitis, based on fundamental research programs, have the potential to provide comparable or greater dollar savings.

The economic impact of pneumococcal pneumonia is also considerable.[6] If, for discussion, an attack rate of 5 persons per 1000 per annum is accepted, then there will be 1,000,000 cases of pneumococcal pneumonia in this country each year. If it is assumed that ten working days at a cost of $23 per day are lost by 75% of those stricken and that half the afflicted are hospitalized for five days at a cost of $100 per day, then the economic cost in terms of hospitalization and lost productivity from illness is on the order of $420,000,000 per year. These estimates do not include lost productivity from death among those of working age or the economic impact of pneumococcal otitis media. The latter illness is predominantly a disease of infancy and early childhood and may be followed by significant impairment of hearing in as many as a third of those afflicted in socioeconomically deprived populations. No data on attack rates of pneumococcal otitis media are available, but, from what is known, it may be inferred that they are high.

The "what if" research for vaccines that will be effective against pneumococcus, *Hemophilus,* and meningococcus in adults has been done. For use in children, most "what if" questions are still unresolved—e.g., the optimal age of administration, the duration of protection, whether the polysaccharides should be modified to give longer-lasting immunity or to be effective at earlier stages, etc. However, such research cannot be funded unless the proposed budget is enlarged, and consequently the next step, the "how to" research, may be impossible.

As mentioned above, the cycle of rubella (measles) epidemics in the United States seems to have been broken by nationwide use of rubella vaccine. The epidemic expected during the early 1970s did not appear, marking the first break in the usual cycle of 6 to 9 years at which rubella epidemics have occurred since statistics on the disease began to be compiled in New York City 45 years ago. National records have been kept for a much shorter period, but the New York City records probably parallel those of the nation as a whole. Thus the last epidemic, which struck in 1964, resulted in the birth of at least 20,000 severely affected infants. Unfortunately, vaccination programs still fail to reach many children. Current figures show that only 60% of children one to 4 years old and only 80% of those 5 to 9 years old are immunized, a level that is too low to protect pregnant women. And yet, the budget proposed by the Ford administration did not provide funds for the Center for Disease Control to furnish vaccine to states, even though the government pays less than a dollar a dose for the vaccine, in contrast to the cost of institutional care for one child affected by congenital rubella, which is $12,000 or more per year.[7] Obviously this is not fiscal "saving" but in fact both medical and fiscal nonsense. Indeed, the Carter administration has recommended that funds be provided to make vaccine for this and other immunization programs available to all children within the next 3 years.

## WHAT ARE THE PROSPECTS FOR FISCAL SAVINGS FIVE TO TEN YEARS FROM NOW?

About ten years ago it was shown that two types of lymphocytes are involved in the immune response. One type of cell makes certain serum proteins that specifically attack foreign substances (antigens). These proteins are called antibodies and are easily detectable in serum. The other kind of immune cells—called T cells because they are derived from or influenced by the thymus—synthesize no such substances in the serum. Nonetheless, T cells (and various subpopulations thereof) are responsible for protection against cancer, against the so-called autoimmune diseases (where immune processes attack the body's own tissues), for kidney graft rejection, for protection against parasites (parasitic diseases such as schistosomiosis and leishmaniosis are still the world's most prevalent diseases), and for a whole variety of known and probably an even greater number of unknown biologic functions.

During the past five years it has become apparent that the interaction of T cells with antigen results in the liberation of a whole host of factors (about three dozen are known at present) with various biologic activities (a partial list is shown in Table III).[8] None of these factors, collectively termed *mediators of cellular immunity*, has thus far been purified, so that their exact function within the body is still unclear. Nonetheless, it appears that some act to prevent proliferation of cancer cells or of parasites or certain viruses; others kill the tumor cells; still others attract to the area of the foreign antigen scavenger cells, which in turn break the foreign antigen, whether it be a mutant cell, parasite, fungus, etc., into smaller fragments which can be digested and destroyed. Purification of these substances will demand relatively small funds (say $5 to $10 million), but once purified, at least some of them will undoubtedly become very useful adjuncts in the treatment of various infectious and parasitic disorders, autoimmune diseases, malignancies, and so forth.

Another recent development is the discovery of the existence of "immune response genes," certain ones of which appear to be linked to the ability of the body to defend itself against certain diseases. It seems highly likely that research in this field may provide information that will be useful for identifying individuals or groups who have genetically de-

**Table III.** Mediators of Cellular Immunity Elaborated by Sensitized Lymphocytes after Addition of Antigen[a]

---

1. Skin permeability factor[b]
2. Chemotactic factors for macrophages
3. Macrophage migration inhibitory factor (MIF)
4. Macrophage activating factor (same as MIF?)
5. Chemotactic factors for other leukocytes (neutrophils, eosinophils, basophils, lymphocytes)
6. Granulocytic migration inhibitory factor (LIF)
7. Growth inhibitory factors (clonal inhibitory factor, proliferation inhibitory factor)
8. Lymphocytotoxin (toxic for all cells other than lymphocytes)
9. Osteoclast activating factor
10. Collagen synthesizing factor
11. Interferon
12. Mitogenic factor(s) for lymphocytes

---

[a] Two to three dozen mediators have been tentatively identified in studies of lymphocytes in cell culture. It appears that many of these substances might be isolated and, perhaps, used for therapy of a number of different diseases. However, further basic research will be required.
[b] A heuristic explanation for the roles of some of the factors listed is as follows: (1) Skin permeability factor dilates the capillaries in the skin, making it easier for cells involved in the immune response to reach foreign substances (antigens) that have entered the body tissues; (2) chemotactic factors attract macrophages (which engulf and destroy foreign cells or parasites, or break them into pieces small enough for the immune system to handle); (3,4) MIF prevents the macrophages from migrating away from the foreign cells while they are being engulfed; (5) chemotactic factors attract other blood cells which break down and release enzymes that attack viruses, proteins, etc.; (6) LIF prevents those cells from moving away; (7) growth inhibitory factors prevent "transformed" (cancer) cells or foreign organisms from dividing and thus increasing in mass; (8) lymphocytotoxin kills "transformed" cells and foreign oraganisms; (11) interferon inhibits, at least in animals, the growth of viruses, both those that cause cancer and those that do not; (12) mitogenic factors cause lymphocytes to divide and thus start the process over again—i.e., this is an amplification mechanism.

termined susceptibility to various diseases before the diseases actually occur, or for early diagnoses when symptoms are vague, so that appropriate treatment can be started when it is most effective, in the early stages of the disease.

## WHAT WILL BE THE EFFECTS ON THE QUALITY OF LIFE?

Much attention has focused in the past several years on cancer, heart disease, and stroke. Although mortality from those diseases far exceeds that from all others, it is of considerable interest that if one considers morbidity, the total number of hospital days due to just one constellation of infectious diseases alone (namely, respiratory infections) is far greater (about threefold) than those for cancer, heart disease, and stroke combined. Furthermore, the population affected in terms of loss of days from usual productive work (or from school) is far younger than those of the cancer and heart disease category, where a significant majority are in the retired group. Thus the financial implications of the still unconquered respiratory diseases are even greater than those of the "high priority" diseases. Furthermore, if one considers impact on the quality of life—for example, the impact of a child with allergic asthma on the entire family— the adverse impact here is undoubtedly far greater than the adverse impact of the individual with a coronary, whose children are probably grown and who statistically is probably in a group where Medicare covers hospitalization costs.

## CONCLUSIONS

It is extremely disturbing that the Administration budget requests in most recent years for "non-targeted" research, which has provided such great fiscal benefits, have called for absolute decreases rather than increases. For example, our total annual health bill for 1977 was in the neighborhood of $160 billion, yet the total proposed NIH budget was $2.8 billion, of which only about one-third was for fundamental ("what if") research. This must be regarded as fiscal irresponsibility. The current proposals are more reasonable but nonetheless have not kept pace with "scientific inflation" (inflation in the prices of scientific equipment and supplies has far outstripped the general inflation rate).

Any corporate manager running a $160 billion-a-year enterprise, would, I suggest, devote at least 5% of his total budget to research.[9] I believe this figure (5% of health costs) would be a reasonable one for the NIH, rather than the current figure (less than 2%), since the benefits to be derived will touch many if not all present and future citizens.

Second, great efforts must be made to prevent the so-called rollercoaster effect of rapid changes in federal funding. Some sort of continuity for long-range funding, so that adequate plans can be made and research teams not disrupted only to begin rebuilding several years later, is obviously highly desirable if not mandatory for continued progress.

Third, the percentage of approved grants funded varies markedly from one NIH institute to another. For example, it is my impression that, at least until several years ago, the National Cancer Institute was funding approved grants with priorities of 4.0 (about 85% of the grants approved by NCI, on a scale where 1.0 is the best and 4.5 is the worst), whereas institutes such as Child Health and Human Development and Allergy and Infectious Diseases were able to fund only those new grants with priorities of approximately 1.5, or about 10% of the grants approved. Thus one institute was funding projects of much lower scientific quality than the vast majority of scientifically better grants that were not being funded because of budget limitations in the other institutes. Clearly, some consideration should be given to reducing the discrepancies between the percentages of approved grants funded by different institutes—for example, so that 35 to 50% of all grants with sufficient scientific merit to warrant approval would be funded.

In the case of the National Institute of General Medical Sciences, which has devoted significant effort toward the elucidation of basic disease processes, the mechanism of genetic exchange and genetic disorders, drug action, and biomedical engineering, appropriations permitted payment of 57% of approved competing awards in 1976, and of only 29% in 1977. In addition, in the Institute of Child Health and Human Development, if President Ford's proposed FY 1976 budget had been approved, it is estimated that funding of new grants would have been reduced to at best 10%. Competing renewals (of grants that have reached the end of the period for which they were awarded but for which a continuation is requested) would have been reduced to only 12%. And even worse, noncompeting yearly renewals (of grants that have not reached the end of their award periods—usually three to five years—and for which funds have been promised) would have been reduced to 63%, as opposed to the present *automatic* renewal. This would be an unprecedented breach of faith with the biomedical research community. It would mean that many promising research programs (37%) initiated within the preceding one to three years would of necessity be dismantled, and that established investigators would suffer a disastrous loss of continuity in their programs. Moreover, funds spent during the first phases of a three- or five-year grant (for initial equipment costs, personnel training, etc.) would be wasted. This "penny-wise pound-foolish" approach, which strikes me as being both fiscally irresponsible and morally indefensible, must be avoided under the new Administration. The most likely results of such irresponsibility would be a loss of faith in the federal funding process for biomedical research, loss of many established investigators from biomedicine for other areas (e.g., specialty practice or industry), and the loss of a vast majority of promising young students with potential for contributions to biomedical research, who would undoubtedly choose other professions. Another source of loss of potential contributors to basic biomedical research is cutbacks in funds for predoctoral training grants and individual fellowships—30% in the current year and an additional 10% reduction scheduled for next year. This undoubtedly will be markedly disruptive for current training programs, and will discourage bright and promising motivated individuals from pursuing biomedical research careers.[10]

Fourth, we urge that NIH funds allocated for health care delivery, so that newer methods of health care can be made available to a greater percentage of the population, be distinguished as separate from NIH research funding, since the general population apparently regards the NIH budget as totally devoted to biomedical research. Research in health care delivery is indeed necessary for upgrading of health care, and should be continued or expanded, but the cost thereof should not be balanced against biomedical research and biomedical research training costs. Indeed, each should perhaps be balanced against other forms of government-sponsored research; for example, what is the research value, or the dollar value for that matter, of sending a man to the moon for yet another time or to Mars, or of research on an SST? I urge that despite the increased funds for "how to" (applied) research, funds for the "what if" (basic) research continue at at least the same level. Had funds been awarded according to OMB criteria back in the late 1940s in an attempt to conquer polio, we would now probably have the world's best respirator and polio would still be with us. Dollars for "what if" as well as "how to" research must continue to be provided now so that in future years we will not have to say "if only."

In conclusion, I believe that in recent years the budgets proposed by the Administrative Branch of the Federal Government for the NIH have not reflected sound fiscal policy, as shown by the benefit-cost analysis presented here. It is hoped that the Congress, after its long and arduous deliberations, will arrive at a budget that will be more realistic in meeting current and future biomedical research needs and thus reducing the future costs of health care delivery in our country.

## REFERENCES

1. Fudenberg, H. H., 1972, The dollar benefits of biomedical research: A cost analysis, *J. Lab. Clin. Med.* **79**:353.
2. Fudenberg, H. H., Fiscal returns of biomedical research, *Amer. Rev. Resp. Dis.* **109**:411.
3. Thier, S. O., Where do we go from here? An appeal to reason, *Fed. Proc.* **53**:223.
4. Howie, V. M., 1975, Natural history of otitis media, *Ann. Otol. Rhinol. Laryngol.* **84**:67.
5. Robbins, J. B., *et al.*, 1973, Haemophilus influenzae type b: Disease and immunity in humans, *Ann. Int. Med.* **78**:259.

6. Austrian, R., 1974, Pneumococcal infection, *Prev. Med.* **3:**443.
7. Goodnight, F., 1975, Rubella vaccine breaks 6-9-year epidemic cycle, *Hosp. Tribune* **9**(11):1.
8. Fudenberg, H. H., 1975, Are autoimmune diseases and malignancy due to selective T-cell deficiencies?, *in: Critical Factors in Cancer Immunology* (J. Schultz and R. C. Lief, eds.), vol. 10, p. 179, Academic Press, New York.
9. Schmidt, B. C., 1975, Schmidt talks about what is good and not so good about federal support of biomedical research, *Science* **188:**716.
10. NAS-NRC Panel on Basic Biomedical Science Manpower Needs, May 5, 1977, Washington, D.C.

# 4

# Of Questions and Committees

## PHILIP HANDLER

> . . . the Academy shall, whenever called upon by any department of the Government, investigate, examine, experiment, and report upon any subject of science or art. . . .
> Act of Incorporation, National Academy of Sciences, March 3, 1863

The organizational structure by which this charge is implemented is the National Research Council, as described in the NRC report of 1976.[1] From this unique enterprise there flows a stream of reports to the government and to the American people, concerning subject matter the diversity of which can best be appreciated from the titles of the reports issued in 1976.

The purpose of this introduction is to indicate the kinds of questions considered by the National Research Council, to describe the mechanisms by which the institution, qua institution, takes collective responsibility for "advice" rendered to the government, and to recount some aspects of the life and times of a committee, the working unit of the National Research Council.

The principal business of science is immutable: the quest for truth. It is pursued in gleaming laboratories replete with bizarre glassware, electronic instrumentation, and dancing strip charts; in lonely observatories on mountaintops; in sturdy submersibles at inky depths; on remote plains, deserts, jungles, and at both Poles; in rift valleys; in cultivated greenhouses; and in human habitations. The subjects of these studies are variously found in cores retrieved by deep drilling; in samples found in rocks, bogs, the sea, the atmosphere, the stratosphere, and the moon; in the light reaching us from the outer planets and from the most remote objects in the universe. They embrace the smallest living organisms and ourselves. Innumerable observations and experiments, performed by a multitude of scientists the world over, are codified, analyzed, and correlated until, in the disciplined minds of a relatively small group of creative

Reproduced from *The National Research Council in 1977: Current Issues and Studies,* pp. 3-20. Used with permission of The National Academy of Sciences, Washington, D.C.

PHILIP HANDLER • Chairman, Governing Board of the National Research Council, and President, National Academy of Sciences, Washington, D.C. 20418.

individuals, there take shape the sweeping generalizations, the laws, and the insights that converge into a coherent understanding of the nature of the physical universe, of the nature of life, and of the human condition. The scientists engaged in these endeavors are of that genre who would enthusiastically reply in the affirmative to the question that Benjamin Franklin posed to those of his friends who would join his "club for mutual improvement," the Junto: "Do you love truth for truth's sake and will you endeavor impartially to find and receive it for yourself and communicate it to others?"

Yet other individuals of slightly different turn of mind—scientists, engineers, physicians, agronomists, and so on—have seized upon each fresh understanding in the effort to employ it for the welfare of mankind. The result has been a rich outpouring of new materials, new devices, new conveniences, easier communication, and longer, healthier, and richer lives for those fortunate enough to have been born in the industrialized nations of the world where such developments proceed apace. In the three and a half centuries since Francis Bacon envisioned the scientific enterprise as consisting of the performance of "experiments of light and experiments of fruit" directed at "the enlarging of the bounds of the Human Empire, through the effecting of all things possible," these two complementary endeavors have proceeded in an elaborate counterpoint, each essential to the other. Together, basic research and its applications transformed our civilization.

## NEW GOALS AND PROBLEMS

As the body politic came to appreciate that transformation and began to share the optimism of the scientific community, our nation also expanded its goals. We sought not only to conquer space and increase human longevity, but also to feed the hungry, eliminate disease and poverty, and improve the socioeconomic status of the disadvantaged, while we also undertook to assist "less developed" nations and to secure a genuine peace. These ambitious goals and the nation's intention to seek distributive justice rested in considerable part on the heightened national confidence engendered by the progress of science and the prospect of an ever richer, more powerful science-based technology.

But we were not long to be permitted to enjoy that mood. A welter of problems old and new, large and small, reasonable and unreasonable, began to clamor for public attention. Ever greater consideration is demanded by the larger questions of our time: population growth, energy supply, adequacy of mineral resources, adequacy of the world food supply, climatic change, national security, and the deadliest arms race in history. And our affluence encourages us also to demand that food and drugs be "safe," that industrial practice injure neither the public health nor the environment, that medical research proceed vigorously but without risk to humans, that privacy be protected. Each issue becomes a matter of public controversy, each demands resolution, and many are brought to the attention of the National Research Council. Thus it is the changing agenda of the American people that shapes the agenda of the National Research Council.

## THE AGENDA OF THE NRC

More specifically, what manner of problems are addressed by the National Research Council?

A consistent thread, naturally, is the concern for science itself. What is the status of each branch of science? What resources will be required in the future to assure the strength of the national effort in each field? How shall large-scale projects—e.g., the Global Atmospheric Research Program or the Large Space Telescope—be organized and managed? What is the optimal scientific program for NASA? What priorities should be assigned in various fields of science? Are adequate numbers of new young scientists being prepared? Will there be opportunities for them?

And the great problems of the day. Can one outline a plan whereby the scientific and technical resources of this country can be mobilized to enlarge and improve the world's food supply? What should be the place of nuclear energy in the future economy of the United States? What are the prospects for solar energy, fusion, and geothermal energy? How tightly coupled are the growth of the GNP and that of the energy supply? Can one now predict long-term changes in continental and global climate? What effects will these changes have? How reliable is current knowledge of the magnitude and distribution of mineral resources? How well can one predict the rate of depletion of fossil fuels and of the minerals utilized in the economy? Are economically acceptable substitutes available? How can we prepare for such eventualities? To what extent are we compromising the quality of life of future generations? How can one maintain global surveillance of critical situations? Is the Department of Defense efficiently utilizing the capabilities engendered by new scientific understanding?

There are the innumerable problems created by the less-than-perfect functioning of the complex man-made world. Can local and national transportation systems be rationalized and made to operate economically? Can new technology improve and lower the cost of acceptable housing? What are the prospects for coal gasification, or for desulfurizing coal? How can government policy and the government's R and D capability be used to undergird the industrial economy? Can new technology restore the efficiency of the postal service? Can one devise a national policy to assure to all children food, shelter, clothing, education, and a supportive environment, regardless of parental means? Is new public policy required for management of recreational facilities? Are vocational retraining programs effective?

And the problems of health care. What will be required to assure all Americans access to an acceptable level of health care? What is the effect of the research activity within a hospital setting on the quality of its medical care? What are likely to be future manpower requirements for physicians, nurses, technicians, and research personnel? How can health care be provided to those in sparsely settled, impoverished regions? Is it possible to validate the efficacy of clinical procedures in common use?

## FACTS AND JUDGMENTS

Public concern for the impact of technology is addressed increasingly to the numerous forms and dimensions of "risk." Such matters have long been considered by the National Research Council, and it was out of that experience that I was led to note to the 1976 General Assembly of the International Council of Scientific Unions that

> latterly, a new and large endeavor has arisen wherein scientific understanding is employed to appraise the risks and benefits which may attend the utilization of diverse technologies in current use. The result is not always a wholesome dialogue. Although much is written concerning the scientific method and the ethical code of science, these concepts reduce rather simply to the imperative of honesty, dispassionate objectivity, and the obligation to publish descriptions of one's procedures and findings in such a way as to permit verification.
>
> But to establish "truth" with respect to technical controversy relevant to matters of public policy, and to do so in full public view, has proved to be a surprisingly difficult challenge to the scientific community. To our simple code must be added one more canon: When describing technological risks and benefits to the non-scientific public, the scientist must be as honest, objective, and dispassionate as he knows he must be in the more conventional, time honored, self-policing scientific endeavor. This additional canon has not always been observed by the individual scientists on the public platform. Wit-

ness the chaos that has come with challenges to the use of nuclear power. Witness the cacophony of charge and countercharge concerning the safety of diverse food additives, pesticides, and drugs.

We have learned that the scientist-advocate, on either side of such a debate, may be more advocate than scientist, and this has unfavorably altered the public view of both the nature of the scientific endeavor and the personal attributes of scientists. In turn, that has given yet a greater sense of urgency to the public demand for assurance that the risks attendant upon the uses of technology be appraised and minimized. And what a huge task that is! . . .

The current agenda of the National Research Council affords abundant illustration of the character and dimensions of public risk: What are the relative hazards of vaccines containing live versus attenuated poliomyelitis virus? Are there "hot particles" of plutonium that are more dangerous than the predictions based on the known properties of this element? Are some artificial sweeteners carcinogenic? Do food additives contribute to the hyperkinetic behavior of some children? To what extent do man-made carcinogens contribute to the current incidence of cancer? To what extent do man-made pollutants of the atmosphere and stratosphere endanger the public health?

Frequently, the question requires judgment of risk versus benefit, yet the two are intrinsically incommensurable: Will the electrical and magnetic fields associated with a large antenna to be buried in the earth disorient fish in lakes and streams, or confuse microorganisms that normally move, however slowly, toward the earth's magnetic pole? If so, should that deter construction of an antenna that may be the only means of communication with submerged submarines? Or if it is alleged that genetic manipulation, as by the technique of recombinant DNA, may result in a new organism of highly undesirable properties—even though none has ever been seen— what should be society's response? The question may take other forms. If the calculated odds against the occurrence of a disastrous accident are very large but the possibility of such accident is real and finite, what should society do? For example, how shall one weigh the known risk of 200 deaths per year in coal mine accidents against the statistical chance of perhaps 1 in 10 million of a major accident in a nuclear power plant? If ultrasensitive analytical techniques detect widespread occurrence of extremely minute traces of some industrial chemical known to be injurious in very much larger doses to man or some other inhabitant of the biosphere, how shall one regulate its usage?

Two general challenges recur time and again: If one knows the dose-response, in small experimental animals, of some substance that is injurious to that species, how shall one calculate the extrapolation to humans?

For a given noxious material, is there a threshold of exposure below which it may be assumed that there are no effects? All these, and more, now occupy our attention.

## DEGREES OF RISK

Recent experience has markedly enhanced the public's perception of risk, and it has become more acutely aware that individuals and societies have always been at risk. The public is slowly coming to understand that the term *safe* has no meaning, that one can only deal with the statistics of risk, and that, usually, to ask that risk be reduced to zero is to ask what is both unnecessary and either impossible or achievable only at unacceptable cost. For example, we can presumably live comfortably with the knowledge that the total solanine in one year's intake of potatoes by the average American would be lethal if given in a single dose—or should I not have mentioned it?

Technologies are adopted by society to secure specific benefits. As associated risks are also perceived, public decision must turn on the relative weights assignable, respectively, to the acceptability of the estimated risk and the desirability of the expected benefit. To be sure, rarely can the risks be stated with confidence, and seldom are risks and benefits commensurable. Yet decision is necessary. Such decision must be made by appropriately designated public officials, or, occasionally, by the public itself, guided by an intrinsically unquantifiable value system.

## COMMITTEES

The task of an NRC committee is not so much to resolve each dilemma as to reveal its nature, quantify it whenever possible, make evident the reliability of the available information, and display the alternative courses available to American society. It is commonplace to scoff at "committees," to suggest that the most useful committee has but one member, or to propose that some alternative mechanism should be utilized for the analysis and resolution of questions such as those noted above. It has been suggested that formal adversarial procedures would be more suitable than the committee system for the examination and analysis of technical matters that are the subject of public controversy. But neither the hearing procedures of legislative bodies nor the formal procedures of administrative law judges, of hearing commissioners, or of the court system have been demonstrated to be as effective as a well-constructed committee for the analysis and resolution of complex controversy regarding technical matters.

Contrariwise, there is no evidence that the committee system employed by the NRC fails to arrive at the closest approximation of "truth" that the relevant body of evidence will support. In a general way, one might come to the paradoxical conclusion that a formal adversarial process is useful only for answering those questions that are so limited as to make the inquiry unnecessary; that is, those questions where facts can genuinely be separated from values, as, for example, whether artificial sweeteners are carcinogenic under any circumstances. Rarely are such questions the subject of major public controversy.

Moreover, the task of sorting out the valid from the invalid evidence can be accomplished by simpler procedures, as was demonstrated by the nonscientist hearing examiner for the U.S. Environmental Protection Agency who, for months, listened to the evidence offered, pro and con, with respect to the hazards alleged to attend the use of DDT.

For the great majority of problems that come before the National Research Council, the matter of risk is but one aspect of the question. A useful response requires not only an evidentiary examination to establish the relevant facts and degree of confidence in which they may be held, but also a judgment concerning the significance of those facts when human, social, economic, or political values are made explicit. For example, the question would not be simply whether it is true that the agents employed to flameproof children's sleepwear are mutagenic in a specific microbiological essay, but, also, whether the amounts and the manner in which they are employed are likely to occasion cancer and, if so, with what frequency? Also, are there nonmutagenic substitutes available, are there alternative approaches to protection of children against the risk of fire, how great is that risk, how successful has the fireproofing program been, and so forth? Or, to give another example, not only can the runways at Kennedy Airport be extended to lighten the burden on the New York area airports, but what would be the effects on the ecology of Jamaica Bay and on the residents of surrounding neighborhoods? Decisions concerning regulation of the use of nitrate in fertilizer will require analysis of the quantitative relationship between nitrate dosage and crop yields, the consequence of nitrate finding its way into drinking water, its effect on the ecology of lakes and streams, the relationships of nitrate usage to reduction of stratospheric ozone by nitrogen oxides, etc.

In each case, those performing the analysis must not only attempt an evaluation of the relevant body of information but must also make their values explicit as they portray their findings of fact and their significance. Even well-intentioned scientists who attempt to be objective may give greater weight to those data that tend to support their general views. Controversy rarely consists of dispute concerning the underlying facts; rather it hinges about their interpretation, which is frequently value-laden. Hence, the public is best protected by an analysis conducted by a balanced group and to which those on both sides of a controversy have agreed. To assure that the public interest is held as the foremost objective, no social invention surpasses a well-constructed committee served by a competent professional staff in enabling the decision-making mechanisms of American society to operate in an informed manner.

Most of the questions under consideration in the National Research Council deal with subjects much broader than the specific risks associated with a specific technology. Many, of course, are not concerned with risk, per se. Invariably, however, there is required not only an analysis of the relevant facts, but also a large measure of judgment that may be value-freighted and, hence, must be made explicit. For example, how will we know whether man-made "environmental carcinogens" are occasioning an increased incidence of cancer in our population? Is the current design of a prototype breeder reactor likely to lead ultimately to a commercially successful source of energy? What research programs are most likely to enable capture of solar energy as a major contribution to total national energy requirements? How can the unique flora of the tropics be utilized for local economic development? In what order should new major facilities be provided for research in astronomy? By what procedures should research grant applications be reviewed and grant recipients selected?

Is the staffing pattern of Veterans Administration (VA) hospitals appropriate to their requirements? More to the point, what is the role of the VA hospital system in current American society? Are there measures whereby one might improve the scientific literacy of the general public? And myriad other questions, to be found throughout this report, all of which require not only an incisive analysis of the existing relevant information base, but also a high degree of creativity and professional judgment.

## CRAFTING COMMITTEES

When a question is brought to the National Research Council, it is referred to the appropriate assembly or commission or to the Institute of Medicine. The executive committee of that unit, most of whom are members of the Academies or of the Institute, will inquire whether the question embraces a meaningful body of scientific or technological information, whether it is appropriate for consideration by that unit, whether it is sufficiently significant to warrant the formal attention requested, and whether there is some prospect that the question can be addressed successfully. If the answers are affirmative and the Governing Board of the National Research Council is in agreement, the matter is then made the subject of the standard modality of the National Research Council—a committee.

Construction of effective committees is an art carefully cultivated by those responsible for the operation of the National Research Council. In so doing, they seek the wisdom of experience, familiarity with the matter in hand, expertise in relevant areas, innovative spirit, a balance of contending interests when these are identifiable, and assurance of objectivity and willingness to devote the time and effort commensurate with the task. When the matter is controversial, an effort is frequently made to include one or more scientists of stature who have had no previous connection with the problem and whose personal expertise lies in a quite remote area but who are known to have good judgment and good scientific "taste."

Initiative in committee selection is the responsibility of the chairman of the cognizant commission or assembly. With the assistance of his professional staff, of the members of his executive committee or commission, and of the records in the files of the National Research Council this task is begun. The search network can expand to include recommendations from the staff and members of other executive committees, members of the academies and of previous NRC committees, officers of scientific societies, and many others. The final list of potential members and their alternatives is reexamined in the Office of the Chairman of the National Research Council, using much the same criteria, but with particular attention to avoidance of undue bias. Considerations more relevant to the totality of the NRC structure than to any given committee include: affirmative action with respect to appointment of women and members of minority groups, a reasonable geographical balance, and representation by such major sectors of American society as academia, private industry, government, citizens groups, consumer groups, labor, management, scientific and professional societies, and others.

An illustration of this art is afforded by the Committee on Nuclear and Alternative Energy Systems, engaged in the most complex task ever attempted by the National Research Council. It is cochaired by an applied physicist who is a university professor and an industrial engineer whose company manufactures scientific instruments, both of whom had previously chaired major NRC committees with great success. In all, ten members are from academic institutions, one from a government laboratory, one from the research arm of an oil company, one from an instrument manufacturer, one from a utility company, one from a bank, and one from a law firm. From a disciplinary standpoint, there are five engineers, three physicists, one geophysicist, two economists, one sociologist, one banker, one physician-radiobiologist, one biological ecologist, and one "public interest" lawyer. They live in Arizona (one), California (four), Colorado (one), Illinois (one), Massachusetts (four), New Jersey (one), New York (two), Oregon (one), and Wisconsin (one). In a general way, by my appraisal when the study began, about one-third were negative, perhaps three were positive, and the others were genuinely open-minded concerning nuclear energy. At this writing, it is clear that the ideas that have come to be uppermost in the committee's collective thinking were central to the views of few if any of the committee members when they first met.

The evolution of a committee's own dynamics and style begins at its first meeting; no two committees are quite alike. These initial meetings are tentative experiences, where the members of the committee learn something about their fellows. Formal discussion of their responses to the questionnaire concerning "potential sources of bias" reveals to each other much about the background, values, and views of their fellow members. The committee reviews its charge and work statement, not infrequently modifying both, examines the dimensions of the problem before it, and develops its own modus operandi. At that first meeting, federal agency staff may present the problem as it appears to the government and provide such relevant information as the government may already have assembled.

With the passage of time, as members begin to know each other, responsibilities for specific assignments, such as preparation of position papers, are agreed upon. The staff, charged with securing all available relevant information, is given more specific instructions by the committee. The committee may request appointment of additional members with expertise in relevant areas as yet unrepresented and develop a list of informed individuals whose views should be gathered, either in writing or in person. A schedule is agreed upon, and the committee is then immersed in an intensive new learning experience. Each member gains close familiarity with diverse aspects of the subject material, is surprised by the attitudes of some and by the information provided by others, acquires familiarity with some portion of the material body of law, and increases his or her understanding in previously unfamiliar aspects of science and technology.

In 1976, about two dozen open committee meetings were convened, in conformance with recently adopted institutional policy. This is still a limited experience. In each case, public notice was given and invitations were extended to numerous individuals and groups who, conceivably, might desire to contribute to the specific study. In most instances, the committee gained credibility in the eyes of external interest groups; rarely did the committee gain new information or encounter a new viewpoint, but often it gained a firmer sense of the views held by the interest groups and the nature of public sensitivity to the issues in question.

Slowly, the diversity of backgrounds of the members gives rise to a coherent view of the committee's problem; conclusions and recommendations begin to emerge, almost of themselves, while the deadline appears to be upon the committee before it has hardly begun. Only after members, chairman, and staff have pieced together a rough draft does the committee begin to see what it has wrought.

For the larger, more complex studies, it is particularly valuable for the committee occasionally to convene in an intensive workshop for several consecutive days in virtual isolation, for example at the Academy's summer studies facility at Woods Hole, Massachusetts.

The final draft takes shape. Inconsistencies, flawed arguments, missing information become evident, are debated and repaired. The logical structure of the report is put in place, and there is a last opportunity for the resolution of controversy. All committees seek for consensus, but not for a compromise in which none believe. When individuals or a minority of the committee dissent or hold views that seriously differ from those of the majority, they are encouraged to prepare a "minority statement" to be included in the report itself. Final assignments are accepted, and polishing begins. Where many have contributed portions of the first draft, all must foreswear pride of authorship if the report is to have a consistent style and avoid repetitiousness. Then, one last pass by the committee staff and the chairman and the manuscript is ready for formal review by an independent panel of reviewers.

In most instances, the review process is helpful and without friction. Almost always, reviewers note small flaws, missing arguments, absence of supporting data that are presumed to be available, minor inconsistencies, irrelevant digressions, poor grammar, verbosity, etc., and their constructive criticism is welcomed. Occasionally, however, the reviewers' comments may strike at the validity of the central findings, conclusions, or recommendations of the report. Then, like as not, the committee will demonstrate the strength of its group dynamic by supporting its report and reaffirming positions arrived at by prolonged and sometimes painful deliberation. The chairmen of the committee and of the review panel then exchange memoranda until the difficulty is resolved, sometimes by adoption of the positions espoused by the reviewers, sometimes by accession of the reviewers to the view of the committee, not infrequently by mutually acceptable compromise.

The report is then ready for public release. It has a style and flavor that is unique to the committee but not of any one member. Its conclusions and recommendations derive from that constructive synergism that makes a good committee other than the mere sum of its parts. The work of the committee is completed. The nation benefits from its collective wisdom and simultaneously gains a cadre of individuals, now extraordinarily knowledgeable with respect to the matters to which they have given intensive examination, prepared to be of assistance in the future.

## SOME STATISTICS

In a typical year more than 800 groups—committees, subcommittees, and panels—are at work in the National Research Council. Some are concerned with basic science, some with development problems or engineering applications, and some with the interactions of science and technology with public policy or with far-reaching social questions. They form a pattern that is fluid and ever-changing with the flow of the council's work. In the listing for fiscal year 1976, for example, there appear 145 groups that were new in that year, while 255 that had been listed in 1975 had been discharged.

In midyear, these hundreds of committees and similar bodies were populated by more than 7500 individuals occupying about 8250 "slots" in the structure. Figure 1 shows that more than 40% were in academic life, while 27% were divided about equally between industry and federal agencies. Others work in local or state governments, in private research institutes, or in private practice.

Table I offers approximate representation of the disciplinary backgrounds of those who serve. The fact that a significant number of individuals serve on more than one committee is irrelevant to this analysis in that, were such duplication completely avoided, in general, chemists would be replaced by chemists, engineers by engineers, etc. The totals in several disciplinary categories are heavily influenced by the large advisory structure of the Transportation Research Board of the Commission on

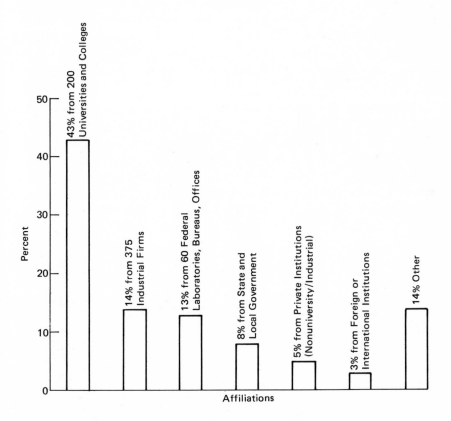

Figure 1. What are the "home" affiliations of the 7500 who serve on NRC committees?

**Table I.** Disciplinary Distribution of the Members of the Committees of the National Research Council

| | Assemblies | | | | Commissions | | | Sociotechnical systems | | Institute of medicine | Total | |
| --- | --- | --- | --- | --- | --- | --- | --- | --- | --- | --- | --- | --- |
| | Behavioral and social sciences | Engineering | Life sciences | Mathematics and physical sciences | Human resources | Natural resources | International relations | TRB[a] | All other | | Number | % |
| Agriculture | — | — | 16 | 4 | — | 66 | 114 | 14 | — | — | 214 | 2.6 |
| Biological sciences | 3 | 23 | 150 | 31 | 77 | 31 | 81 | 14 | 1 | 3 | 414 | 5.0 |
| Medical sciences[b] | 12 | 28 | 455 | 41 | 29 | 90 | 43 | 14 | 70 | 65 | 807 | 9.8 |
| Chemistry | 1 | 22 | 33 | 168 | 31 | 38 | 16 | 84 | 17 | 1 | 411 | 5.0 |
| Earth sciences[c] | — | 23 | 16 | 332 | 21 | 63 | 33 | 84 | 18 | — | 590 | 7.1 |
| Physics and astronomy | 8 | 68 | 14 | 290 | 47 | 16 | 27 | 14 | 11 | — | 495 | 6.0 |
| Mathematics[d] | 5 | 12 | 12 | 83 | 31 | 9 | 6 | 280 | 10 | 5 | 453 | 5.5 |
| Architecture | — | 1 | 3 | 6 | — | 2 | — | 56 | 103 | — | 171 | 2.1 |
| Engineering[e] | 9 | 341 | 26 | 210 | 48 | 50 | 54 | 1400 | 685 | 2 | 2825 | 34.2 |
| Social sciences[f] | 140 | 95 | 29 | 53 | 73 | 34 | 152 | 560 | 69 | 20 | 1225 | 14.8 |
| Law | 6 | 23 | 2 | 6 | — | 15 | 6 | 140 | 30 | 9 | 237 | 2.9 |
| Other | 2 | 36 | 5 | 26 | 11 | — | 11 | 140 | 134 | 13 | 418 | 5.1 |
| Total | 186 | 672 | 761 | 1250 | 368 | 414 | 543 | 2800 | 1148 | 118 | 8260 | 100.0 |

[a] Transportation Research Board.

[b] Includes all branches of clinical medicine; basic medical science, veterinary medicine, public health, etc.

[c] Includes geology, geophysics, seismology, hydrology, meteorology, mineralogy, etc.

[d] Includes statistics, applied mathematics, systems analysis, etc.

[e] Includes all branches of engineering.

[f] Sociology, psychology, economics, anthropology, geography, political science. NOTE: In many cases the disciplinary characterizations overlap, e.g., in biological and medical sciences, electronics specialists may be either physicists or engineers, etc. Also, there was no attempt made to eliminate duplicated counts in cases where an individual serves on more than one NRC committee.

Sociotechnical Systems, which includes large numbers of engineers, economists, and sociologists, as well as a significant number of attorneys.

Of the 7500, more than 200 were foreign nationals. Every state was represented. The distribution by major regions of the country is shown in Figure 2, along with the regional distribution of the nation's population for comparison purposes. In some regions, the proportion of those serving in the NRC was about the same as the proportion of the population; others were larger or smaller. The high ratio for the South Atlantic region is the principal distorting factor. It comes about because the 13%, or so, of the members of the Research Council committees who are federal employees are drawn predominantly from the heavy concentration of federal scientific and engineering agencies in the District of Columbia and nearby Maryland and Virginia. In turn, this occasions the seemingly low ratios of the eastern and western Plains regions, while the highly developed educational and industrial establishments of the Pacific and Middle Atlantic regions match their large populations. The New England region, with educational and industrial development out of proportion to its fraction of the national population, shows the second highest ratio.

Figure 3 shows that about three-fifths of expenditures are for advisory and research activities. The absolute expenditures in these categories significantly understate the magnitude of this effort. No figure is available to indicate the total number of man and woman days contributed by the 7500 volunteers who make this activity possible. As a first approximation each contributes about 10 days per year—some much more—for a grand total of no less than 75,000 man-days per year. Were each recompensed according to the consultant's fee schedule of the federal government, to say nothing of consultant fees in the private sector, the direct cost of this enterprise would increase by perhaps one-third.

Sixteen percent of total outlays go for direct support of fellowships and other arrangements for the support of scholars. About 4% of total expenditures are for formal publications and other media and for conferences and symposia. Twenty-one percent of all expenditures are for the administrative support of the entire enterprise, including the physical plant.

Funds for the operation of the Research Council come principally, but not entirely, from the federal government. About five-sixths of the supporting funds come from federal contracts and grants; the remainder derives about equally between the institution's own internal resources and funds from outside private sources and from state and local governments. Finally, Figure 4 indicates the major departments and agencies of the federal government from which funds were received during fiscal

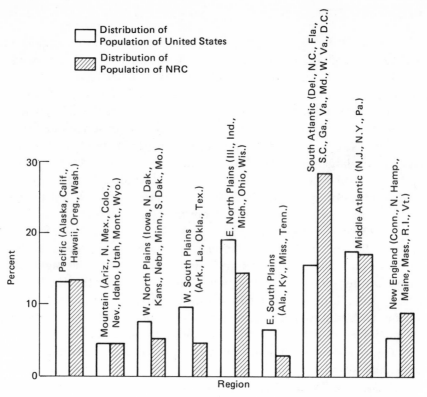

Figure 2. Where do members of NRC committees come from? Ninety-seven percent are U.S. citizens.

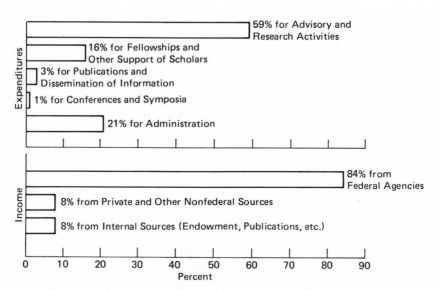

Figure 3. The NAS/NAE/IOM/NRC complex. The sources and uses of its funds.

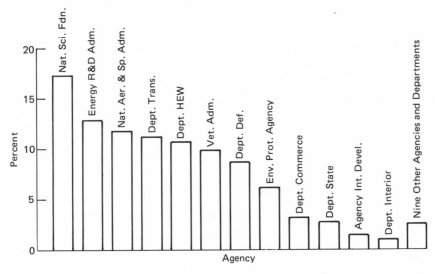

Figure 4. Distribution of funds from federal agencies to the NRC—fiscal year 1976. Total: $47.2 million.

year 1976. Although this picture also changes with the pattern of requests and with changes in our own perception of needs, Figure 4 may be regarded as typical of the sources of financial support of the National Research Council in recent years.

Thus the National Research Council is a unique institution. Through it flows a continuing stream of the nation's most highly talented scientists, engineers, physicians, and other professionals. Their professional lives are enriched by an intensive learning experience while, voluntarily, they serve our nation as only they can.

## REFERENCE

1. Handler, P., 1976, Scientific volunteers in the national service, *in: The National Research Council in 1976: Current Issues and Studies,* pp. 3-22, National Academy of Sciences, Washington, D.C.

# 5

# On the Planning of Science

## LEWIS THOMAS

If there are, as is sometimes claimed, certain matters that human beings are better off for not knowing about, or things that we ought not to be trying to understand, I cannot imagine what these might be. Therefore, I do not propose to get into this line of argument beyond acknowledging that the argument does exist. I take it as axiomatic that science is a useful, intelligent, and productive sort of human behavior, and, as our collective social activities go, it has a considerably better record than most. Moreover, I doubt that it will make a great deal of difference, in the very long run, whether any or even all of us were to decide that science was, for one reason or another, a bad thing and should be voted away. It is now a permanently established part of our social structure, and it will not go away. To be sure, it has only become a dominant part of human behavior during the last 300 years or so, but it represents an explosively successful expression of the most fundamental of all human urges, which is to find out about things. We are not, of course, unique among animals for curiosity in general, but our kind of incessant, compulsive, insatiable need to reach an understanding of nature, and, above all, our instinctive drive to make some kind of sense out of it, surely sets us apart from other forms of life. We seem to have agreed, informally, a few centuries ago, that we were not likely ever to find all the meaning we need by making it up out of our own heads, so we set about doing science, and I believe we will keep at it, for a long time to come.

I believe that science is a good thing for the human mind, and as important for the development of collective human thought as any of the other forms of art that seek meaning. I don't think its influence has yet penetrated the inner layers of our consciousness to the extent that literature has, or painting, or sculpture, but perhaps this is because science is

Reprinted from *Fundamental Aspects of Neoplasia* (A. A. Gottlieb, O. J. Plescia, and D. H. L. Bishop, eds.), pp. 413–421, Springer-Verlag New York, Inc., New York, 1975, with permission.

LEWIS THOMAS • President, Memorial Sloan-Kettering Cancer Center, New York, New York 10021.

still only beginning. I cannot imagine any terminal point in its future, nor any line of inquiry that will prove inaccessible.

I am aware of the dangers of hubris in this line of thinking. We do run certain risks, especially in biologic science, and all of us are aware of them. The new technology that permits the stitching together of DNA from different sources, bacterial, viral, even human, and the possible hazards to life posed by the resulting man-made micromonster, have sent a chill through the microbiologic community, but, by and large, the people who work in this field are sensible and trustworthy, as are the people who support the laboratories concerned, and I am sure that these hybrids will not be handled until there is certainty about their safety. Incidentally, *hubris* is a peculiarly appropriate and perhaps prophetic word here, since it is the etymologic source of the word *hybrid*. Hubris was constructed from two Indo-European roots signifying outrage, and hybrid was originally used to describe the inappropriate offspring of the wild boar and domestic sow. Like many of our oldest words, it carries its own warning.

There are, of course, other kinds of hazards ahead. The press has caught sight of some of them, and we are entering what I hope will be a temporary phase in which science is considered too risky for words. Along with oil spills, strip-mining, and herbicidal warfare, for which science gets blamed, we are also suspected of making plans to clone prominent politicians from bits of their own notable cells, or transplanting heads, or devising drugs to control human behavior to our personal liking. People are becoming fearful of science, and I would too if I thought such things were likely to happen. But I do not.

Set against the possible hazards of new and better science are the self-evident benefits. There are three general categories of benefit, which I would list in the order of their importance to humanity as follows: First, a more comprehensive understanding of nature, and a consequent enrichment of the human spirit. Second, more information that can be used to solve major human problems in the future, and especially problems relating to human disease. Third, a kind of information that can be put to use directly, the minute it is obtained, for practical and beneficial purposes.

The first category, that of understanding and meaning, I do not propose to deal with further here. Although it ranks at the top of my list (or perhaps *because* it is there), I could not possibly deal with it and still have time to discuss the other two categories. And it is these categories about which most of us are deeply worried today, and with which society's decisions about the planning of science are most directly concerned.

I intend to talk about the difference between basic and applied science, for this is actually the center of today's argument. It is a particularly agitated, and agitating, argument in the biomedical sciences, and this year—and I expect for some years to come—it is also, separately, an argument about how science should be carried out in dealing with the problem of cancer.

The great trouble with talking about basic and applied science is that people think you are arranging scientists into social castes, with differing and antagonistic customs and manners. The terms have become loaded with bogus meanings. Basic scientists are always delving into profundities, thinking every inch of the way, fishing up obscure bits of information for which there can be no conceivable use; they are ill-paid for their infinite pains. Applied scientists are well-off, athletic chaps, using other people's research to manufacture things that can be sold at a profit; they are superficial, unmeditative.

Because of labels like these, the terms *basic* and *applied* have lost much of their usefulness, and when they come into general conversation they tend to cause more trouble than they are worth. Nevertheless, I would like to use them for this discussion, on condition that I can make them mean exactly what I want them to mean. They are necessary if you are going to consider the planning of science, and most especially, the funding of science, whether by government, or foundations, or universities, or research institutes. They are, in fact, two entirely different kinds of scientific effort, and it is perfectly fair to call one basic and the other applied, if you're scrupulously fair-minded about values. Unless you manage to keep them separate in your mind, and plan for them as quite different kinds of activity, you run the danger of ending up with no good science at all.

Applied science, then, according to my definition, is the kind of scientific activity that you must engage in when you are entirely certain how an experiment, or a chain of experiments, is going to turn out. The potential usefulness or profitability of the outcome has nothing to do with the matter; the outcome could simply be entertaining or philosophically illuminating, and it would still be applied science if you start out with a very high degree of certainty. To become engaged in this kind of work you have to start out with an orderly and abundant array of indisputable facts, better still, a redundant array, and these facts inform you that the outcome is not just a possibility, or even a probability, but a dead certainty.

There are several outstanding examples of this sort of applied science in biology. The Salk vaccine is a particularly instructive one. The indisputable facts at hand were that there were three types of polio virus, and no more, that all three were good antigens, and that they could be provided in infinite quantities in tissue cultures. Once these things were known, it was an absolute certainty that a vaccine against poliomyelitis could be made for use in humans. This is not to suggest that the work would be easy, or undemanding of high immunologic skill, or any less rigorous and sophisticated than any other set of experiments in biomedical science. Just that it was a certainty, and the work that was then performed by Salk and his associates was a masterpiece of elegant applied science.

The development in the past several years of better and constantly more effective chemotherapy against acute childhood leukemia is another example. It became a certainty, or a near-certainty, that if the right combinations of certain drugs could be worked out, and their administration timed and monitored correctly, the disease could be cured in more children, and the rate of sustained remissions rose from around 20% to around 80% or higher. The work required meticulous attention and great caution, involving a large number of skilled clinical investigators, and the outcome was as had been predicted by the most knowledgeable people in the field. Something like this has also happened in the therapy of Hodgkin's disease and certain other lymphomas and, most spectacularly, in a number of the solid cancers of childhood.

In some respects, this kind of applied research resembles the moon shot, or the proximity fuse, or the hydrogen bomb, and it is fair enough to draw analogies between the planning of biomedical and physical science when you are working at this level. You obviously need a high degree of organization. Management skills are indispensable in both the planning and the doing of the science. The logic of systems analysis may be invaluable. All of the scientists involved are under an obligation to work together in team fashion, and everyone must stick closely to an agreed schedule.

It is a distinguishing characteristic of any really great piece of applied science that, if it doesn't turn out the way it is supposed to, this comes as a shock and a surprise. Something really quite awful must have gone wrong.

In basic science, everything is precisely the opposite. The shock, and the surprise, come when the experiment *does* turn out as you hoped. Instead of certainty about the outcome, you start out with a very high degree of uncertainty. It is all right to pretend confidence, and to go around your laboratory bragging that this or that experiment is fated to come out as you predict, but if you always have the nagging, uncomfortable hunch that you're on the wrong track, you're doing basic science, under my classification.

Generally speaking, the uncertainty of basic science is due to the fact that what is being looked for is really an idea that will fit with another idea, a connection and a meaning, perhaps a mechanism, and when you are dealing with work of this kind you have to rely on your imagination. It is a form of gambling, but the great difference from real gambling is that if you are lucky, and win, your first thought has to be that maybe you're wrong after all.

You can measure the quality of the work by the intensity of your own surprise. Any really significant piece of new information about nature is bound to be a surprise. Sometimes, if you have a winning streak, the surprise will simply be your own astonishment at being right. At other times, it will be surprise that something else turned up; instead of coming out the way you hoped, the experiment revealed something else, totally unexpected, unpredicted, and unpredictable. There are, of course, two ways of looking at this kind of event: One is to persuade yourself that the unexpected information is, in fact, an irrelevant triviality; the other is to realize that your whole program has just been derailed and you are now entrapped in a completely new approach. Whichever, you can't leave it there, sitting in your notes; you are now obliged to run it down.

Well, how do you plan and organize this kind of science? I really have no answer for this, except that I am absolutely certain that you can't turn it, just by wishing, into what is primarily a management problem, with the solutions now dependent upon the proper kind of organization charts, team deployment, systems analysis, and neat labels inside sequentially arranged boxes with big arrows and little arrows running back and forth between them. The way you do it, I suspect, is to find a bunch of very bright and very imaginative investigators, pack them together in quarters as crowded as possible, consistent with free breathing, and hope for the best. It may be very important to pay more attention to the design of the corridors than has been customary for most institutions. Corridors should have reasonably comfortable structures to lean against or sit on, and plenty of blackboard with inexhaustible chalk supplies. I sometimes wonder if we are in need of so many clocks in our hallways, or, for that matter, any.

You need skilled, hardworking committees to arrange the doing of applied science, and the success of the outcome may very well depend on the quality of committee planning. On the other hand, committees, even small committees composed of the brainiest people in town, can be the death of basic science. Not always, of course; once in a while it happens that a committee member will cry out in anguish because a new idea has just fought its way up into his consciousness, but the chances are statistically better, in my opinion, that the idea would have come sooner and with greater clarity if he'd been away from the committee, stumbling down the corridor, or staring out of his laboratory window, or maybe in the shower.

The really good ideas, the sudden intuitive perceptions of connections between seemingly unrelated bits of information, the sudden overwhelming revelations that make a scientist worry seriously about what would happen to the fate of the world if he were hit by a truck on his way to work, occur in individual minds, and they cannot be programmed or planned.

If I am right about these things, then the most important and difficult step in the planning of science is to decide where the problem stands on the issue of certainty. If you have lots of good hard facts, all pointing plainly to a predictable outcome, it makes no difference how difficult the technologic steps or how sophisticated the instruments required: If you line up the investigators in the right order and lay out the work in a properly systematic fashion, you get what you want, sooner or later. But if you make a mistake at the outset in your evaluation of the certainty of the position, and if what you are really in need of are good hunches and flashes of intuition, it will be a disaster. If you try to organize basic science in this manner you'll get nothing out of it except more uncertainty in an endless, impenetrable series of committee reports, all equally depressed and depressing.

I have a strong hunch that most of the important and interesting problems in biomedical science today, including the problem of cancer, are predominantly matters of high uncertainty. There is an abundance of new and fascinating information, and there are a good many enticing theories concerning the key issues of etiology, the fundamental mechanisms underlying neoplastic transformation, the possible role of immunologic reactants, the nature of viral transformation, and even new approaches to chemical control of neoplastic cells. But, despite the richness of the new information, and the increasing speed with which it is being accumulated, I do not sense any general feeling of certainty at this time about any fundamental aspect of the cancer problem. It seems to me a completely safe prediction that, if and when the time comes, when there is a general and comprehensive answer to the problem of cancer, this will be an event of overwhelming surprise; indeed, I would go so far as to predict that the first reaction of most of us will be, "But that is impossible!" Needless to say, the almost immediate second reaction in some quarters may be, "Ah yes, that is really what my group has been saying for some time," but the very first response will be dumbfoundment. And how do we make plans for that?

Meanwhile, there are important parts of the problem that lend themselves nicely to the most exacting methods of applied science right now, and there will be more of these in the years just ahead, if we are lucky. We need to develop better techniques of assessment so that these can be recognized quickly, and capitalized on—like the childhood leukemia story, for example. But there are not many, not yet, and we must not make the mistake of trying to force them into existence before their time.

A similar situation exists for most of the other major human diseases. There is a limited number of problems where certainty has already led to major achievements in applied science; the outstanding example is, I suppose, the development of the whole field of antibiotic therapy for bacterial infections. For the most part, however, we are in unknown territory, engaged in a running hunt, and we will have to rely on the same chaotic, disorderly, spontaneous, unmanageable, and uncontrollable manifestations of the human intellect that have brought the natural sciences to their present stature over the last couple of hundred years.

Even though it isn't yet clear just how it worked, it hasn't worked out all that badly. We stumbled our way into chemistry, and evolution, quantum mechanics, and relativity turned up, genetics evolved with a life of its own, microbiology blundered its way along from 1875 into the era of antibiotics, and, here today, all unplanned for and unpredicted, are molecular biology, immunology, neurophysiology, and, who knows, experimental psychology.

It is normal and healthy for scientists to be impatient, but impatience is a hazard for the planners and policy-makers who do their best work in an atmosphere of optimistic quiet. Perhaps the wisest thing of all for us to agree upon, for the time being, would be a public acknowledgment that our predecessors in science have started, long before our own time, a job that will never, ever be finished. Cancer will be solved, to be sure, as soon as the right ideas drift to the surface in the right minds, and we need to make sure that the right minds are there and ready, with an ample supply of even brighter young minds being trained to follow on, for there will always be more new things to find out about, and there will be no end to the enterprise.

We owe an enormous debt to the past, but we have an even greater obligation to the future. We must concede that the future exists, and that there is a tremendous amount of highly important work to be done, which we will never know anything about and cannot even guess at today. This requires of us more humility than we are accustomed to display, and we must dig deep to find it.

In summary, I'd like to itemize a few matters that are at the top of my own list of things to be apprehensive about; where I think we might run into various sorts of trouble in the planning of science over the next few years. I should perhaps emphasize, for quite obvious reasons, that I am speaking now about biomedical science in general, and not necessarily about the cancer program or any of the other special research projects with which the federal government is currently concerned. Also, I wish to stipulate that these are my own views as a private citizen, and no other person or persons, or governmental body, living or dead, can be blamed for them.

Item: Committees should not be charged with a responsibility for generating research ideas. It is fitting and proper for committees to act as peer review bodies, to assess the quality of scientific ideas as well as scientific work, but it is a violation of nature for a committee to sit down and try to think up bright ideas for other scientists to work on.

Item: Before you organize scientists into interdisciplinary, interinstitutional, or international teams, with detailed instructions and protocols for each worker, you had better be absolutely certain that you have a solid, concrete objective in mind, and that all participants are in agreement about the value of the objective as well as its reachability. If you deploy teams of scientists, not as individuals but as teams, in a highly structured, systematic way, with the intention or even the hope that something now unforeseen will turn up, or that brand new ideas about brand new mechanisms will somehow come to light, you are committing everyone concerned to an entirely novel and still untested way of doing basic science, and you should know this. It worked marvelously well for landing on the moon, but I doubt that if you were starting from scratch it would have uncovered the syphilis spirochete, or the function and structure of DNA, or even aspirin.

Item: Whatever you do, make sure that the scientists who are given responsibilities for solving significant problems are able to take pleasure from their work. This means accepting the fact that the exceptionally good ones, who will move things forward, are really wild men, involved in one of the wildest of all the instinctive activities that humans can become engaged in. It is a form of social behavior, subject to a certain kind of control, immensely responsive to encouragement and support, insatiable in its demands for ever-increasing sums of money, and incalculably productive when it goes well. But the transport of information from mind to mind is dependent on what we have always called trains of thought, and it is important to remember that these, like ordinary trains, can be stalled, derailed, or sent off to the wrong destinations or even lost altogether, depending upon the way the system is working. Therefore, before we permit major interventions and transformations of a system that has worked with reasonable success in the past, we should go cautiously and apprehensively, looking over our shoulders every step of the way.

Reasonable success, indeed. We are entitled to celebrate the body of science as one of the greatest of all human accomplishments, and we can do this without any risk of seeming to boast, provided we make it clear that we are describing the whole science, and all its history. Where we get ourselves into deep trouble is by seeming to claim that science is something we just invented, around, say, two decades ago, and, having invented it, we're about to figure out some really neat ways of doing it better and quicker. We didn't invent it, and we haven't really discovered any qualitatively different ways of doing it yet, and we certainly can't claim to understand how the system works. The best we can do, if we want to improve it, is to continue reminding ourselves of the principle features of the scientific structure that we have inherited from our forebears. It is a legacy passed straight down from the longer, more ancient tradition of *scholarship,* and it includes honesty, the endlessly rewarding and uniquely human gratification that comes with the opportunity to tell someone else everything you know about something new and important, the pleasure that come from surprise, and certain congenial habits of work: these include meticulousness, self-criticism, skepticism, an obsession with making notes, and references to the work of predecessors; in short, rigor. With these we obtained Faraday, Maxwell, Gibbs, Pasteur, Ehrlich, Metchnikoff, a tremendous list of today's luminaries too long to mention, and heaven knows who tomorrow. With so many other things in doubt, it is comforting to know that the tradition is so old and so powerful, and that, whatever today's weather, it is certainly here to stay.

# 6

# Influence of NIH Policy Past and Present on the University Health Education Complex

## ROBERT Q. MARSTON

### INTRODUCTION

NIH is a mission-oriented agency whose mission is health. The Institutes have a particular responsibility for the health implications of the biomedical research they support. However, it is also useful to consider other aspects of this research. First, a significant contribution is made to science generally. Second, most would agree that biomedical science constitutes one of the most dynamic of the scientific areas today. Then, there is the significant relationship of biomedical research to the university.

The advances made by university-based scientists since the creation of the NIH have resulted in contributions never before possible in an atmosphere of teaching, patient care, and research activity. This relationship was expressed best in recent years by Clark Kerr in his 1972 address before the Association of American Medical Colleges. He characterized biomedical science as the dominant intellectual drive in the university as a whole. In his words, "The health sciences are now the most important single part of all higher education in the United States."[1]

Biomedical research is very important for this nation and for the world, not only from the pragmatic standpoint of its contributions to health, but also as a "civilizing endeavor." Specifically, it is a humanizing activity—although biomedical science has its share, but no more than its share, of the "arrogance of science." Frederick T. Gates, talking about the Rockefeller Foundation, said that "as medical research goes on it will find out and promulgate as an unforeseen by-product of its work new moral laws and new social laws, new definitions of what is right and wrong in our relations with each other. Medical research will educate the human conscience in new directions and point out new duties."[2] It is this intellec-

ROBERT Q. MARSTON • President, University of Florida, Gainesville, Florida 32611.

tual thrust, this unfolding of new horizons in the biological sciences, which has bonded the universities and the NIH since the end of World War II.

Biomedical research has revolutionized the entire health establishment and all educational programs for health professionals. In turn, the intensive study of human disease has led to discoveries of basic life processes of great importance far beyond the field of medicine itself.

Thus the decision to couple closely a mission-oriented federal agency with the universities of the nation, and more especially with their health centers, has exploited effectively the common interests of both. In no other area, with the possible exception of the Land Grant movement, has the relationship of our federal government to universities been so close and the results so mutually beneficial.

John Sherman, on behalf of the Committee on the National Medical Policy of the American Society for Clinical Investigation, reviewed recently the organization and structure of the NIH and needs for the future. The abstract of that review states:

> In the assessment of domestic federal programs and the agencies responsible for them, few have been as frequently and highly praised as the National Institutes of Health (NIH). Contributing to that success in part is an unusual organization and structure. Based on a series of semi-autonomous, disease-oriented program divisions supplemented by several support units with a co-ordinative function performed by the Director, NIH, a remarkable and essential combination of administrative stability and flexibility, as well as scientific and political acceptability, has emerged. The changing environment in which NIH now functions, however, suggests the need for a greater degree of intra-NIH and extra-NIH program integration and co-ordination. Concomitantly, there must be more consistent federal policies, a clearer definition and understanding of "technology transfer" and additional resources for the directors of NIH and the individual institutes.[3]

## POLICY INFLUENCES

Against this self-evident assertion of mutual dependence and mutual benefits between NIH and universities, it is useful to examine the influence of selected NIH "policies" on university-based science and scholarship, on university educational programs, on university organization and management processes, and on university issues outside the biological-science-related areas.

First should be considered, however briefly, the most important policy decision of all: the direct involvement of the federal government in the health field and the choice of the universities to implement this federal involvement.

Three factors laid the groundwork for a significant increase in federal support of health-related research following World War II: (1) resistance to the federal government becoming involved in any other aspects of health care, (2) the role science had played in the winning of World War II, and (3) the nationwide appeal for research on dread diseases.

The choice of the universities, rather than research institute models of other nations, recognized the success that foundations, volunteer health organizations, and some federal agencies had had with the grant-in-aid process and the eager responsiveness of medical schools and universities to the idea. The utilization of peer review groups to play a significant role in the selection process allayed much apprehension. Such a union, at that time at least, effectively blunted fears of inappropriate federal intrusion into health matters or into the universities.

The timely infusion of increasing federal support made it possible for scientists in university medical centers across the nation to exploit the explosive opportunities to advance knowledge in the biological fields. Every medical school developed a science base capable of making meaningful contributions and on many campuses the health center became the model for excellence of scholarship for the entire university.

All in all, the university-NIH relationship has been good for America, for the world, and for universities. However, problems have emerged as funds have become more constrained: the one-sided nature of federal-university "contracts" resulting in vacillating levels of funding from year to year; a decrease, if not obliteration, of peer review; increasing turnover of federal personnel involved in the federal review process; and the lack of clear consistent policies are especially threatening and frustrating to universities with their long-range multipurpose goals. There have been specific criticisms raised by some concerning the NIH influence. Among them are that it has (a) led to a preponderance of science-based, rather than patient-based, doctors, (b) contributed to overspecialization, (c) detracted talent and money from what some consider to be the real health problems, (d) disrupted the integrity of the university by creating semiautonomous units on campus with primary loyalties to NIH rather than to the university, and (e) intruded, or may intrude, along with other federal agencies, inappropriately into the prerogatives of the university. The validity of such criticisms is sometimes debatable. It is debatable especially in view of the overall achievements of the NIH-university complex.

The NIH and land grant experiences have become the two most useful large-scale models to examine when exploring the interfaces between the universities and the federal government in research, education, and delivery of limited direct services. The strengths and weaknesses of the relationship should and will be reviewed continuously in the future.

## LEVEL AND CONSISTENCY OF SUPPORT

The annual recurrences of NIH budget requests being reduced at the higher levels of the Executive branch under a series of Presidents and then raised by Congress above the original requests demonstrates the basic difficulty in determining how much is enough, for what, and to be determined by whom.

The issue was drawn most keenly and dramatically in the Johnson/Nixon budget in 1968, which also happened to be the Shannon/Marston NIH budget year. In exchange for a tax increase required by the Vietnam war, an $8 billion expenditure reduction was required by Congress. NIH obviously had to shoulder its share. Although the NIH budget resumed growth in subsequent years, especially in selected areas such as cancer and heart disease, the message went across the nation that "soft dollars" really are "soft dollars." However, by that time in history the issue from an earlier age—Will the University pick up the salary of a faculty member who loses a grant?—was no more than a persistent side issue. Medical schools had become dependent on NIH for their continued existence in education and in patient care, as well as for research. The request from the health centers was for consistency of support, institutional support, and disaster grants, along with the usual request for more money.

Several policy issues grew out of this experience, each with significant influence on universities. (1) There was added impetus to launch an augmented cancer crusade in order to rekindle public enthusiasm for biomedical research, among other purposes. (2) There were intensified efforts, especially in the Office of Management and Budget, to contain NIH programs. (3) There were serious questions raised concerning the method of support, not only for research but for health manpower as well, which was also the responsibility of NIH at that time.

## THE CANCER CRUSADE ISSUE

The National Cancer Program stimulated interest and vigorous debate about science policy and federal policy that will be continued throughout the world for many years. A full discussion of the cancer issue is beyond the scope of a chapter on the influence of NIH policies on academic medicine. However, this program and the debate preceding its establishment provided sharp insight into the more general questions of targeted and applied research, accountability required in return for federal support, and (a subject close to the heart of all at the university) the relative role of scholars and scientists in determining the conduct of science and scholarship.

The cancer program was announced in his State of the Union message by President Nixon in January 1971. He recommended an "intensive campaign to find a cure for cancer," asked for an additional $100 million for cancer research, and stated: "I will ask later for whatever additional funds can effectively be used. The time has come when the same kind of concentrated effort that split the atom and took man to the moon should be turned toward conquering this dread disease. Let us make a total national commitment to achieve this goal."[4]

In December President Nixon signed the National Cancer Act of 1971. Congress had debated the issues, especially in committees chaired by Senator Kennedy of Massachusetts and Congressman Rogers of Florida. Rogers in the House of Representatives and Senator Nelson in the Senate were especially effective in modifying earlier proposals in a direction more acceptable to the academic community.

This excerpt from the House Committee Report reflects the concern of those universities:

> The subcommittee members became particularly impressed with testimony and other public expressions of interest from several members of the scientific community who supported an intensified program but were deeply troubled by the implications of removing the National Cancer Institute from the National Institutes of Health. In addition to receiving expressions of alarm from scores of national organizations, including the American Medical Association, the American Hospital Association, and the Association of American Medical Colleges, practically every significant scientific body in the United States supported the concept of maintaining the federal cancer research effort within the NIH. Several recipients of the Nobel prize in medicine, including a Nobel laureate whose award was based on his treatment of cancer patients, expressed oppostion to the approach contained in the Senate-passed bill. Heads of 72 medicine departments of medical schools throughout the country expressed opposition to certain provisions of S. 1828. Thirteen members of the faculty of Harvard Medical School, each long associated in cancer research or the treatment of cancer patients, publicly opposed the course of action contemplated in the Senate-passed bill.[5]

In view of the close relationship between NIH and the academic community, it is not surprising that this view coincided closely with statements made by the director of NIH, in opposing the creation of a separate cancer authority by emphasizing the fact that "the basic lack in the cancer problem is fundamental knowledge of life processes, not developmental capability or central coordination, and in placing greater faith on the investigator-generated grant mechanism than on the federally-directed contract mechanism to achieve significant progress."

In the debate between the NIH-University coalition biomedical community and those favoring a cancer crusade there is no question where the general public stood. Ann Landers stimulated more than a million responses to a statement in her column in May 1971 asking for support of the cancer crusade. Later she thanked her readers with these comments:

> It will not be enough merely to utilize the existing machinery for cancer research.
>
> The existing machinery has been around since 1937 and it is a jungle of red tape. The proposed National Cancer Authority would be an agency similar to the National Aeronautics and Space Administration which put the first man on the moon. If we had stayed with "the existing machinery" it is doubtful that we would have reached our national goal.
>
> The answers to the scourge of cancer can and will be found. I say a massive, unified assault on this killer disease is long overdue.[6]

A near "compromise" was finally reached, whereby, although the National Cancer Institute remained under the NIH, the NCI budget was separately developed and presented through the NIH Director and the Secretary of HEW, both of whom retained only the right to comment on it. The Director of NCI was appointed by the President, but reported to the NIH Director. In addition, a three-man panel was appointed to report directly to the President on the progress of the cancer program. In actual practice, NCI functions administratively like all the other institutes of the NIH.

Seven years after the Presidential announcement of an intensified cancer program the level of support for cancer has risen dramatically—the upward thrust being largely due to public interest. However, the basic questions of targeted versus applied research and the best organizational arrangements to achieve desired science goals remain subjects for debate. There has been recently, for instance, a thrust by the American Association for Medical Colleges to reestablish the full authority of the NIH director over all the institutes, including NCI. Fortunately, the perceived overpromise for a quick solution to the cancer problem seems to have subsided while solid, steady progress in cancer and biological science research generally continues under the administrative support and guidance of NIH.

On the crucial debate about the separate nature of the NCI the issue seems resolved, at least in the mind of the current Director of the NCI, Dr. Authur Upton, who said recently:

> I report to NIH Director Don Frederickson, Assistant Secretary Richmond, and Secretary Califano just as any other Institute Director. Regarding the so-called budget bypass, it is a great advantage for NCI to be able to submit its budget directly to the White House and the Office of Management and Budget but within this administration cancer-program matters have been delegated directly to Secretary California. So now HEW is much more in the picture.

## CATEGORICAL INSTITUTES

In a totally rational world a nation would be expected to support all of science in the National Science Foundation programs at a higher level than science relating only to health, which is supported through NIH. Yet for much of the recent life of these two agencies the NIH budget has been triple the NSF budget.

The appeal of the categorical disease label is, and has been, more popular with the general public because it is easier to identify with, as was dramatically reemphasized in the great cancer debate. Even so, NIH itself has resisted the creation of additional categorical institutes and supported vigorously the need for noncategorical research for the last 15 years—not, however, with complete success. Despite this NIH opposition to further fragmentation, a compelling argument can be made for the fact that support of disease-oriented research across a broad area, as implemented by NIH, has resulted in benefits beyond simply the generation of more money.

The influence of the categorical approach on academic health centers has been predictable and, although to a considerable degree desirable, the lack of sufficient support in less visible areas of biomedical science has taken its toll. However, the degree to which there is an imbalance between specialized and general medicine, science-based medicine, and compassionate broad-based medicine cannot be adjusted by curtailing NIH programs.

The fact must be faced that although the policy of categorization has furthered science and scholarship, it has been at the price of fragmentation of the educational programs and university organizational and management processes.

## MECHANISM OF SUPPORT

*Institutional versus Project Support.* No policy issues have been followed more closely by the rest of the university than the basic issue of the conditions under which federal funds have been granted for general support of education versus research in academic health centers.

NIH has long maintained that prudent investment of federal funds to achieve specific research results requires a strong and stable research environment beyond the specific needs of any given project. Yet each year the debate between "buying a product" versus the intelligent support of a national research effort continues. Thus uncertainty about the continuation of and the level of general support programs through the General Research Support Grants has been especially troublesome to universities.

However, this failure to firm up federal intentions concerning institutional support based on level of research effort has had less influence on universities than the decade-long debate about federal support of education in the health field. Symbolic of this debate has been the organizational focus of the Federal Health Manpower Program. When first established, the Health Manpower Bureau was an independent component of the Public Health Service. Then it was attached to NIH for five years, but again separated. During the period while health manpower was under the aegis of NIH, many policy issues were debated in the context of overall federal support for academic health centers.

There was general anticipation that the capitation type of institutional support would be long-term, tied to few conditions, and provide an instructive model for federal support in other areas of higher education. Indeed, one of the ironies of history is that the failure to establish capitation as an entitlement was at one time due more to the contest between the President and Congress on the power to withhold the release of funds than on substantive disagreement over the policy of continuing institutional support.

Today it is clear that much uncertainty surrounds health education capitation grants as a useful model, since the conditions for receipt of such funds have been burdensome, restrictions or conditions for use have increased or become overcumbersome, and serious questions about continued efficient applicability have been raised. Finally, the universities are deeply concerned with curricula revisions written into conditions for capitation awards in dentistry and pharmacy and with the admission standards of U.S. citizens attending foreign medical schools being mandated.

What happened? One could contend that the academic health community was naive to believe that federal dollars would be spent for other than the achievement of highly visible national purposes as perceived by the federal government. Furthermore, significant federal support of higher education is a much more complex question than how best to meet a transient need to increase health manpower. In addition, the establishment of any new, long-term fixed commitment of tax dollars runs counter to the whole mood of the American people.

From the university standpoint, the one-sided nature of the "bargain" was apparent the very first year. For instance, the academic health centers admitted 100% of the increased number of students required but were funded at the 86% level.

The "disaster grant" period did not help the institutional support cause either. About half of the medical schools claimed and received federal dollars for bailout of "financial disaster." NIH's recommendation to phase out such grants did not alleviate concern that unrestricted capitation grants might not give schools the financial stability envisioned.

Based on the NIH experiences, one can only conclude that the climate for institutional support for universities is less likely or desirable from both the federal and the university standpoint than it was only a few years ago.

*Centers.* The research center concept raised major problems for an academic health center. Long-term stability of support has to be balanced against fragmentation of efforts and the acceptance of significant intrusion into the internal affairs of the institution.

From the federal standpoint the center is the quickest way to disperse large sums of money and responsibility and to focus sharply on federally perceived needs. Clearly, the center concept helps the NIH more than it helps the university. The British Medical Research Council and our own Atomic Energy Commission and Veterans Administration approach of running a federal activity adjacent to a university should be considered as an alternative to some large center grants.

*Moral Commitment for Continuing Grants versus New Grants.* A basic NIH policy issue has involved the relative support of new grants versus the continuity of research support. In this dilemma, there are two truths: (1) A reasonable number of new grants—often proposed by new, young investigators selected in open competition—is essential to progress in the biomedical sciences, and (2) serious science requires long-term support. The NIH study section approach made it possible for the young scientist to obtain a grant when his chairman's proposal was given a lower priority. Too, from time to time the work of every scientist is reevaluated as applications for new grants or for competing renewal grants. Thus consistent recent policy has been that some level of support for new grants is essential.

In the post-1968 budget years, a major policy issue was the fate of long-term support, i.e., the year-by-year "downward negotiation" of noncompeting continuation grants. Noncompeting continuation awards for each year within the prescribed award period provided the investigator with the assurance of funding for a time frame in which significant results could probably be achieved. Continued funding was assured during this period as long as there was reasonable evidence of continued progress and the absence of significant problems.

However, under the cutbacks required by the 1968 budget, it was necessary to recover funds already "committed" to noncompeting continuation grants. Initially this was viewed as a one-time event. However, with continued tight budgets, the practice of administratively reducing such grants was continued in subsequent years. Each year the concern of the NIH increased. We determined to draw the issue sharply in the early 1970s at a meeting with Elliott Richardson, then Secretary of HEW.

Perhaps 40 to 50 of the top level administrators in DHEW were present. The Assistant Secretary for Health advised continued "downward negotiation" of these noncompeting continuation grants to make funds available for population research and other urgent needs.

The meeting started very badly. Some hinted that the proposal to discontinue this money-saving practice contributed to the growing feeling that the appetite of NIH was insatiable. Fortunately, Secretary Richardson was called to the White House, so we recessed. When he returned and the meeting resumed, he said this grant program was a matter of great concern and he was prepared to spend as much time as was necessary to understand the issues and to make an intelligent decision. The debate, largely between Secretary Richardson and the director of NIH, continued for about 4½ hours.

The issues were: (1) Had the "fat" really been extracted from grants awarded in the pre-1968 period? (2) Had the negotiation process substituted federal employees' judgment for the judgments of study sections and councils concerning allocation of resources needed to continue the research? (3) Could serious research be conducted effectively under the conditions of year-by-year review of the level of support?

Secretary Richardson concluded about 8:00 p.m. that the NIH position was valid and that there would be no more across-the-board "downward negotiation" of noncompeting continuation grants.

The influence of this policy decision for academic health centers was important for several reasons. It decreased the intrusion of the federal bureaucracy into peer review processes. It diminished the uncertainty of funding. It eliminated the dilemma of the individual scientist and an NIH administrator negotiating the project-by-project balance between university support and NIH support. Finally, it recognized the fact that serious science cannot survive under a plan of year-by-year support.

*Training Grants.* Training grants and program project grants are in the intermediate area between project grants and centers in that they involve broad evaluation of the research environment and a commitment of resources for a period longer than the project grant but shorter than for centers. They are basically supportive of the university environment in such a way as to derive optimum value for dollars spent. They are, therefore, both desirable mechanisms of support viewed either from Washington, from the campus, or from the standpoint of the individual scientist.

With the exception of the basic research project grant, no other aspect of NIH programs fit so well into the university setting as did the NIH training grant. The peer review process assured both student and university administration of the quality of the program. The training grants merged research and education ideally. The period of support and phasing in and out of programs protected the interests of students and institutions.

However, the inherent logic of supporting the entry of new investigators into the federally supported research arena and the reemphasis of the importance of the noncompeting continuation grants at NIH made the training grants more vulnerable in the search for places to cut the controllable aspects of the federal budget. The extent to which the attack on the NIH training grants was a cost containment rather than a policy issue is, at the least, unfortunate, especially in the context of this chapter.

There are reasonable questions beyond simple cost containment. One of the earliest policy questions was how many training grants should there be in a given area of science. In general, experts could relate reasonably well such factors as total funds available, size and complexity of the field, and number of suitable environments for training and arrive at rational estimates of the number of grants needed. As funds become constrained the estimated number needed almost always exceeded the funds available. An earlier expectation that every medical center would have a number of training grants—perhaps even one in every major area—became less likely as competition became keener.

Difficult decisions were involved in determining when to close out existing training grants in order to release funds to establish new grants or to adjust to increased costs.

These and other pragmatic and substantive issues became secondary issues when in the early 1970s the Office of Management and Budget proposed repeatedly the phasing out of training grants as a matter of policy. The role of federal training grants in the nation's science programs continues to be debated.

The beneficial influence of training grants on academic institutions is quite clear from years of congressional testimony. However, the uncertainty, not only of funding level, but also of basic policy has created problems for universities.

*Clinical Trials.* Clinical trials raise identical problems for academic health centers and for NIH itself. Who shall pay the high costs? Which clinical trials are a natural extension of the role of academic health centers and NIH and which are problems of cost containment? What are the ethical constraints?

The specific impact of NIH policies on academic health centers in the development of clinical trials in the past is more easily defined than those previously discussed. Because they tend often to be multiple institutional, long-term, carefully programmed, and adequately financed, universities can make intelligent choices to participate or not to participate. A basic concern of both NIH and the universities is that resources not be diverted from other areas of important biomedical science to support high cost clinical trials.

Many assume that the development of some form of national health insurance, as is the case in Great Britain today, will absorb some part of the patient care cost now borne by NIH. However, a national health insurance program could generate demands for clinical trials designed to eliminate eligibility for reimbursement for procedures and treatment which are costly and have questionable benefit. Such clinical trials do not fall within current NIH or university interest or expertise.

Funding matters aside, clinical trials may lack the intellectual excitement, the sharp conclusions, and the opportunity to modify experiments in process intelligently and easily characteristic of other types of research. Furthermore, ethical constraints may be unusually complex and physician-patient acceptance of the results controversial.

Yet, despite the fact that clinical trials do not fit as neatly into the central theme of the NIH-university tradition, there are still compelling reasons that such research be done and done well. Furthermore, our expanding and complex society increasingly calls on the university to help solve practical problems in economics, engineering, political science, and many other areas, in addition to the more traditional ones of agriculture and medicine. Such activity in the public interest is an appropriate university function within intelligent limits of scope and type of programs to be undertaken and when its basic integrity of the university is protected.

The conditions for participation in outreach and service programs are different from the conditions for university involvement in more central basic research and scholarship. These conditions must be recognized and considered when such programs are proposed. First, such programs should involve full-cost reimbursement, since they are largely in the public interest. Second, they should not be at the expense of other NIH-university research. Third, they should be well within the expertise of the resources of the universities.

## WHO SHOULD DETERMINE SCIENCE POLICY?

For that segment of research support that comes from the public treasury, the ultimate decision on biomedical research priorities is primarily the responsibility of society. Having said this, one must add that the notion of "society as a whole" is an amorphous concept, which obviously includes the scientific community, as well as other components. Determining what society's priorities are is by no means a simple and straightforward task. The problem translates into: "Who speaks for society?" and "What are the processes by which 'society' makes its decision?" The voices claiming to speak for "society" are many and discordant—executive branch, Congress, the press, both laymen and professionals, major study groups. All of these groups have their say and, eventually, a decision results which we conventionally agree to refer to as a "decision of society."

A critical question is: How does society get the expert advice it needs? Whatever societal desires may be postulated, an indispensable datum for decision on priorities is the best possible scientific and technical estimate of what the possibilities and the probabilities of success are. Thus, in the planning stages, responsible public administration requires a careful weighting of expert scientific advice. In the execution phase—that is, after society has delivered its mandate and specified the level of intensity at which the mandate is to be pursued—those charged with carrying it out must be allowed to use their best scientific and technical judgment (bolstered, of course, by sophisticated advice) to ensure an optimal return on investments.

Perhaps the issues of who should decide can be sharpened by quoting two sources that start at the opposite end of the debate. The first one is a statement made by Frank Carlucci when he was undersecretary of HEW:

> There are two schools of thought. . . . One says that a public agency should be a primary advocate of the special group of citizens that it serves. The other holds to the belief that a public agency must serve first and always the broad public interest, and take its direction and policy from the duly elected leader of the executive branch of government—be he president, governor, mayor or county supervisor. My beliefs, and those of Secretary Weinberger, rest clearly with this latter view. To me, public advocacy by a public agency is outright chaos. Sooner or later it places that agency in an adversary position with the chief executive. [7]

This is in stark contrast to the statement of the First Minister of Health of the United Kingdom in speaking about the need to establish a Medical Research Council which was independent of government. He spoke as follows:

> A progressive Ministry of Health must necessarily become committed from time to time to particular systems of health administration. . . . One does not wish to attach too much importance to the possibility that a particular Minister may hold strong personal views on particular questions of medical science or its application in practice; but even apart from special difficulties of this kind, which cannot be left out of account, a keen and energetic Minister will quite properly do his best to maintain the administrative policy which he finds existing in his department, or imposes on his Department during his term of office. He would, therefore, be constantly tempted to endeavour in various ways to secure that the conclusions reached by organized research under any scientific body, such as the Medical Research Committee, which was substantially under his control, should not suggest that his administrative policy might require alteration. . . . It is essential that such a situation should not be allowed to arise, for it is the first object of scientific research of all kinds to make new discoveries, and these discoveries are bound to correct the conclusions based upon the knowledge that was previously available and, therefore, in the long run to make it right to alter administrative policy. . . . This can only be secured by making the connection between the administrative departments concerned, for example, with medicine and public health, and the research bodies whose work touches on the same subjects, as elastic as possible, and by refraining from putting scientific bodies in any way under the direct control of Ministers responsible for the administration of health matters. [8]

The basic question is how best to arrive at sound decisions on priorities for biomedical research which will take cognizance of the wishes of society as well as the realities of science. The interests of both the NIH and academic medicine require that the realities of science remain dominant in the determination and in the implementation of policy.

## TARGETED VERSUS BASIC RESEARCH

NIH continues to be urged by the Federal government and society to solve, through science, the health problems of the world. Universities are urged to expand outreach and service programs to improve their public image and to solve promptly the problems of society. Both face the dilemma of trying to pay court to the diverse pressures.

The public, confronted by the assurance of Walter Cronkite nightly, "That's the way it is today," believes there are, or will be, simple answers to complex problems. There are, of course, no simple answers to complex problems—only intelligent decisions as to how to approach them. The NIH and universities concur that almost always the really important answers arise from basic research. In short, experiments come out as they come out, not as we would like for them to come out.

There is room for honest debate about the balance between targeted and basic research, but the debate has not been especially keen within the NIH-university community because both favor, in general, basic research.

Indeed, it is this emphasis on the "state of the art" in science as the starting point for all policy decisions which may be overlooked by those viewing the NIH-academic medicine relationship. Brief comments about four substantive issues of the early 1970s illustrate the differing influence of the science base. There are the decisions made on to what extent funding should be directed toward L-Dopa, cancer, sickle cell anemia, and intervention trials.

L-*Dopa.* The basic work on L-Dopa was carried out, as is almost always the case, under stimuli unrelated to the control of the symptoms of Parkinsonism. The introduction of the issue was presented at NIH through a film developed by Columbia University documenting chronic bedridden patients arising and walking, following controlled dosages of an amino acid that, in the levorotatory form, is found in the broad bean. It was one of those rare clear-cut experiments which all scientists long for but all too seldom see. The question facing NIH was how best to get the results of this scientific advance to patients. Would/should NIH underwrite the cost of pharmaceutical plant conversion to develop and produce adequate supplies of synthetic L-Dopa? In this clear-cut example, the question had to be asked whether adequate funds should be transferred by NIH for the needed clinical trials, FDA clearances, and additional research. In the face of a sure bet, the answer clearly was yes. As it turned out, in this particular case, allocation of the funds for these purposes was not required.

*The War on Cancer.* Although already discussed earlier in this chapter, the debate returned again and again to the basic question of the science base in the war on cancer. Was knowledge about basic processes sufficient for a crash program? Almost everyone agreed that, while there were promising leads, adequate basic knowledge was, in fact, lacking. Despite this deficiency, the American people became convinced that they wanted a "War on Cancer," which is their right in our democratic society. Significant strides forward have been developed and much good has come as a result of this public interest and the resulting encouragement for many, many scientists to try harder. There is no doubt that there will be more progress in the future. Those who worried about possible overpromise or diversion of resources from other areas still worry. Yet, when national interest runs so high in a particular area of disease control, it cannot go unheeded.

*Sickle Cell Anemia Program.* The sickle cell anemia issue stood in contrast to the war on cancer. The problem of cancer covered such a broad area of science that almost any general prediction had and has some chance of success. On the other hand, not only was sickle cell anemia a disease well understood in modern genetic terms—the locus of the amino acid defect, the physical chemical nature of the hemoglobin problem—but the one new experimental observation, i.e., the effect of urea on sickle cell hemoglobin, was easily resolvable within existing technology and available resources. Because of political issues, the NIH was informed that the budget for research on this disease would be increased from approximately \$2 million to nearly \$15 million. To its credit, NIH resisted such an unrealistic increase in a field of limited scientific opportunity.

The L-Dopa story is characteristic of penicillin and immunizing vaccines in that in such cases the benefits are so clear compared to the destructive aspects of the disease that a high probability of success is predictable fairly early on. Such breakthroughs as exemplified in the L-Dopa case are appreciated by scientist and layman alike, and the public has come to expect more and more such dramatic achievements.

However, the problem of sickle cell anemia is an example of our ability to survey an area of science and predict with confidence the limited prospects of rapid progress. Such negative assessments usually are not well received by interested segments of the public. Science cannot, simply by concentrated dedication, solve everything. For instance, despite the urgency of the world population problem, despite the unexpected phenomena of the effect of copper when added to IUDs, it was clear in the late 1960s that no outstanding advances in the contraceptive field would occur over the next five years. Also, the negative results of the oral antidiabetic trials is one more example of the understandable reluctance of professional and layman alike to see their hopes unrealized by the results of science. To repeat, "Experiments come out as they come out, not as we want them to!"

*Intervention Trials.* The fourth issue demonstrates, among other things, that if one chooses a broad enough area of knowledge, at an average state of progress, the results will be a mixed bag of successes and failures.

Following a number of long-term epidemiological studies, of which the Framingham study is one of the best known, it becomes clear that individuals with hypertension and high serum fats, and who smoked, had eight times the probability of a heart attack compared to individuals without these risk factors.[9]

The key question was: Would discontinuation of smoking, control of hypertension with the effective drugs at hand, and/or the control of cholesterol by diet and drugs decrease the risks of heart attacks and, if so, by how much?

Early feasibility studies established the fact that the costs of so-called intervention studies were likely to be high; one figure was $40 million a year to try to find answers to only *some* of the questions. Yet, for a problem of this magnitude for the American people, the costs were justified. The problems to be faced were the prospect of obtaining valid answers for asymptomatic individuals requested to submit to years of "treatment" and surveillance which might be of questionable value if there were mild deviations and which might also pose moral or ethical questions. Could the scientist really consider withholding advice and treatment which, on the best evidence available, although not proven, seemed desirable? Could he afford not to? Could one avoid the ethical question by an intensified interaction program to be compared to conventional treatment by practicing physicians?

In spite of the problems, it has been possible to launch a number of programs which should provide useful information and which still take into consideration problems of the type we faced several years ago. It is also important to note that, even at this early date, there may be seen some decline in cardiovascular disease in the United States. Some believe this decrease is associated with changes in life-style, including smoking, eating, and exercise habits. The decline exists for whatever reason.


## SUMMARY

There is no question but that NIH programs and policies have changed over the basic nature of academic health centers and the universities of which they are now such an integral part.

For the most part these changes have served well both the universities and the NIH by (1) producing biomedical research unmatched in the world or in previous history, (2) producing scientists and scholars in numbers and in quality needed to exploit effectively expanded opportunities in the biological sciences, (3) revolutionizing the education of physicians and other health-related workers, and (4) revolutionizing the practice of medicine.

Almost every NIH policy has strengthened university-based science and scholarship. The peer review system of study sections and national advisory councils has provided education and communication and intellectual stimulus of great and historic value. The intramural program on the NIH campus, in addition to scientific contributions which are the best in the world, has provided a national "balance wheel" and a worldwide information focus of very great value to universities everywhere.

However, predictably as one moves away from the primary science-based health goals of NIH, the impact on universities and their academic health centers has been mixed.

1. The reporting burdens arising from the Fountain Committee hearings on NIH in the mid-1960s have been counter to the basic thrust of universities. Current audit processes which seem to place a higher premium on paper work than the achievement of national goals are destructive. The substitution of rules for reasons serve neither the nation nor its universities.

2. University organization and management processes have been

challenged by NIH programs and policies. On balance, probably every university has suffered, to some degree, a loss of opportunities to blend effectively the full force of strengths in the biological sciences because of the fragmenting effects of NIH programs and policies.

3. The impact of NIH policies on university educational programs has been debated greatly. However, the issues are really drawn on a canvas much larger than that covered by health science or education in the health professions. Neither can substitute for the broader issues of national health insurance or the relative priority of medicine versus other social desirables. In the restrictive sense, education in the health professions tends to be a bit less defensive, more objective, and possibly more effective than the average across the university as might be expected in any area with augmented resources.

4. The most difficult summary is the impact of NIH policies in university issues outside of the biological sciences. Within hours of the writing of this sentence, a reasonably happy conclusion has been written to the *cause célèbre* of potential inappropriate federal intrusion into the universities' affairs. U.S. medical students in foreign medical schools will not be forced past our admission committees, as seemed possible at one time.

At no time in our national history, except at our very beginning, has concern in our society been so high about a burdensome government unresponsive to the needs of the people.

Concern for health, dread diseases, and unrealistic hopes in the power of science have been inherent in the growth of NIH and of academic health centers. For a while, the appeal of comparable "glamor programs" elsewhere in the university seemed reasonable. Today there are three major shifts from a glamor approach: (1) A world of constrained physical resources, including energy, may well place health and education in a different priority from a world of endless growth. (2) The world of the 60s suggested a program that may cure a problem. The world of the 70s and 80s restores the responsibility to the individuals. Heart disease and stroke may have decreased because of changes in the life-style of individuals. (3) Our understanding of basic life processes continues. Many of the problems deemed insoluble even a few years ago may very well be soluble in a few decades.

The message these trends reveal to NIH and universities is the need to focus on the basics—the university equivalent of the national cry for the three Rs in elementary education.

# REFERENCES AND NOTES

1. Kerr, C., 1972, Enlarging human capability: The central role of the health sciences, *J. Med. Educ.* **47**:843-50.
2. Gates, Frederick Taylor, born Maine, N.Y., July 2, 1853, conceived the idea of the Rockefeller Institute for medical research, of which he was president of the Board of Trustees until his death. *The National Cyclopaedia of American Biography*, vol. 23, pp. 250-251.
3. Sherman, J. F., 1977, The organization and structure of the National Institutes of Health, *N. Engl. J. Med.* **297**:18-26 (Abstract).
4. Nixon, R. M., State of the Union message, January 22, 1971, Weekly Compilation of Presidential Documents, January 25, 1971.
5. *The National Cancer Attack Act of 1971*, House Report 92-659, pp. 10-11.
6. Wright, D. S., Professor of Political Science and Public Administration at the University of North Carolina at Chapel Hill and Visiting Research Scholar, International Institute of Management, Berlin, Germany, 1977, Government and the crusade against dread disease: The case of hunting a cure for cancer in the United States, Discussion paper series, International Institute of Management-Wissenschaftszentrum, Berlin, dp/77-42, p. 74, quoting Ann Landers, May 1971.
7. Carlucci, Frank Charles, III, born Scranton, Pa., October 18, 1930. Undersecretary of DHEW 1974-75. *Who's Who in America*, 1976-77, p. 508.
8. Addison, C., 1970, *quoted in: The Development and Organization of Scientific Knowledge* (H. Himsworth), p. 102, William Heinemann, Ltd., London.
9. Framingham Study, Framingham, Mass., an epidemiological investigation of cardiovascular disease. [Bethesda, Md., U.S. Department of Health, Education and Welfare, National Institute of Health-U.S. Government Printing Office.] Study under direction of National Heart Institute, 1976, *Popular Names of U.S. Reports: A Catalog* (3rd ed.), (compiled by Bernard A. Bernier, Jr., Katherine F. Gould, Porter Humphrey), Serial Division Reference Department, Library of Congress, Washington, D.C.

# 7

# Much Ado about Recombinant DNA Regulations

## WACLAW SZYBALSKI

There is no truth on earth that I fear to be known.

Thomas Jefferson

The right of freedom of speech and press includes not only the right to utter or to print, but the right to distribute, the right to receive, the right to read . . . and **freedom of inquiry**, freedom of thought, and freedom to teach. . . indeed the freedom of the entire university community. . . .

U.S. Supreme Court in *Grisvold* v. *Connecticut*, 1965, *U.S. Reports* **381**:482.

## INTRODUCTION

Evolution shapes the form and activity of all living organisms in response to the environment in which they exist. Chemical changes in DNA, the long threadlike molecule composed of four kinds of bases coding for the genetic message, are responsible for almost all the hereditary changes that are the basis of evolution. These genetic changes are either localized mutations, where one or a very few bases are deleted, added, or substituted by other bases, or more extensive changes where whole functional genes or gene clusters are deleted, added, or exchanged.[1] If one compares information contained in DNA to a book or a large set of volumes, such mutational changes correspond to adding, deleting, or exchanging individual letters, words, sentences, or entire pages of information.

It often is very beneficial for an organism to acquire new genes, and many mechanisms developed naturally to perform such genetic exchanges. Most frequently whole blocks of genes are exchanged during the process of genetic recombination between two members of the same species. This mechanism is so important in higher organisms that their reproduction completely depends on sexual genetic exchange. Thus sex is essential for higher organisms, whereas primitive species seem to do well without it.

Several mechanisms also developed in nature to transfer genes between species by the so-called illegitimate recombination process. In this

WACLAW SZYBALSKI • McArdle Laboratory for Cancer Research, University of Wisconsin, Madison, Wisconsin 53706.

way all species can share any new gene that might be beneficial under certain circumstances. Special DNA sequences called IS and specific enzymes, usually in cooperation with plasmids or bacteriophages, can carry genes from species to species.[2] This process happens all the time and probably evolution largely depends on it. Most of the natural processes of genetic exchange can also be utilized by man under controlled conditions, and much of the development of agriculturally important plants and very beneficial domesticated animals is the product of such human intervention.

A new method, the *recombinant DNA technique,* was recently added to many existing methods of carrying out genetic recombination under laboratory conditions. This method is scientifically important because it permits more precise and more efficient use of genetic recombination, and therefore makes the research safer, more relevant, and much less expensive. This technique, because of its precision and ease can provide the answers to several crucially important biological problems within a few months or years instead of centuries.

As with many other important human achievements, the development of the recombinant DNA technique also created some controversy because society is usually conservative and apprehensive of new developments. In this chapter I shall first describe the principles of the recombinant DNA technique, next describe its benefits in relation to the purely hypothetical risks, and then discuss the political developments leading to legalistic regulations and restrictions based on irrational fears and resulting in greatly misplaced priorities. It would help the reader of this chapter if he were first to become acquainted with some general reviews and chapters on recombinant DNA and related subjects[3-19] and also refresh his memory of some fables, such as the one about killing the goose that laid golden eggs, *The Emperor's New Clothes* of Hans Christian Andersen, and the movie *The Bridge over the River Kwai.* I leave it to the reader's imagination to find the analogies between the present developments and these fables and fiction.

## THE RECOMBINANT DNA TECHNIQUE

The recombinant DNA technique is a new method that permits incorporation of fragments of foreign DNA into the genome of an organism.[5,6] If one imagines that a genome consists of a very long thread, this technique corresponds to cutting the thread and splicing into it a piece of thread from another organism.

Normally, the system used in conjunction with the recombinant DNA technique is composed of three elements, (a) a host cell, (b) a vector, and (c) a cloned DNA fragment. This chapter will deal only with systems based on *Escherichia coli* host cells and two kinds of vectors, namely, bacteriophage λ and plasmid DNA. At this time the great majority of research projects employing the recombinant DNA technique are based on these systems.[5,6]

## HOST, VECTOR, AND CLONED DNA

The *E. coli* K-12 host is a laboratory strain of bacteria which over 50 years ago was derived from the normal inhabitant of the intestinal tract. However, it has lost its ability to colonize the gut[20] and, as all *E. coli*, has little capacity to propagate in nature outside the gut. Thus its only true habitat is the laboratory, where it is cultivated on special media. Out of this K-12 strain new mutants were developed which, as will be discussed later, have a far more reduced ability (by over one hundred millionfold) to survive even temporarily in the gut or elsewhere in nature.[21]

A vector is a much shorter DNA genome that can replicate rapidly in *E. coli* K-12 cells and hence produce a large number of identical copies, up to several thousand per cell. Another useful property of a vector should be the simplicity of its isolation in pure form, free of host components. It is convenient to insert the DNA into such a vector because that permits producing a large amount of cloned DNA from a limited number of host cells.

Two kinds of vectors are presently used in conjunction with the *E. coli* host: (a) bacteriophase λ and (b) plasmids.[22,23]

*Bacteriophage* λ is a parasite of *E. coli* that infects the cells and reproduces in them, forming 100 to 1000 new phage particles per cell, and in the process kills the host cell. Phage λ can also establish "peaceful coexistence" with the host,[4] but the so-called EK2 strains[24,25] of λ used in the recombinant DNA technique can only kill the host cells. The killed cell either lyses and releases into the medium a large crop of phage particles or retains the phage in the lifeless cell shell. Thus the phage particles, which consist of pure DNA packaged in a protein coat, can be easily harvested in very large quantities and the DNA can then be readily extracted and purified.[24,25]

*Plasmids* are small circular DNA molecules that replicate autonomously and hence can be present in very large quantities in a cell.[23] There are methods to induce their rapid replication, which leads to death of the host cell, e.g., by chloramphenicol treatment. Operationally, there is much similarity between replication of plasmid DNA and phage DNA in the host cell, with the main difference that the DNA of most phages has the capacity to direct its own packaging into phage particles while obligatorily killing the host cell. Because plasmid DNA is produced in large quantity and consists of identical small circles, it is comparatively easy to purify free from the very long and tangled host DNA and from cells and cellular debris. Up to 3000 plasmids can be produced per bacterial cell.[18,21,23]

Cloned DNA fragments are produced by fragmentation of any DNA. The DNA can be from lower organisms, as bacteriophage or bacteria (prokaryotes), or yeast (lower eukaryotes), from plants, animals, and even man (higher eukaryotes).

### COMPARATIVE SIZE OF DNA IN HOST, VECTOR, AND CLONED FRAGMENT

The length of DNA is usually measured in base pairs or in daltons. The length of the E. coli host DNA is about 5 million base pairs, of the various λ vectors, about 35,000 to 50,000 base pairs, and of most cloned DNA fragments, 1000 to 10,000 base pairs. The length of most plasmid vectors varies from 5000 to 100,000 base pairs.[2] Therefore, the length ratio of the cloned DNA to the bacterial host DNA is only 1:5000 to 1:500. Thus the bacterial host carries only a tiny amount of the foreign cloned DNA, which corresponds to either less than one gene or at most a few genes.

### CONSTRUCTION OF CELLS CARRYING RECOMBINANT DNA

The recombinant DNA technique usually consists of the following steps[14,18]:

1. The DNA to be cloned is cut into many fragments, generally using a special enzyme, a sequence-specific restriction endonuclease. A given fragment is then selected for insertion into the vector.

2. The vector DNA is cut in a specific place by the same enzyme.

3. Since the enzymes normally used produce cohesive ends, the DNA fragment can be easily inserted into the vector DNA and then they are permanently spliced together using another enzyme called ligase.

4. In this manner a recombinant DNA molecule is produced that consists of the vector DNA and the linearly inserted cloned DNA fragment.

5. Such a recombinant DNA can now be introduced into the host cells, by a so-called transformation (for plasmids) or transfection (for phage) process.

6. Providing the recombinant DNA has retained its capacity for replication, it will propagate within the host and the cells will either die, producing a crop of bacteriophages, or become permanently associated with the plasmid, depending on which of the two kinds of vectors was used.

7. DNA cloned in the bacteriophage vector can now be produced in large quantities by infecting new batches of host bacteria, which die while releasing a new crop of phages. This system is a *two-component* system,[24,25] which normally does not lead to production of live host bacteria stably associated with cloned foreign DNA.

8. In the case of recombinant plasmid DNA, a stable association between the plasmid and the host bacterium is formed. Therefore, this is a *one-component* system.[5,6,23,25] Recombinant DNA is produced by propagating the bacteria and in the case of *Col*E1-based or λdv*cro*ts-based plasmids can be further amplified by, e.g., chloramphenicol or heat treatment, respectively, which leads to host cell death.


## BENEFITS OF THE RECOMBINANT DNA TECHNIQUE

Existing methods used in molecular biology permit the detailed study of genes and their functions in very primitive organisms, e.g., small bacteriophages, the DNA of which contains between 5000 (coliphage $\phi$X174) and 50,000 (coliphage λ) base pairs. Bacteriophage λ can naturally pick up and incorporate into its genome small fragments of *E. coli* DNA, thus enabling study in great detail of any particular gene or gene cluster (operon) of this bacterium. In this manner a large amount of basic biological data was obtained for several *E. coli* operons, including *bio, lac, gal, ara, trp*, and several others.[3,4,23] Having a large quantity of isolated DNA of one gene or operon also permits its most detailed study, i.e., sequencing and decoding of the chemical gene structure. Moreover, the gene activity in vitro under controlled conditions, including RNA and protein synthesis, can be conveniently studied for isolated operon DNA and compared with the in vivo activity.

Unfortunately, such detailed study was nearly impossible with *eukaryotic* organisms, including higher animals and man, because their DNA is up to 100,000 times more complex than that of phage λ and no simple method was available to isolate, propagate, and study only one or a few genes. At present, however, the recombinant DNA technique makes such study possible and practical. Thus the major practical advantage of the recombinant DNA technique is the ability to fish out a DNA fragment corresponding to only one-millionth of the, e.g., human genome, reproduce it in large quantity, and study it in detail, as was done before only for a few bacterial (*prokaryotic*) genes and operons. This opens up immense opportunities for research, some of which have already been realized.[13,14,15,26-35] Such research will lead to the understanding of higher organisms, their normal or abnormal gene functions, their hormonal and other controls, their pathology, including neoplastic and other diseases, and many other theoretical and practical applications, some of which will be listed below.

## ISOLATION OF INDIVIDUAL EUKARYOTIC GENES

Several eukaryotic, including human, genes have already been cloned. These include genes of yeast and *Drosophila* flies,[28,29] genes responsible for production of ovalbumin, the main component of egg,[33] globin and immunoglobulins,[34] the main blood and immunity components, and several hormones, including insulin,[35] somatostatin,[26] somatomammotropin, and growth hormone.[32]

## EXAMPLES OF BASIC SCIENTIFIC BREAKTHROUGHS ACCOMPLISHED ALREADY OR IN THE FORESEEABLE FUTURE

1. The cloning of a large number of *Drosophila* fly genes has given deep insight into the structure of eukaryotic chromosomes and their chemical composition.[28]

2. The cloning of many yeast genes has permitted the determination of which of them function in *E. coli* cells.[29] It is also possible to study the fine genetic structure of this simple eukaryotic organism by recombinational analysis, using crosses between the phage λ vectors that carry the yeast genes.[30] This opens up the amazing possibility of studying within *one day* the genetics of higher organisms, whereas a conventional genetic study of one eukaryotic cross would normally take *many months or years*.

3. The cloning of globin genes and of yeast tRNA has led to the unexpected major discovery that often there are untranslated sequences right in the middle of the gene.[31]

4. The genes coding for several hormones, including human hormones, have been completely sequenced, and thus their code is now broken; this will obviously further our understanding of hereditary diseases affecting these hormones and of disorders involving other human proteins.[32-35]

5. The synthesis of the human hormone somatostatin by the *E. coli*

host has already been accomplished,[26] and two gallons of E. *coli* culture, worth less than a few dollars, produced more of this hormone than could be previously obtained by painstaking extraction from a half million sheep brains. Synthesis of other important and very difficult-to-obtain human hormones and proteins could be accomplished by this technique in the foreseeable future.

6. The synthesis of human proteins by recombinant bacterial strains will lead to development of new branches of the pharmaceutical industry. Moreover, the systematic mutational modification of cloned genes coding for human proteins could lead to development of powerful new pharmaceutical agents.

7. Great progress has been made, thanks to the recombinant DNA technique, in understanding the structure of genes that code for immunoglobulins,[16,34] the proteins responsible for immunologic defense against many diseases and used in passive immunization procedures.

8. Powerful new vaccines much safer than the present ones could be developed by cloning genes coding for important antigens and antibodies. Pure antigens or human immunoglobulins (antibodies) specific for a given antigen would be much safer and often more effective than partially inactivated or mutationally weakened microorganisms or natural sera, which at present are used in the immunization process. There is also hope for the efficient synthesis of interferon, a natural agent of great promise in virus and cancer therapy.

9. The recombinant DNA technique should lead to vast improvement of fermentation technologies and to creation of new technologies that would supply us with scarce materials and food products.

10. This technique could relieve the present gas and liquid fuel shortage by permitting their efficient production from organic wastes and coal.

11. Great ecological benefits could be realized through the development of microorganisms that efficiently oxidize thin layers of crude oil spilled on the water surface.[36] Many other kinds of pollution, e.g., by chlorinated hydrocarbons, could also be effectively dealt with by development of special microorganisms.

12. Great agricultural benefits could be derived from detailed study of the genes involved in nitrogen fixation or in synthesis of essential nutrients, followed by practical application of such knowledge.[13,16]

This list of benefits, both enriching human knowledge and serving practical ends, could be made much longer and more detailed, but that is not the purpose of this chapter.

## CONCERNS ABOUT THE HYPOTHETICAL RISKS OF
## RECOMBINANT DNA RESEARCH

The recombinant DNA technique was developed at a time when the general awareness of the untoward effects of many technologies, especially those leading to environmental pollution and affecting health, had become quite an important political and social issue. Since most scientists readily understood the great significance of this technique, the question was immediately raised whether recombinant DNA activities could create any biological hazards. The main scenario considered at that time was that insertion of foreign genes into the E. coli host could convert it to a dangerous epidemic pathogen which might spread throughout the population in the form of an uncontrollable plague. This scenario was conceived mainly by molecular biologists and biochemists who understood the molecular and biochemical principles of the technique but had not enough knowledge about the epidemiology of infectious diseases, especially of diseases caused by the so-called enteric microorganisms, which include E. coli. As will be discussed later, these apprehensions have no factual basis, but at the time they appeared plausible to uncritical scientists, especially in view of the popular and widely read science fiction novel entitled The Andromeda Strain.[37]

Two major developments converted these early apprehensions into a real issue. These were a letter signed by the co-chairmen of the 1973 Gordon Conference on Nucleic Acids (June 11-15, 1973, New Hampton, N.H.)[38] and a letter from Berg et al.[39] As a result of these letters the National Academy of Sciences sponsored an international meeting in Asilomar, California, February 24-27, 1975, with its summary statement published in Science,[41] and the director of NIH established the Recombinant DNA Advisory Committee.[13] A large amount of publicity was created by the above events, which converted the scientific developments and ensuing scientific discussion into a public issue. The controversy was aided by the pronouncements of a few prominent or vocal scientists, who for reason of their political or other beliefs, but without much knowledge of the subject, voiced strong opinions about the possible apocalyptic consequences of the recombinant DNA technique.[42-45] Since the press and other popular media like to deal with sensational and thus newsworthy subjects, many headlines and articles appeared, some stressing the dangers of laboratory-created monsters, borrowing heavily from folklore tales and science fiction.[46-48] These media activities were appealing enough to frighten some segments of the general public and hence to start several political developments on the federal, state, and local levels.

I shall first briefly discuss the activities of the NIH Advisory Committee leading to the issuance of the guidelines, then assess the current scientific outlook on the hypothetical risks, and finally consider the present and proposed regulations and legislation and the dangers of such regulatory activities.

## THE NIH ADVISORY COMMITTEE AND THE GUIDELINES

The NIH Advisory Committee with the rather long and not entirely logical name of NIH Recombinant DNA Molecule Program Advisory Committee (see ref. 13) was established on October 7, 1974, to provide advice to the Secretary of the Department of Health, Education and Welfare (HEW), the Assistant Secretary for Health, and the Director of the National Institutes of Health (NIH).[49,50] This committee was established in accordance with Section 301 of the Public Health Service Act (42 U.S.C. 241), in which "the Secretary of H.E.W. is directed to conduct research, investigations, experiments, demonstrations and studies relating to the causes, diagnosis, treatment, control and prevention of physical diseases and impairments in man." The function of the committee was to advise "concerning a program (a) for the evaluation of potential biological and ecological hazards of DNA recombinants of various types, (b) for developing procedures which will minimize the spread of such molecules within human and other populations, and (c) for devising guidelines to be followed by investigators working with potentially hazardous recombinants."

The first meeting of the committee was held on February 28 and March 1 in San Francisco, California, and the original membership included DeWitt Stetten (NIH), chairman; eleven members: E. A. Adelberg (Yale University), E. H. Y. Chu (University of Michigan), R. Curtiss, III (University of Alabama), J. E. Darnell, Jr. (Rockefeller University), S. Falkow (University of Washington), D. R. Helinski (University of California, San Diego), D. S. Hogness (Stanford University), J. W. Littlefield (John Hopkins Hospital), J. K. Setlow (Brookhaven National Laboratory), W. Szybalski (University of Wisconsin), and C. A. Thomas, Jr. (Harvard Medical School); and the executive secretary, W. J. Gartland, Jr. (NIH). This group included only scientists, less than half of them actively employing the recombinant DNA technique in their research; the others were more or less familiar with this subject. As the work proceeded, more members were added, some representing important but underrepresented scientific areas (e.g., plant sciences), some to represent small colleges or to be sympathetic and attune the views of some radical groups, like Science for People, and some who were not scientists but represented the areas of ethics, law, and government.[49] Unfortunately, the area that was the main concern of the committee, i.e., the possibilities of epidemic dangers of recombinant DNA carried by enteric organisms, was highly underrepresented in the committee, especially after the early resignation of S. Falkow.

Perhaps because of that, but mainly due to political realities and the consequent sense of urgency, the committee did not address itself to its primary assignment, i.e., "evaluation of potential biological and ecological hazards of DNA recombinants," but tacitly assumed that valid reasons exist for "developing procedures which will minimize the spread of such molecules (i.e., recombinant DNA) within human and other populations, and for devising guidelines." In the meantime the recommendations of the 1975 Summary Statement of the Asilomar Conference on Recombinant DNA Molecules[13,41] were adopted as the guidelines for the accepted laboratory practices in this field of research.

The first draft of the guidelines, based on the original Asilomar Statement, was prepared by the subcommittee consisting of D. S. Hogness, chairman, E. H. Y. Chu, D. R. Helinski, and W. Szybalski. W. E. Barkley of NIH was a consultant to the subcommittee on physical containment and W. J. Gartland, Jr. of NIH served as executive secretary. This draft had little if any factual basis but was an uneasy compromise between divergent beliefs of the members on the relative importance of the biological and political dangers and what the response to them should be. Two types of containment were proposed in this draft, namely, biological containment graded EK1, EK2, and EK3, based only on the E. coli K-12 host and its vectors, and physical containments P1, P2, P3, and P4. The experiments were divided into many classes based mainly on taxonomical criteria and then, without any convincing scientific reasons[51] but mainly following "intuition" and the hastily conceived Asilomar statement,[41] they were assigned to specific classes of containment.

The first draft of the guidelines emerged as a very conservative document. The subcommittee believed that this had to be so in order to allay the general apprehensions and was assured that the guidelines represented only a code of good laboratory practices that would not be converted into any regulations. Actually, one of the main motives for creation of the guidelines and their very conservative nature, far beyond any scientific reasons, was the assurances that such guidelines would *prevent* any imposed regulations or legislation.

The first draft was considered during several subsequent public meetings of the advisory committee, with their conservative features first slightly downgraded and then again upgraded in response to many outside pressures and considerable input of many individuals and political groups.[50,52] The final deliberations included a public meeting on February 9-10, 1976, convened by the director of NIH, including his special advisory committee with additional broad lay participation,[50] and a subsequent meeting of the Recombinant DNA Advisory Committee on April 1-2, 1976. This was followed by publication of the first official version of the guidelines in the *Federal Register* on July 7, 1976, as decided on by the director of NIH and including his detailed introductory comments.[53] In these comments a first hint of the possible general regulations is contained, since the director first states that "it is my hope that the Guidelines will be voluntarily adopted and honored by all who support or conduct such research," but at a different place one reads that "considerations of their [the guidelines'] *conversion to regulations* can proceed with continuing review of their content and present and future implications." It is also stated that "the scientific community generally urged that there be no Federal regulations" and that "many who opposed changing the proposed Guidelines into Federal regulations expressed concern for flexibility and administrative efficiency, which could best be achieved, in their view, through voluntary compliance."[53]

The publication of the guidelines had some positive but also serious negative effects on research. The positive effect was that it quieted the controversy surrounding the use of the recombinant DNA technique, but the negative effects included: (a) great waste of the time and effort of the investigators and of the members of the local biohazard committees and of national committees because of the adversary nature of the complex bureaucratic process for securing permission for often already funded research; (b) substantial delays in some research, especially that which required EK2 biological containment and P3 physical containment, since EK2 systems and P3 laboratories became available only sometime after promulgation of the guidelines; (c) virtual prohibition of all research which depended on EK3 biological containment and P4 laboratories since neither are as yet (i.e., January of 1978) available; (d) great waste of funds on building and designing P3 and P4 laboratories, even though there is no real need for them other than legalistic requirement by the overconservative guidelines; (e) creation of general disrespect for the guidelines by those who clearly realize that they are not based on sound scientific considerations; and (f) delaying or denying to the public the benefits of important biomedical and other research.

After the first guidelines were issued on June 23, 1976, the Recombinant DNA Advisory Committee started revising these guidelines and the new proposal was published in the *Federal Register* on September 27, 1977.[54] There are several important changes in this new proposal based on the premise that "everything we [the committee members] have learned tends to diminish our estimate of the risk associated with recombinant DNA in *E. coli* K-12. Nevertheless, the revised Guidelines continue to be deliberately restrictive, with the intent of erring on the side of caution." This "intent of erring" was a deliberate and a very extreme statement, and its purpose was to reflect major social and political pressures clouding sound scientific judgment which did not justify many restrictive requirements of the guidelines, even in their new less-inclusive form.

The major innovations in this new proposal are as follows: (a) inclusion in the guidelines only of organisms containing recombinant DNA and not the recombinant DNA itself; (b) a new definition of recombinant DNA as "molecules consisting of segments of DNA from different genomes which have been joined end-to-end outside living cells and have the capacity to infect some host cells and be maintained therein"; (c) a new concept of *novel* recombinant DNA (as first proposed by W. Szybalski, who was chairing the sessions of the Recombinant DNA Advisory Committee that were devoted to formulating the Introduction) and that the guidelines "pertain only to novel recombinant DNAs, here defined as molecules that consist of segments of any DNA from *different* species that are *not known to exchange chromosomal* DNA by natural physiological process." Thus the new guidelines would in general exclude research involving "those combinations of DNAs (viral, extrachromosomal, or chromosomal) which are not considered novel. In general, recombinant DNA molecules formed from any combination of DNAs will not be considered novel when all the components are derived from genomes known to replicate within the organism used to propagate the recombinant DNA." The purpose of this change was to exclude from the guidelines all those kinds of recombinant DNAs which are constructed from DNA components known to naturally coexist in one cell and even recombine; (d) several less major changes were introduced in the section on experimental guidelines, including (i) the possibility of specific exemptions pertaining to "experiments that are not to be performed"; (ii) lowering the "shotgun" experiment requirements for some important experiments, e.g., to P3 + EK2 for DNA from uninfected cells

of primates and man; (iii) lowering by one step the containment requirements for purified DNA and characterized clones by the action of local
institutional biohazards committees (IBC), and the further possibility of
lowering by more than one step by the NIH Office of Recombinant DNA
Activities (ORDA); (iv) authorization for "judicious and *flexible* interpretation of these Guidelines" by the Director of NIH; (v) consideration of
new host-vector systems and the new designations HV1, HV2, and HV3
analogous to EK1, EK2, and EK3, the latter applied only to *E. coli* K-12
host-vector systems.

This new proposal underwent further scrutiny during a public meeting of the special Advisory Committee to the Director of NIH on December 15 and 16, 1977.[55] This committee was broadly based and included
about 20 persons representing environmental health and safety, clinical
medicine, human genetics, virology and medical microbiology, immunology, plant pathology, chemistry, environmental groups, college
administration, theological ethics, students, technicians, members of institutional biohazards committees, private lawyers, public law officials,
law educators, and foreign scientists in the field of molecular biology.
Moreover, there were 12 invited witnesses representing labor, the environmental lobby, industrial and academic research, and several public
witnesses, also representing these areas. The draft of the revised
guidelines was generally approved by the committee members, but several interesting and revealing points came out during the two-day discussion, in which criticism centered on the frequent use of political instead of
scientific considerations and the lack of proper justification that led to the
overly restrictive nature of several sections of the proposal:

1. It became clear that the hypothetical risks were greatly exaggerated and that the guidelines were much too restrictive.[56]

2. There was uniform agreement that the recombinant DNA technique employing EK1 or EK2 vectors does not present any practical risks
of epidemics. Consequently, this led to requests to exclude from the
guidelines most of the novel recombinant DNA research based on these
*E. coli* K-12 vectors.[57]

3. The committee members strongly criticized the unreasonable and
inflexible restrictions pertaining to the cloning of viral DNA and resulting in delays of risk assessment, e.g., for *E. coli*-cloned polyoma DNA. It
was learned from the foreign representative that because of this inflexible
application of the guidelines U.S. research on risk assessment is lagging
far behind European research.[58]

4. It became clear that the present guidelines are a historical acci-

dent, and if based on the present assessment of safety there would have been neither any serious warning similar to that issued by the signatories of the 1974 "moratorium" letter,[39] nor any Recombinant DNA Guidelines.[57] Moreover, Dr. J. Watson,[59,60] as one of the signers of the original "moratorium" letter, offered an apology to society for this act, stating that probably it was the "silliest thing" he did in his life.

5. During questioning of witnesses by the committee it became clear that many restrictive parts of the proposed guidelines have no scientific basis but were adopted due to political considerations, mainly to appease some vocal pressure groups.[46,47,59,60] The committee recommended that these sections, especially the section on cloning viral DNA,[61] should be revised to allow much more moderate and scientifically justified containment conditions.

6. The risks of the recombinant DNA technique based on the EK1 or EK2 host-vector system were estimated as much less than one minor ailment (e.g., upset stomach) per whole world per 10,000 to 100,000 years when 10,000 to 100,000 laboratories carry on such research. This kind of risk is of no practical concern.[57]

7. Very strong and characteristic opinions were expressed by the Nobel laureate J. Watson,[59,60] who very convincingly discounted all the hypothetical dangers of recombinant DNA of any practical significance. He characterized the guidelines and the whole hearing as "nonsense" and remarked that this was supposed to be a great dialogue between scientists and the public, but he cannot think about a worse subject for dialogue, because there is nothing significant to discuss[60] about the hypothetical dangers of recombinant DNA. Referring facetiously to the Whole Risk Catalog,[60] which he is preparing, he said that under letter D he lists many items starting with dogs, doctors, and dioxin, but DNA is very far down on this list. The hypothetical dangers of recombinant DNA are so slight that he should rather worry about being licked by a dog[60] and perhaps we should first design guidelines and legislation to guard us against the latter risk.

8. The dangers and high monetary and social cost of the regulations, especially of restrictive ones, were also emphasized. The dangers included (a) lost or delayed benefits to mankind, (b) prolongation of the time when lives are still unnecessarily shortened or lost and human misery extended, (c) expensive and stifling bureaucracy, (d) incentive for young researchers to treat with disdain the NIH guidelines because they have no valid scientific basis, and (e) misleading the public and legislative

bodies, which are used to equating restrictive regulation with the presence of real hazards and not imaginary risks that not only are nonexistent but cannot be even rationally postulated, as was clearly stated by Dr. A. Campbell.

9. The NIH administration was criticized for not including enough pertinent data, e.g., the transcript of the Falmouth Risk-Assessment Conference of June 1977, into the Federal Register issue that carried the new proposal for the revised guidelines, and for not supplying the justification for this new proposal until a rather late time. [61]

Despite the presence of many witnesses who in the past were quite vocal in condemning recombinant DNA research, their criticism was now very muted. They agreed that the scenarios of epidemics caused by insertion of foreign DNA into E. coli K-12 are of no concern, [62] and their isolated pleas for making the guidelines more restrictive were exposed as unrealistic or unreasonable during questioning by the members of the committee, especially by well-informed legal experts, including Mr. Peter Hutt, former counsel of the FDA, and Mr. Dennis Helms, Assistant to the Attorney General of New Jersey.

The guidelines proposal will now have to be revised accordingly by the Recombinant DNA Advisory Committee and its final form will be decided on by the director of NIH.

## PRESENT ASSESSMENT OF THE SAFETY OF THE RECOMBINANT DNA TECHNIQUE

### RISK ASSESSMENT

This assessment is directed only toward research applying the E. coli K-12 EK1 and EK2 systems, because it represents the great majority of research based on the recombinant DNA technique and because several safety aspects of these systems have been evaluated. [63] For the bulk of this research, whether involving novel or not novel DNA, the risks are nonexistent from the practical point of view. By the latter statement it is meant that the risk is much less than one minor and nonepidemic ailment per 10,000 to 100,000 laboratories carrying on the research for 10,000 to 100,000 years.

How was such a figure derived? The possibility of an epidemic is a product of at least four probabilities: (1) the probability that by introduction of foreign genes E. coli K-12 would acquire some pathogenic property, i.e., toxin production, (2) the probability that a laboratory worker becomes exposed to a sufficiently high dose of such an *E. coli* K-12 system, (3) the probability that this novel *E. coli* K-12 or a vector carried by it could become implanted in the intestinal tract (or some other part of the body) of the laboratory worker, and (4) the probability that it could be spread through the population in an epidemic manner.

These four independent factors are all usually under control of very many finely adjusted gene activities, which *E. coli* K-12 is lacking and which would have to be acquired one by one, as discussed below.

1. It is very hard to imagine that random cloning of individual genes or operons from many organisms like *Saccharomyces* yeast, *Drosophila* flies, mice, or even humans could produce a pathogenic *E. coli* strain, since only a finely adjusted combination of genes, the product of long evolution, might have such an effect. The exact probability is hard to guess, but it certainly is infinitesimal and present experience shows that cloning of DNA in *E. coli* in an average of 100 laboratories for the last five years did not produce any such *E. coli* pathogen.

2. For enteric organisms, usually a massive dose is required for a successful infection. Standard microbiological practices and avoidance of mouth pipetting make such accidental ingestion very unlikely, perhaps less than once per 100 laboratories per year.

3. The colonization of the intestinal tract of normal laboratory animals and of humans was studied and it was shown that even ingestion of large numbers of *E. coli* K-12 does not result in permanent implantation of this laboratory strain.[20] In the case of the *E. coli* K-12 EK2 host, the intestinal tract of even germ-free animals generally could not be colonized.[64] Furthermore, not even one of the ingested 100 billion coliphage λ vectors could be recovered in human feces.[65] In the over-two-year study in a laboratory that has handled *E. coli* K-12 and several transmissible R-type plasmids without any special precautions, no case of either colonization by *E. coli* or of transmission of any plasmid to the normal bacterial flora was found during monitoring feces of the laboratory workers every second or third day.[66] Since plasmids currently used in recombinant DNA research show a million times lower transmissibility and the *E. coli* K-12 EK2 host is 100 million times less likely to survive, the latter study on the implantation component alone shows that the chance of any intestinal illness in a laboratory worker is much less than one per 10,000 laboratories working for 10,000 years. This estimate does not even take into account any special physical containment equipment, which even if very cumbersome and expensive adds only another safety factor of 100 or 1000, which

will be meaningless in view of the already infinitesimally low probabilities of any infectious disease.

4. The epidemic spread of highly pathogenic enteric organisms such as those causing cholera or typhoid fever is not observed anymore in technologically developed societies, since it requires repeated and widespread ingestion of water or food heavily contaminated with fresh fecal matter. Moreover, not a single true epidemic occurred during the last 100 years which originated from laboratory-cultivated pathogens, some quite dangerous, in a very large number of hospitals and public health laboratories throughout the world, many being operated under rather primitive conditions.[13] Whenever isolated cases of laboratory infections were observed, none were due to *E. coli* but instead most were mainly due to airborne respiratory infections rather than to enteric infections.

Multiplication of only those probabilities for which some estimates could be given led to unanimous agreement by participants of the 1977 Falmouth Risk-Assessment Workshop[63] "that *E. coli* K-12 cannot be converted into an epidemic pathogen by laboratory manipulations with DNA inserts." Certain doubts expressed during this conference on the possibility of the transfer of plasmid vectors from *E. coli* K-12 to more robust intestinal bacteria were now answered by the over-two-year study of Petrocheilou and Richmond,[66] who showed that this scenario was not realized under normal laboratory conditions, using the "worst-case" kind of plasmids. Analogous calculations and conclusions were presented by Holliday.[67]

As far as the environmental risks are concerned, *E. coli* in general and especially the K-12 strain poses no practical risks whatsoever, since it is known not to be capable of propagating efficiently in the natural environment such as soil or surface waters. This property permits the use of *E. coli* as a sensitive indicator of *recent* fecal environmental contamination because it *rapidly disappears* when the source of contamination is eliminated.

## BIOLOGICAL CONTAINMENT

Two steps of biological containment are currently available with *E. coli* K-12 systems, namely EK1 and EK2. In the EK1 system the *E. coli* K-12 host should be free from conjugative plasmids and foreign phages. In those EK2 systems that employ λ phages,[25,68] the host survival is reduced by special mutations and the phages carry several mutations that preclude their stable association with the host and their survival in nature. In the EK2 plasmid system,[68] the host is a K-12 derivative extremely impaired in its survival, and the plasmids are of the nontransmissible type, which have vanishingly low capacity to be naturally transferred to another less disabled host. All these genetic impairments of the EK2 systems result in less than one chance per 100 million that any escaping recombinant DNA vector could survive in nature. This additional and immense factor of biosafety is superimposed over the already safe K-12 EK1 system, which was discussed in this section.

## OTHER SAFETY FEATURES

Another measure of safety is exemplified by the synthesis of somato-statin by *E. coli* K-12 carrying a recombinant DNA plasmid. In this case the protein produced is an *inactive* hybrid of bacterial protein and somatosta-tin.[26] Only subsequent harsh chemical treatment of the isolated protein with cyanogen bromide releases the biologically active hormone. This safety principle could be applied to many biologically active proteins when produced with the aid of the recombinant DNA technique.

## EVOLUTIONARY SIGNIFICANCE

Apprehensions were expressed that the recombinant DNA technique might lead to crossing of species barriers, an event that never occurs in nature, and that such tampering with "evolutionary wisdom" is un-wise.[43,45] However, it was stressed by others that *E. coli* has ample opportunities to pick up foreign DNA under natural conditions[7-9] since it is endowed with both cutting and splicing enzymes, and it was recently shown that this process can occur in nature.[69] Watson termed this fear of "illegitimate sex" as "very silly."[60]

## REGULATIONS AND LEGISLATION

The original purpose of the Asilomar statement and of the guidelines was to specify a code of good laboratory practices designed for applications of the recombinant DNA technique. This code was to be generally accepted and used by all laboratory workers, as was both traditional and very effective in other areas of microbiology, especially in clinical and public health laboratories that routinely study real pathogens. The guidelines were supposed to relieve all apprehensions about the recombinant DNA technique, especially since the assessment of risks, as described in the previous section, indicated that from a practical point of view the risks were nonexistent. After all, how could our society, which tolerates such pleasurable activities as smoking and automobiles, both leading to death of hundreds of thousands every year, be concerned about a danger corresponding to less than one minor intestinal ailment per 10,000 to 100,000 years, especially when associated with very beneficial research leading to improvement of health and human welfare.

However, the apprehensions created by the mass media together with political considerations led to a situation contrary to simple scientific logic. Not one or two but many various legislative and regulatory proposals, some of extremely restrictive and punitive nature, are now being considered by federal, state, and local legislative bodies and authorities.

*How Did It All Start?* On the federal level the first step toward enforcement of the guidelines was taken by the NIH administration and by other government granting agencies. Thus the guidelines were converted from a voluntary code of good practices to regulations.[13] The conditions of receiving government funds to carry on research involving the recombinant DNA technique were: (a) approval of the research plans and procedures, including containment facilities and monitoring, by the local Institutional Biohazard Committees and the National Study Groups, and (b) filing in the Memorandum of Understanding and Agreement (MUA) that all research will conform to the guidelines. The penalty for improper conformance, it was understood, would be loss of the financial support on which the research depends. Since such enforcement of the guidelines applied only to most of the government-sponsored research, the next step was the efforts[70-75] to create means for enforcing the guidelines on all activities involving the recombinant DNA technique.

It must have been somehow erroneously decided that research using recombinant DNA, even when creating no risks, must be different from all other biological and chemical research, and upon the recommendations of the Interagency Committee on Recombinant DNA Research (see ref. 13, Appendices I and J, and ref. 71), a legislative proposal was developed under HEW Secretary Califano. This administration bill was introduced on April 6, 1977, by Senator Kennedy (see ref. 13, Appendix N) but then quickly transformed into Senate bill S.1217.[72,73] It also formed the basis for House of Representatives bill H.R. 7897 sponsored by Congressman Rogers.[74,75]

*What Are the Main Features of These Two Legislative Proposals?* Both the Senate and House versions of these bills[72-74] are very restrictive and punitive, although, as will be later described, Senator Kennedy has recently withdrawn his support of S.1217. Both bills start with the findings, which first indicate some potential benefits of the recombinant DNA activities but then make very exaggerated statements that "microorganisms containing recombinant DNA could spread throughout the United States and to other countries, adversely affecting human health, the environment, industry and agriculture" (in S.1217), or that "recombinant DNA may present a risk of injury to health and the environment, and there is a risk that such organisms and viruses may spread quickly and without warning to persons, agricultural plants and products, and other items in or affecting commerce" (in H.R. 7897). These statements, on which the whole legislation is based, obviously are incompatible with the risk assessment as discussed in the previous section.

Both bills then conclude that "it is essential in the public interest that the health and welfare of the Nation be protected from such risk" by regulations specified in the bills.

*What Is the Nature of These Regulations?* The facility in which research will be carried on has to be *licensed,* and to apply for such a license (valid for only two or three years) it would be necessary to meet many conditions and to proceed through a lengthy bureaucratic process. The applications would have to be very long, including "a detailed description of the activities to be conducted" (S.1217) or "a thorough description of each recombinant DNA activity to be conducted under the license (including applicable *research hypotheses, designs,* and *protocols*)" (H.R. 7897). Many other conditions would have to be met, including maintenance of detailed medical records, certification of training, monitoring programs, etc. The detailed applications would have to be published in the *Federal Register* (S.1217), and any application review would also be published in the *Federal Register* (H.R. 7897).

After a lengthy review process each application would be approved or disapproved either by a special Federal Commission (S.1217) or by the local Institutional Biohazard Committees, which furthermore would be followed by review on the Federal level by the Secretary of HEW in case of research requiring containment equivalent to P3 or higher (H.R. 7897). The composition of the Commission and Committees is prescribed, requiring a majority of nonscientist members (S.1217), which would have to make highly technical decisions. A special Commission is also proposed in H.R. 7897 which would "conduct a study as to the appropriateness of continuing recombinant DNA activities," "identify the basic ethical and scientific principles," "conduct a comprehensive review and critique," and "make recommendations to the Congress and Secretary of HEW." The purpose of both bills would be first to enforce the NIH guidelines and then to design new rules and regulations specifying how the research should be carried out.

*What Is the Mode of Enforcement of These Bills?* The first kind of enforcement would be the denial, revocation, suspension, or limitation of a license. After the license is issued, the research would be policed by the organization of Federal inspectors, which could enter the facility "upon presenting appropriate credentials" and inspect the "equipment materials, containers, records, files, papers, processes, controls, facilities, and all other things." "No inspector shall be required to obtain a search warrant or warrant for seizure" prior to "entering, inspection or seizure of recombinant DNA." If an inspector "finds material he has reasonable cause to believe is a hazardous product of recombinant DNA activities [the degree of hazard is not defined] he may . . . seize . . . or destroy the material" (S.1217). Analogous inspections are proposed by H.R. 7897 by inspectors appointed by the Secretary.

*What Kind of Punitive Measures Are Proposed?* The penalties for violation of any requirement are fines and imprisonment. In the case of H.R. 7897 the fines are up to $50,000 per day of violation and up to one year of imprisonment, also for each day of violation, but not more than a total of ten years of imprisonment. The highest fine is for knowingly or willfully violating the regulations, e.g., (a) conducting any recombinant DNA activity without license, (b) failing to establish and maintain records, (c) failing to make reports or to provide information, among others. If I read it correctly,[74] "any person who knowingly (or willfully) fails to make a report" on time and delays it for ten days may be liable to a fine up to $500,000 and ten years imprisonment. The punitive measures of S.1217 are lower and amount to only up to $10,000 per day of violation, together with license revocation, suspension, or limitation. There are many other aspects of the enforcement and punitive measures, which would require much more space to discuss in detail.

*State and Local Legislation.* In addition to federal legislative proposals, many state and local bills and ordinances have been either considered, proposed, or even passed. Most of them are restrictive and quite damaging to research, but examples of the positive approach do also exist. For instance, the Dane County Board (county-elected government unit that includes the town of Madison, where the University of Wisconsin is located) proposed the following resolution[76]:

> Whereas, mankind now stands on the threshold of a vast new field of knowledge involving the inheritance and genetics of life, and
> Whereas, this threshold has not been achieved overnight, but, rather through painstaking and tedious research beginning at the turn of the century, and
> Whereas, mankind stands to gain through the understanding of diseases

such as hemophilia, sickle cell anemia and cancer; the improvement of agriculture and most importantly, increases in basic knowledge,

Therefore be it resolved that the Dane County Board of Supervisors does
hereby approve and encourage further research into the field of Recombinant
DNA and hereby opposes attempts to curtail this important area of endeavour,
and

Be it further resolved that a copy of this resolution be sent to Dane County's Congressional delegation.

On the other hand, the mayor of the City of Cambridge, Massachusetts, the site of Harvard University, has adopted a very hostile and irrational attitude, best expressed by his letter, which borders on the ridiculous.[77]

However, the ordinance adopted by the City of Cambridge did not
reflect the nonsensical views of the mayor but still is more restrictive than
even the first published version of the NIH guidelines.

Space does not permit the discussion of other examples of state and
local regulations.

*What Was the Reaction of the Scientific and Other Communities to These
Legislative Proposals?* Among most scientists and other persons who were
familiar with the recombinant DNA technique and took time to study the
bills, the initial reaction was of utmost surprise and disbelief. For instance, the letters to the Congress of the overwhelming majority of participants in several Gordon conferences held in the late summer of 1977
(including the same conference on Nucleic Acids which in 1973 requested
the study of the safety of recombinant DNA research) now voiced grave
concerns about the legislation. The letter from the Nucleic Acids Conference[78] stated: "We are concerned that the benefits of recombinant DNA
research will be denied to society by unnecessarily restrictive legislation.
. . .   We feel that much of the stimulus for this legislative activity derived
from exaggerations of hypothetical hazards of recombinant DNA research that go far beyond any reasoned assessment. . . . The experience
of the last four years has not given any indication of actual hazard. Under
these circumstances, an unprecedented introduction of prior restraints on
scientific inquiry seems unwarranted."

The participants of the Gordon Conference on Biological Regulatory
Mechanisms sent a similar petition to every member of the Congress,[79]
stating

. . . that the bills (H.R. 7418, now 7897 and S.1217), if enacted, impose unjusti-
fiable control over many important areas of scientific inquiry. The result would
be to deny to society and to our country the substantial benefits anticipated for
this research. The experience of the last four years is important. Despite in-

creasingly vigorous search to identify precisely the degree and nature of any actual public health hazard, no indication of actual danger has been uncovered. Instead, many conjectured dangers have been shown not to exist.

The premise (legislative findings) on which these bills are based: "that there is risk that such organisms and viruses [created by the research] may spread quickly and without warning to persons, agricultural plants and products . . . " derives from exaggerations of the hypothetical hazards of recombinant DNA research that go far beyond reasoned assessment.

It is evident to us as scientists that dramatic advances in fundamental knowledge have already emerged from the application of these techniques. We are concerned that the legislative measures under consideration will set up bureaucratic machinery so inflexible and unwieldly as to severely inhibit the development of many fields of knowledge.

Under these circumstances, an unprecedented introduction of prior restraints on scientific inquiry and technological development seems unwarranted and imprudent. It would be unwise to legislate hazard where hazard has not been shown to exist and indeed shown to be improbable. We believe that the proposed legislation might well deprive society of needed improvements in public health, agriculture, industry and environmental protection on behalf of fears that are not rationally based on concrete risks.

This resolution was signed by 140 participants of the conference, and since then about 1000 more persons spontaneously signed this petition with a list of these additional signatures sent to Representative H. O. Staggers, chairman of the House Interstate and Foreign Commerce Committee.

Participants of another conference devoted to virology[80] wrote to Congress on June 27, 1977: " . . . we are concerned that pending legislation to regulate recombinant DNA research will severely curtail advances in our field and associated practical applications of great potential benefit. . . . There never has been any evidence that recombinant DNA poses a hazard to human health or to the environment. . . . We believe that enactment of special legislation to regulate recombinant DNA is unnecessary and unwise." The bills (H.R. 7418, now 7897 and S.1217) "are punitive to the point of intimidation; they establish cumbersome and time-consuming procedures; and the regulatory committees provided for are to consist largely of persons without expertise in the field to be regulated. Passage of either bill in its present form is likely to restrict research in the United States, and as a result impede promising biomedical, pharmaceutical, and agricultural applications."

These excerpts illustrate only a small sample of the reaction to the proposed legislation, which also includes a report of the president of the National Academy of Sciences,[81] an essay on conditions for prohibiting research,[82] and resolutions of many scientific societies, among others.

This reaction of the scientific community received fair coverage by the press and other media, of both the regular[83] and "underground" kind.[84]

At present there are three main approaches used by the opponents of the legislation: (a) opposition to any kind of regulations because they are based on the wrong premises, (b) support of legislation that will have a strong preemption clause as to protect the research from oppressive state and local regulations, and (c) supporting the lesser of any two evils. Because of the latter approach, the Rogers bill H.R. 7897 was initially favored over the S.1217 of Kennedy, and this early but at present unwarranted attitude seems to still be reflected in some recent actions.

*What Was the Response of the Congress?* Perhaps the first significant response was that of Senator G. Nelson,[85] who was the only member of the Senate Committee on Human Resources to vote against S.1217. He states: "I am concerned that S.1217 is unnecessarily burdensome and detrimental to the future of this important biomedical research." He concludes that S.1217 "sets a bad precedent for future restrictive regulation of biomedical research in general. The compliance provisions and paperwork are excessive, possibly unworkable, and particularly burdensome for small businesses. The potential for obstructing research and impeding progress in conquering diseases appears to be much greater than the benefits accruing to the public through provisions of this legislation." Also, Senators Eagleton and Chaffee filed somewhat critical supplemental views on S.1217.[73]

Subsequently, Senator G. Nelson introduced an amendment[86] to S.1217, cosponsored by Senator Moynihan, in the form of a substitute bill which certainly is superior to both S.1217 and H.R. 7897. However, its findings do not assess the risks correctly, it still requires cumbersome licensing, and it provides undesirable enforcement and punitive measures.[86]

The other actions in the Senate include:

1. A major statement by Senator A. Stevenson, Chairman of the Subcommittee on Science and Technology and Space,[87,88] in which he strongly criticizes S.1217, summarizes the history of the concerns about recombinant DNA and the dramatic change in perception of the hypothetical risks. He expresses deep concern also about the freedom of scientific inquiry rooted in the first amendment to the U.S. Constitution, and the Senate's "responsibility to safeguard the conduct of scientific research from unnecessary and unreasonable governmental interven-

tion." He suggests that no legislation on recombinant DNA be enacted until the next session and announces a public hearing of the Subcommittee on Science, Technology and Space "to develop further the relationship between proposed legislation of recombinant DNA research and the constitutional protection of scientific research from unwarranted governmental intervention."

2. These hearings were held on November 2, 8, and 10, 1977, and included testimony by the president of the National Academy of Sciences, the Director of NIH, the President's Science Advisor, and panels of scientists, lawyers, ethicists, representatives of scientific societies, environmentalists, and representatives of industry. The proceedings of these hearings were published (see refs. 94, 95).

3. In a dramatic move on September 28, 1977, Senator Kennedy withdrew his support from S.1217, originally sponsored by him (which was already reported out from his subcommittee and from the Committee on Human Resources), because of the changing assessment of risks of recombinant DNA and the projected lack of necessary votes to pass the bill.[88]

4. Instead of S.1217, Senator Kennedy was planning to introduce a very short interim bill designed only to endorse the NIH guidelines, but its early draft[89] still contains its original findings, which are at odds with the present assessment of the risks. This proposal does not contain a preemption clause. Moreover, his plans include creation of a commission which would evaluate the state of the art and propose future legislation.

5. Senator H. Schmitt (R-NM) introduced a more general bill (S.2267), which would establish a two-year nongovernmental study commission to evaluate the risks and benefits of research in general and of the recombinant DNA technique in particular.[90,91]

In the U.S. House of Representatives there were fewer changes during the last few months, since Congressman Rogers and his staff were tenaciously supporting their bill H.R.7897,[74] which was reported out of Rogers's Subcommittee on Health and the Environment but was blocked in the Committee on Interstate and Foreign Commerce by its chairman, H. O. Staggers, who is preparing a simple new bill with more realistic findings which endorses the NIH guidelines and includes a strong preemption clause against local regulations. Any House bill emerging from the Commerce Committee would most probably have to go through the R. Thornton Subcommittee and the Committee on Science and Technology chaired by Congressman O. E. Teague, who already has held extensive hearings on the recombinant DNA technique.[92]

*What Is the Present (December 1977) Status of Legislation?* This simplified review of Congressional activities shows the tremendous change in attitude caused by active involvement of informed members of the scientific community in the legislative process. Whereas as late as in August 1977 it appeared to many political "experts" that the restrictive legislation would rapidly and almost unanimously pass through both Houses, at present one major bill (S.1217) has been transformed into a short amendment,[89] several more appropriate and much simpler bills have either been introduced or are in preparation, and the last bastion of restrictive legislation (H.R. 7897) has probably no chances for passage or even reaching the floor of the House. One may conclude that, as the end of 1977 approaches, the recombinant DNA legislation is in disarray.[91] From a logical point of view this should not be surprising, since the legislative proposals represent an effort to protect the public from "dangers" that do not exist from the practical point of view.

*What Would Be the Ideal Form of Legislation?* In view of the present benefit/risk assessment and the absence of any proven dangers, there is little if any reason for legislation of recombinant DNA activities. However, the public concerns, the enforcement of the NIH guidelines within some but not all research areas, and the unpredictable local legislative activities, all act as incentives for creating federal legislation.

If proposed, such legislation should be very simple and limited to the following features:

1. There should be a strong preemption clause regarding all state and local regulations.

2. The legislation should encompass recombinant DNA activities in all sectors and at first should mandate comprehensive benefit/risk assessment studies similar to those proposed by Senator Schmitt.[90]

3. On the basis of such studies, special advisory committees should design several sets of guidelines, each for individual areas of recombinant DNA activities, separately for research (medical, agricultural, ecological, industrial, etc.), for agriculture and for manufacturing activities (pharmaceutical, chemical and fermentation industries, agriculture, etc.) The guidelines should be very simple, creating no interference with research and including only those kinds of novel recombinant DNA experiments where the risks are possible to define, e.g., actual synthesis of potent polypeptide toxins or known serious pathogenic properties of the particu-

lar host-vector system. Most of the novel recombinant DNA experiments employing well-explored host-vector systems (e.g., *E. coli* and EK2 vectors) should be outside any regulations.

4. Filing of a simple one-page registration form with the NIH Office for Recombinant DNA Activities should be the only requirement for research activities. Such registration should (a) list names and addresses of all investigators, (b) specify the species and kind of DNA cloned, (c) specify the host-vector system, (d) specify physical containment, (e) state the purpose of the experiments, (f) state the period covered by the registration, and (g) include a statement that the specific guidelines will be followed. Such registration would have to be filed just prior to the initiation of the experiments, but no specific approval would be required (see ref. 55, Comments, pp. 45-47).

5. The NIH Office for Recombinant DNA Activities and the special advisory committees that designed the guidelines should follow the registered research and *promptly* modify the guidelines and other requirements, relaxing them when no risks materialize or strengthening them when new evidence indicates that some hypothetical dangers might likely materialize. Thus the regulations should incorporate a procedure for *variances* from the regulations on either an ad hoc or a class basis.[70] Such variances permit instant flexibility, while at the same time preserving adequate public protection.

6. The legislation should have a sunset clause.

## DANGERS OF LEGISLATION AND REGULATIONS OF THE RECOMBINANT DNA TECHNIQUE

In a democratic society, the purpose of regulations is to protect the public from clearly defined risks. For example, legislation and ensuing regulations are designed for protecting from the danger of death or injury by the automobile or other machines and tools; from poisoning by toxic or carcinogenic chemicals, drugs, or foodstuffs; from injury by various sources of radiation; and from many other agents that were shown to be harmful. However, society has chosen to limit these regulations as to either tolerate some harmful agents or reduce the harm to tolerable levels instead of completely eliminating it. One could question the soundness of some of these decisions: (a) For instance, why is an activity as useless and harmful as smoking tolerated and even subsidized? (b) Why is the use of alcohol, which leads to addiction in 20% of users, not only socially acceptable but even glorified in books, periodicals, movies, and television? (c) And why is the automobile, which kills 50,000 Americans each year, which maims many more, which pollutes our environment, and which depletes scarce fuel resources, idolized and promoted as a symbol of the good life? Apparently, not only the risks but also a risk-to-benefit ratio govern the social acceptance of risks, even when the benefits are very questionable.

Against this background, the regulation of recombinant DNA activities, for which no risk was ever demonstrated and for which the hypothetical risks are of no practical concern, appears totally at odds with the accepted response of our democratic society to other risks. Obviously, what governs the reasons for regulations are not the practical risks but public apprehensions or rather misapprehensions about the risks. Thus we are treading here on very dangerous ground, trying to regulate imaginary dangers where no practical dangers exist. This kind of regulation was possible under totalitarian rule when the edicts of the dictator were not allowed to be questioned, or in medieval times when superstitions and religious dogmas were of ultimate importance. The only recent example of official application of safety measures against purely speculative dangers was the quarantine of the astronauts returning from the moon voyage.[9] This measure was contrary to common sense and to simple scientific fact that microorganisms pathogenic to man could not have developed under inhospitable lunar conditions and in the absence of the human host. As predicted, such quarantine was proved unnecessary but was quite costly. Monetary costs, however, seemed to matter little in the Apollo program.

At this time of declining support for science, the costs of unnecessary regulatory activities could be quite detrimental to scientific research and thus should be carefully considered and compared with the redeeming aspects of any regulations.

The dangers of legislation and regulation as pertaining to recombinant DNA could be classified into several broad groups, which will be discussed in more detail: (a) political dangers, including loss of some of our constitutional freedoms, creation of laws that invite disrespect, and misleading of the public; (b) depleting and misdirecting fiscal and human scientific resources; (c) fostering bureaucracy and policing basic scientific research; (d) denying or delaying the benefits of research to society; (e) misdirecting legitimate environmental concerns and other beneficial measures.

## POLITICAL DANGERS

*Freedom of inquiry.* The concept of the freedom of inquiry has been developing for several hundred years, and one hopes we have reached the point where no scientific ideas and concepts will be restricted simply out of fear of the ideas themselves. As cited at the beginning of this chapter, the freedom inquiry is guaranteed by the First Amendment to the U.S. Constitution. Any abridgment of this freedom is a very grave matter, and certainly should not be exercised under the pretext of protecting the public from totally unproven hypothetical risks. This was eloquently stressed by Senator Stevenson,[87] DeWitt Stetten, deputy director of science, NIH,[93] and the president of the National Academy of Sciences, Dr. P. Handler.[94-96] Also, as far back as in 1894, the Board of Regents of the University of Wisconsin made a statement treasured by the students and faculty: "Whatever may be the limitations which trammel inquiry elsewhere, we believe that the Great State of Wisconsin should ever encourage that continual and fearless sifting and winnowing by which alone the truth can be found," as stressed in Smithies's testimony.[97] We need to accept no constraints other than those absolutely essential and well documented.

*Laws that invite disrespect.* Since the proposed regulations concerning the recombinant DNA technique have no sound scientific basis, but mainly express the beliefs and concerns of not well-informed persons, they would not be generally accepted by knowledgeable scientists and would therefore require strong enforcement to the point of intimidation. This point was already stressed by Hopson, who observed that "among young graduate students and postdoctorates it seemed almost chic not to know the NIH rules."[98] History is replete with examples of fights against unreasonable rules, and it would be tragic to deliberately create new such examples. Not everybody will be inclined to follow the example of Socrates, who sacrificed his own life in respect for the law.

*Misleading the Public.* Setting a precedent for regulating and enforcing regulations against risks that cannot be documented would invite many more such laws against any activity simply disliked by any outspoken group or political organization. The dangers of such actions to our democratic systems are obvious. Moreover, regulations always beget more regulations, despite the present public outcry against excessive regulations.[99] Such laws would also mislead the public and might result in serious apprehensions and fears, since the existence of regulations might be equated with the existence of real dangers. As stated by Handler,[96] it is a difficult problem for the layman, even an interested one, who has not been professionally close to the field of recombinant DNA, "to obtain some sense of where the bulk of informed opinion really lies, to distinguish statements of facts from assertions and indeed from science fiction."

Several books that pertain to recombinant DNA were recently published.[100] They provide some useful information but also some misinformation (especially Howard and Rifkin, reviewed by Szybalski), as pointed out by the reviewers.[100] Especially pertinent to the subject of this subsection are the reviews by Brenner, Harris, May, and Medawar.[100] The Nobel laureate Medawar sympathizes "with laymen and legislators who are trying to make sense of this whole strange farrago of pipedreams and nightmares."[100] But he states that "for their excess of fearfulness, laymen have only themselves to blame, and their nightmares are a judgement upon them for a deep-seated scientific illiteracy which manifests itself in two ways": (1) the public allow themselves "to be dupes of that form of *science fiction* which is our modern equivalent of the Gothic romances," and (2) "even educated laymen have no idea of the very wide gap between *conception* and *execution* in science," with the execution already depending on "political" decisions. He stresses that all great advances in civilization are based on *confidence,* and that "short of abolishing the scientific profession altogether no legislation can ever be enforced that will seriously impede the scientists' determination to come to a deeper understanding of the material world."[100]

*Other Political Dangers.* Politicizing science is another danger, since it leads to a new kind of adversary relationship and detracts scientists from their primary goal of pursuing knowledge. It invites scientists to turn informers and to accuse each other in the name of hypothetical risks or political beliefs, as occurred, e.g., during the "trial-in-absentia" press conference called by Mr. Leslie Dach at NIH on December 15, 1977, as reported by the media.[101] Even the legislative drafts invite informing, by stating "whenever a bona fide request for an inspection is made by any person . . . , that there is a hazardous product of recombinant DNA activities present, an inspection shall immediately be conducted" [S.1217, Sec. 1806(e)(2)].[72,73] The danger of intimidation by such wholesale "immediate" inspection is obvious. Another example is Senator Stevenson's hearings,[94,95] where scientists, who employed the safest plasmid in their very beneficial and practically risk-free research on cloning of the insulin genes, were chastised[102] for using their best judgment, simply because due to bureaucratic delays the safer plasmid, though approved by the advisory committee, was not finally certified until several months later.[103] When referring to these incidents,[94,95,98,101] J. Watson said "we have had enormous attention paid to people having evaded the Guidelines" and facetiously compared the scientific significance of the guidelines to that of the tiddlywinks game, by remarking "we should be careful of the federal penalties we impose on people who cheat at tiddlywinks."[60]

Furthermore, history teaches us about the many dangers of politicizing science, with examples being the activities of the Holy Inquisition and the tribulations of Copernicus and Galileo Galilei, the infamous Scopes trial pertaining to the teaching of evolution, and the Lysenko affair.[7,9,83] These few examples show how dangerous it is to base laws on metaphysical, theological, and mystical grounds, or on some political doctrine. Drawing absurd analogies to science fiction, like the novel *The Andromeda Strain,*[37] or the series of movies on the Frankenstein monster, is also a poor reason for legislation, and it invites ridiculous actions, as the already cited letter from Cambridge mayor Vellucci,[77] and the attempt to regulate nature itself.

## DEPLETING AND MISDIRECTING FISCAL AND HUMAN SCIENTIFIC RESOURCES

Since scientific resources are not unlimited, regulations would cause a serious decrease in many beneficial scientific activities. The direct cost of administering and enforcing the regulation would run into many millions of dollars (see the estimates in ref. 73) charged directly or indirectly to the scientific budget. Physical containment facilities are very expensive, even if unnecessary, and the cost of regulated research would skyrocket.[104] Even more damaging would be the loss of the productive time of many scientists, who now would have to fill out myriads of forms, defend their research, and participate in unnecessary committee work and other bureaucratic activities.[85] This would lead to another more permanent danger, namely that many young scientists would avoid the areas of research fraught with such controversial regulations and their intellectual contribution to this important area of science would be permanently lost. The result would be the crippling of an important and beneficial area of human endeavor.[40,51]

## FOSTERING BUREAUCRACY AND POLICING BASIC SCIENTIFIC RESEARCH

As far as research is concerned, most of the bureaucracy at present is associated with distribution of funds. The regulation of recombinant DNA activities would add several novel dimensions to the bureaucracy, namely, licensing, scrutiny, and approval of each experiment and inspections, enforcement, and general policing of the daily laboratory routine. Obviously, this is not only distasteful but also unworkable for the very sensitive creative process.[86,87] It appears easy to expose the true dangers of a surrealistic scenario, in which eager inspectors are trying to identify and control the imaginary risks while enforcing the regulations by "seizing and destroying" the "dangerous" recombinant DNA and reporting lax scientists to the judicial authorities. In this context, Zimmerman in his analysis of the legislative alternatives sponsored by the House of Representatives points out that the inspections, as proposed by legislative drafts, "sound bureaucratically ominous" and that the "inspectors trooping into a University research lab would no doubt be welcomed with the warmth and cordiality befitting a midnight raid by the Gestapo."[105]

## DENYING OR DELAYING THE BENEFITS OF RESEARCH TO SOCIETY

Many substantial benefits of the recombinant DNA techniques were already listed. Denying or delaying any of these would exact a high price in lives needlessly shortened or lost and in prolonged human misery. Many examples could be cited but just one will be mentioned, namely, research on safe and effective vaccines, which are unavailable at present. For instance, no vaccine exists for Herpes II virus, which causes a very painful, debilitating, dangerous, and rather common disease, especially in women.[57] The traditional approach, i.e., the use of attenuated or killed Herpes II as a vaccine, would be very risky and unacceptable because the virus transforms cells in vitro, indicating its carcinogenic potential. On the other hand, the recombinant DNA technique could be the means of producing either a pure, well-defined, and safe antigenic complex or specific antibodies, the latter to be used for passive immunization. Unfortunately, the present guidelines either prohibit such studies or make them very cumbersome. Many examples of other vaccines and lifesaving human proteins, which would be studied or produced by applying the recombinant DNA technique, could be cited.[13]

As discussed by Eisenberg,[19] there is a great similarity between the current recombinant DNA controversy and the criticism encountered by

Louis Pasteur in his work on developing the antirabies vaccine. The following excerpts are cited from the article entitled "M. Pasteur's Dog Kennels," as published in 1884[106]: "M. Pasteur is not lucky. The city of Meudon has already vigorously protested against the creation of the dog kennels of this eminent scientist. Now the surrounding communes also protest . . . [and] appeal to the Senate in order to stop the realization of this project." If these protests (similar to present-day local ordinances against recombinant DNA activities) had succeeded, the development of vaccines might have been blocked or delayed. This historical perspective and analogy are quite frightening.

## MISDIRECTING LEGITIMATE ENVIRONMENTAL CONCERNS

The uncontrolled increase in our population and in industrial activities seriously threatens our environment and hence the quality of life. The environmental concerns are very real and of utmost importance. The recombinant DNA technique could be useful in solving certain environmental problems, by adapting microorganisms to destroy specific pollutants or by permitting conversion of "dirty" chemical technologies to "clean" enzymatic ones. In the latter context, any improvement in the efficiency of biological nitrogen fixation would decrease our reliance on the chemical synthesis of nitrogen fertilizers.

It is erroneous and tragic, therefore, that several respectable environmental movements, e.g., the Sierra Club and the Environmental Defense Fund, spend their time, funds, and effort to publicly oppose research employing the recombinant DNA technique and to advocate restrictive regulations.[55,73,94,107] This is a shocking example of misdirected and misplaced priorities, where resources are limited and the need for saving our environment so great. This is also an example of how the public and environmental groups were misled by scenarios of imaginary dangers, whereas it is well known, as already discussed, that *E. coli* species are not endowed with the capacity to propagate in nature outside the gut, and *E. coli* K-12, especially EK2, is adapted neither to the gut nor to environments other than special laboratory media.[20,63]

## ADDENDUM

### TWO NEW 1978 LEGISLATIVE PROPOSALS

Representatives Staggers and Rogers introduced new bill H.R. 11192 on February 28, 1978 (Recombinant DNA Act), and Senator Kennedy proposed another bill in the form of an amendment to S.1217 on March 1, 1978 (Recombinant DNA Act of 1978). Since these two proposals have much in common, they can be discussed together. Their main purpose is to temporarily extend the NIH guidelines to all sectors and convert them into regulations, while at the same time to establish a commission to study recombinant DNA research and propose future regulations.

The findings section of these bills stresses the great benefits of the research but still draws attention to the epidemiological dangers of recombinant DNA by stating that "there is a risk that any such potentially hazardous organisms or viruses may spread quickly and without warning to persons, agricultural plants and products, and other items affecting commerce," although such epidemiological dangers are now known to be nonexistent. It would be pathetic to include in the bills a patently incorrect assessment, and this needlessly alarming statement should be deleted.

While specifying the original version of the NIH guidelines of July 7, 1976, as the basis of the legislation, the bills permit the Secretary of the HEW to modify the guidelines and to exempt "any recombinant DNA activity which the Secretary finds does not present a significant risk to health or the environment," providing that such changes and their basis will be published in the *Federal Register*. Any such change, however, might take years, as based on the present experience with modifying the NIH guidelines. Therefore, instead of incorrectly assuming that a given human activity is guilty of being dangerous until proven otherwise (which is against the spirit of any responsible legislation), the proposal should be changed by requiring the secretary first to assess the risks of both (a) the recombinant DNA activities and (b) withholding the benefits due to time-consuming regulations. "Only those recombinant DNA activities which the Secretary finds do present significant practical risks to health and the environment" should then be included in the regulations based on H.R. 11192 and S.1217. It would be ridiculous and tragic to regulate and hamper beneficial research for many years to come where no practical risks exist, other than imaginary scenarios currently persisting only in the minds of a few alarmists.

The secretary would have to issue regulations concerning procedures for registration of the projects and their enforcement, and this would probably become an expensive and wasteful bureaucracy, as judged from the present attempts to enforce the NIH guidelines. Penalties up to $5000 per each day of violations will be assessed against persons who would "fail or refuse to (a) establish and maintain records, (b) make reports or provide information, or (c) permit entry or inspection."

Both bills provide for creation of special inspection teams, with inspectors not required to obtain search or inspection warrants, allowed to take samples of recombinant DNA materials or to "order the recombinant DNA or materials detained" if the inspector has reason to believe that a violation occurred or that the research "presents a significant risk to health or the environment." It is difficult to imagine how the inspectors would assess the significance of imaginary risks that do not exist from the practical point of view. No expertise exists for assessing and handling imaginary dangers since the Middle Ages or witch hunting and trials of the past centuries.

The main differences between the bills are in the preemption clause and in the composition of the Commission. H.R. 11192 proposes that no state or its subdivisions "may establish or continue in effect any requirement for the regulation of recombinant DNA activities," unless they follow a special procedure, show a good cause, and their application is approved by the Secretary of HEW. There is no such preemption clause in the amended S.1217, an omission which might invite new local regulation.

The "Commission for the Study of Research and Technology Involving Genetic Manipulation," as proposed in S.1217, shall consist of 11 members appointed by the Secretary of HEW with a majority of six "who are not and have never been professionally engaged in biological research." Within 30 months the Commission should present a report to the Secretary of HEW, concerning (a) the "current state of knowledge of the dangers," (b) "evaluation of whether the Federal guidelines are needed and, if needed, whether they are adequate," (c) "likely directions" of the research and its risks, (d) "role of the public" and local governments, (e) long-term applications in "medicine, pharmacology, immunology, industrial fermentation and agriculture," (f) "ethical, moral, social, economic and political implications," and (g) "current and anticipated industrial applications."

The Commission, as proposed in H.R. 11192, shall consist of 13 members selected by the Secretary of HEW "from individuals distinguished in the fields of medicine, law, ethics, the biological, physical and environmental sciences, philosophy, humanities, health administration, government and public affairs." The 30-month deadline and charges are similar, but without specifying "evaluation of whether Federal guidelines are needed" (as in the S.1217 amendment), but stressing more "the need for an expansion of the scope of such controls."

As already mentioned, any charge to the commission should include not only evaluation of the risks of the recombinant DNA activities, but also of potential damages caused by unneeded regulations and ensuing bureaucracy. The waste of taxpayers' money; prolongation of human misery due to delays in highly beneficial medical, environmental, agricultural, and other applications; crippling of research by misdirecting of the efforts and discouraging scientists (especially the young ones) from entering the field; and the general damage to the freedom of inquiry—all should be carefully considered and evaluated by the commission.

As compared with the analogous 1977 legislative proposals, the new bills appear more reasonable on first sight but will most probably result in very restrictive and highly bureaucratic regulations, as already happened in the case of the regulations designed to enforce the present NIH guidelines. Bill H.R. 11192 has already been reported out of the Interstate and Foreign Commerce Committee with only a few amendments and out of the Committee on Science and Technology. [107a] No action has as yet been taken in the Senate. It is too early to predict whether this unneeded legislation will be adopted and in what form, especially since H.R. 11192, if approved by the House with the present strong preemption clause, most probably will not be acceptable to Senator Kennedy. [108]

## NEW 1978 NIH GUIDELINES

Very profound changes in the proposed guidelines were revealed and discussed during the April 27-29, 1978 meeting of the NIH Recombinant DNA Advisory Committee (RAC). These include (1) drastic downgrading of the physical containment, especially for cloning of viral DNA, (2) excluding from the guidelines all cloning in E. coli host-vector systems of DNA from those species that exchange their genes or plasmids with E. coli, (3) analogous exclusion for other prokaryotic host-vector systems, (4) delegation of the M.U.A. approvals to the local Institutional Biosafety Committees without the necessity of delaying research until receiving approval from the NIH, and (5) authorization for the Director of NIH to exempt from the guidelines all other classes of recombinant DNA that "do not present a significant risk to health or the environment" on the recommendation of RAC after appropriate notice and opportunity for public comment. Very significant also was a profound change in attitude toward the hypothetical risks, as expressed both by the NIH Administration and the RAC members. In his introduction Dr. D. S. Fredrickson, Director of NIH, stressed that no dangers have materialized and urged RAC members to make recommendations based only on scientific appraisal and not on apprehensions. He also stressed the latest assessment of the hypothetical risks for viral recombinant DNA[109] and asked that the guidelines be downgraded accordingly. The resignation statement[110] of the venerable chairman of RAC, Dr. DeWitt Stetten, was also very revealing and moving. He admitted being greatly troubled by many aspects of the attempts to regulate recombinant DNA research, starting with the Asilomar Conference, which he compared to a religious revival meeting, and ending with possible legislation. Another "religious" aspect was the criticism that early drafts of the NIH guidelines violated the "spirit of Asilomar."

The new draft of these guidelines was just published,[111] and after a 60-day period for public comment, including public hearings on September 15, 1978, and then another discussion within RAC, its final version should be signed by the Director of NIH and published in the *Federal Register* sometime in November 1978. Hopefully, in a few years all regulations governing use of the recombinant DNA technique in basic research will be abandoned.

## ACKNOWLEDGMENTS

The author is greatly indebted to many persons who supplied him with pertinent information, unpublished manuscripts, legislative drafts, and who critically read the manuscript or its parts. I am afraid that this list is far from complete, but I would like to thank Dr. Philip H. Abelson, Dr. E. S. Anderson, Dr. Daryl Banks, Dr. Jon Beckwith, Dr. Paul Berg, Dr. Fred R. Blattner, Dr. Robert Bock, Dr. Tom Brock, Congressman Clarence J. Brown, Dr. Robert H. Burris, Dr. Daniel Callahan, Dr. Allan Campbell, Representative Dr. Tim Lee Carter, Dr. Stan N. Cohen, Dr. Roy Curtiss, III, Dr. Peter Dans, Dr. Bernard D. Davis, Dr. L. Eisenberg, Dr. Lynn Enquist, Dr. Stanley Falkow, Congressman James J. Florio, Dr. S. Formal, Dr. Donald S. Fredrickson, Dr. Rolf Freter, Dr. Jonathan Gallant, Dr. W. J. Gartland, Jr., Dr. P. Gemski, Jr., Dr. S. L. Gorbach, Dr. C. Grobstein, Dr. H. Halvorson, Dr. Philip Handler, Dr. Phil E. Hartman, Senator S. I. Hayakawa, Mr. Dennis Helms, Esq., Congressman Harold C. Hollenbeck, Dr. Lawrence Horowitz, Dr. Thomas H. Jukes, Senator Edward M. Kennedy, Dr. Jon King, Dr. Arthur Kelman, Dr. P. Leder, Dr. James M. McCullough, Dr. Lois K. Miller, Dr. Bruce Molholt, Dr. Mario Molina, Representative Charles Mosher, Mr. Don Moulton, Senator G. Nelson, Dr. Thomas C. Nelson, Ms. Nan Nixon, Speaker Thomas P. O'Neill, Jr., Dr. F. Ørskov, Dr. Gail Pesyna, Ms. Nancy Pfund, Dr. Lennart Philipson, Mr. J. Thomas Ratchford, Dr. Bill Reznikoff, Dr. M. H. Richmond, Congressman Matthew J. Rinaldo, Congressman Paul Rogers, Dr. Judith Robinson, Dr. Wally Rowe, Dr. William J. Rutter, Congressman David

Satterfield, Congressman James Scheuer, Senator Harrison H. Schmitt, Dr. Julius Schultz, Senator Richard S. Schweiker, Dr. Margery Shaw, Dr. Maxine Singer, Dr. Ann Skalka, Congressman Joe Skubitz, Dr. Dieter Soll, Congressman H. O. Staggers, Mr. John Stewart, Dr. Hans DeWitt Stetten, Senator Adlai E. Stevenson, Dr. Bernard Strauss, Congressman Ray Thornton, Dr. John Tooze, Dr. LeRoy Walters, Dr. R. W. Watkins, Dr. James Watson, Congressman Henry A. Waxman, Dr. Charles Weiner, Dr. Charles Yanofsky and Dr. Burke Zimmerman. Special thanks for editing this chapter are due to Dr. Elizabeth H. Szybalski. This chapter was prepared during the tenure of National Cancer Institute Grant CA-07175.

## REFERENCES AND NOTES

1. Ayala, F., The stability of biological species, in ref. 16, pp. 90-97; Shapiro, J. A., 1977, DNA insertion elements and the evolution of chromosome primary structure, *Trends in Biochem.* **2**:176-180; Szybalski, W., and Szybalski, E. H., 1974, Visualization of the evolution of viral genomes, *in: Viruses, Evolution and Cancer* (E. Kurstak and K. Maramorosch, eds.), pp. 563-582, Academic Press, New York.

2. Bukhari, A. I., Shapiro, J. A., and Adhya, S. L., eds., 1977, *DNA Insertion Elements, Plasmids, and Episomes*, Cold Spring Harbor Laboratory, Cold Spring Harbor, N.Y.

3. Watson, J. D., 1976, *Molecular Biology of the Gene*, 3rd ed., W. A. Benjamin, New York.

4. Campbell, A. M., 1976, How viruses insert their DNA into the DNA of the host cell, *Scientific American* **235**:102-113.

5. Cohen, S. N., 1975, The manipulation of genes, *Scientific American* **233**:3-11; Helling, R. B., 1975, Eukaryotic genes in prokaryotic cells, in: *Stadler Genet. Symp.* (Columbia: University of Missouri) 7:15-36.

6. Cohen, S. N., 1977, Recombinant DNA: Facts and fiction, *Science* **195**:654-657; Sinsheimer, R., 1977, Recombinant DNA, *Ann. Rev. Biochem.* **46**:415-438; Abelson, J., 1977, Recombinant DNA: Examples of present-day research, *Science* **196**:159-160; Primrose, S. B., 1977, Genetic engineering, *Sci. Progr. Oxford* **64**:293-321; Murray, K., 1976, Biochemical manipulation of genes, *Endeavour* **35**:129-133.

7. Davis, B. D., 1976, Evolution, epidemiology, and recombinant DNA, *Science* **193**:442; Davis, B. D., 1977, The recombinant DNA scenarios: Andromeda strain, chimera, and Golem, *American Scientist* **65**:547-555; see also ref. 92, pp. 251-259.

8. Lederberg, J., 1975, DNA splicing: Will fear rob us of its benefits? *Prism* **November**:33-37.

9. Szybalski, W., 1977, Safety in recombinant DNA research, *Gene* **1**:1-2.

10. Grobstein, C., 1977, The recombinant-DNA debate, *Scientific American* **237**:22-33.

11. Philipson, L., and Tiollais, P., 1977, Rational containment of recombinant DNA, *Nature* **268**:90-91.

12. Singer, M., 1977, A summary of the National Institutes of Health (USA) Guidelines for recombinant DNA research, *Gene* **1**:123-139.

13. National Institutes of Health, Office of the Director, *Final Environmental Impact Statement on NIH Guidelines for Research Involving Recombinant DNA Molecules*, Parts 1 and 2, DHEW Publication (NIH) 1489 and 1490 (Bethesda, Md.: NIH, October 1977); Grimwade, S., 1977, Recombinant DNA, *Nature* **270**:291.

14. Beers, R. F., Jr., and Bassett, E. G., eds., 1977, *Recombinant Molecules: Impact on Science and Society*, Raven Press, New York.

15. Schultz, J., and Brada, Z., eds., 1977, *Genetic Manipulation as it Affects the Cancer Problem*, Miami Winter Symposia Series, Vol. 14, Academic Press, New York.
16. *Research with Recombinant DNA*, 1977, An Academy Forum, National Academy of Sciences, Washington, D.C.
17. Singer, M. F., 1977, The recombinant DNA debate, *Science* **196**:127.
18. Recombinant DNA Issue, 1977, *Science* **196**:159-221.
19. Eisenberg, L., 1977, The social imperatives of medical research, *Science* **198**:1105-1110.
20. Williams-Smith, H., 1975, Survival of orally administered *E. coli* K-12 in alimentary tract of man, *Nature* **255**:500-502; Anderson, E. S., 1975, Viability of, and transfer of a plasmid from *Escherichia coli* K-12 in the human intestine, *Nature* **255**:502-504.
21. Curtiss, R., III, Pereira, D. A., Hsu, J. C., Hull, S. C., Clark, J. E., Maturin, L. J., Sr., Goldschmidt, R., Moody, R., Inoue, M., and Alexander, L., Biological containment: The subordination of *Escherichia coli* K-12, in ref. 14, pp. 45-56.
22. Szybalski, W., 1976, Genetic and molecular map of *Escherichia coli* bacteriophage lambda (λ), *in: Handbook of Biochemistry and Molecular Biology* (G. D. Fasman, ed.), 3rd ed., Nucleic Acids, Vol. II, pp. 677-685, CRC Press, Cleveland.
23. Levin, B., 1977, *Gene Expression*, Vol. 3, *Plasmid and Phages*, Wiley, New York.
24. Szybalski, W., Safety of coliphage lambda vectors carrying foreign genes, in ref. 14, pp. 137-150.
25. Enquist, L., and Szybalski, W., 1978, Coliphage lambda as a safe vector for recombinant DNA experiments, *in: Viruses and Environment* (E. Kurstak and K. Maramorosch, eds.), Academic Press, New York.
26. Itakura, K., Hirose, T., Crea, R., Riggs, A. D., Heyneker, H. L., Bolivar, F., and Boyer, H. W., 1977, Expression in *Escherichia coli* of a chemically synthesized gene for the hormone somatostatin, *Science* **198**:1056-1063.
27. Efstratiadis, A., Kafatos, F. C., and Maniatis, T., 1977, The primary structure of rabbit β-globin mRNA as determined from cloned DNA, *Cell* **10**:571-585.
28. Glover, D. M., White, R. L., Finnegan, D. J., and Hogness, D. S., 1975, Characterization of cloned DNA from *Drosphila melanogaster*, including one that contains the genes for RNA, *Cell* **5**:149-157; Grunstein, M., and Hogness, D. S., 1975, Colony hybridization: A method for the isolation of cloned DNAs that contain a specific gene, *Proc. Natl. Acad. Sci. USA* **72**:3961-3965.
29. Struhl, K., Cameron, J. R., and Davis, R. W., 1976 Functional genetic expression of eukaryotic DNA in *Escherichia coli*, *Proc. Natl. Acad. Sci. USA* **73**:1471-1475; Cameron, J. R., and Davis, R. W., 1977, The effects of *E. coli* and yeast DNA insertions on the growth of lambda bacteriophage, *Science* **196**:212-215; Carbon, J., Ratzkin, B., Clarke, L., and Richardson, D., 1977, The expression of yeast DNA in *Escherichia coli, in: Molecular Cloning of Recombinant DNA*, pp. 59-72, Academic Press, New York.
30. Struhl, K., and Davis, R. W., 1977, Production of a functional eukaryotic enzyme in *E. coli*; cloning and expression of the yeast structural gene for imidazole glycerol phosphate dehydratase (*his3*), *Proc. Natl. Acad. Sci. USA* **74**:5255-5259; and personal communication.
31. Williamson, B., 1977, DNA insertions and gene structure, *Nature* **270**:295-297.
32. Seeburg, P. H., Shrine, J., Martial, J. A., Baxter, J. D., and Goodman, H. M., 1977, Nucleotide sequence and amplification in bacteria of the structural gene for rat growth hormone, *Nature* **270**:486-494; Shrine, J., Seeburg, P. H., Martial, J. A., Baxter, J. D., and Goodman, H. M., 1977, Construction and analysis of recombinant DNA for human chorionic somatomammotropin, *Nature* **270**:494-499.
33. McClements, W., and Skalka, A. M., 1977, Analysis of chicken ribosomal RNA genes and construction of lambda hybrids containing gene fragments, *Science* **196**:195-197; McReynolds, L. A., Catterall, J. F., and O'Malley, B. W., 1977, The ovalbumin gene: Cloning of a complete ds-cDNA in a bacterial plasmid, *Gene* **2**:217-231.

34. Tonegawa, S., Brack, C., Hozumi, N., and Schuller, R., 1977, Cloning of an immuno-globulin variable region gene from mouse embryo, *Proc. Natl. Acad. Sci. USA* **74**:3518-3522.

35. Ullrich, A., Shine, J., Chirgwin, J., Pictet, R., Tischer, E., Rutter, W. J., and Goodman, H. M., 1977, Rat insulin genes: Construction of plasmids containing the coding sequences, *Science* **196**:1313-1319.

36. Friello, D. A., Mylroie, J. R., and Chakravorty, A. M., 1976, Use of genetically engineered multi-plasmid microorganisms for rapid degradation of fuel hydrocarbons, *in: Proceeding of the Third International Biodegradation Symposium* (J. M. Sharpley and A. M. Kaplan, eds.), pp. 205-214, Applied Science Publishers, London.

37. Crichton, M., 1969, *The Andromeda Strain*, Knopf, New York.

38. Singer, M., and Soll, D., 1973, Guidelines for DNA hybrid molecules, *Science* **181**:1114.

39. Berg, P., Baltimore, D., Boyer, H. W., Cohen, S. N., Davis, R. W., Hogness, D. S., Nathans, D., Roblin, R., Watson, J. D., Weissman, S., and Zinder, N. D., 1974, Potential biohazards of recombinant DNA molecules, *Science* **185**:303; and *Proc. Natl. Acad. Sci. USA* **71**:2593-2594.

Personal communications from the signatories and their close associates point to various motives behind this letter, which include genuine concern, ambition to be a cosigner of a historical document, eagerness to demonstrate the social responsibility of biologists in contrast to the failure of atomic physicists to issue a similar warning, delaying the imminent participation of a large number of scientists in this field, and "liberal guilt."[40] With the present better knowledge of the benefits versus the virtual absence of any practical risk, such a letter would not have been written, at least not for the *E. coli* K-12 host-vector systems.

40. Watson, J., 1977, In defense of DNA, *The New Republic*, June 25, pp. 11-14.

41. Berg, P., Baltimore, D., Brenner, S., Roblin R., and Singer, M. F., 1975, Summary statement of the Asilomar conference on recombinant DNA molecules, *Proc. Natl. Acad. Sci. USA* **72**:1981-1984; *Nature* **255**:442-444; *Science* **188**:991-994.

42. Cavalieri, L. F., 1976, New strains of life—or death, *The New York Times Magazine*, August 22, pp. 8-9, 58-59, 62, 64, 67-68.

43. Sinsheimer, R., 1975 Troubled dawn for genetic engineering, *New Scientist* **October**:148-151.

44. Wald, G., 1976, The case against genetic engineering, *The Sciences* **16**:6-11; and the answer by Ptashne, M., 1976, The defense doesn't rest, *The Sciences* **16**:11-12; see also ref. 92, pp. 239-247.

45. Chargaff, E., 1976, On the dangers of genetic meddling, *Science* **192**:938-940.

46. Auerbach, S., 1976, Scientists split on rules for genetic experiments, *The Washington Post*, February 10, A2; Beware of those who muck about in genes, *The Economist* **26**:79; Bishop, J. E., 1976, Stiff curbs on gene-transplant research are urged by Michigan University panel, *The Wall Street Journal*, March 23, p. 12; Curbs put on tinkering with genetics, *Globe-Democrat*, St. Louis, Mo., June 24.

47. Faculty to oversee safety standards in genetic research, *The New York Times*, December 28, 1975, p. 30; Fried, J. J., 1975, Is science creating dangerous new bacteria?, *Readers Digest* **107** (December):133-136; Fried, J. J., 1975, Bacterial experiments offer promise—and danger, *The Sunday Sun*, Baltimore, October 12, pp. 1-3; Hubbard, R., 1976, DNA research and path of prudence, *The Boston Globe*, July 1, p. 18; Kifner, J., 1976, Creatior of life experiment at Harvard stirs heated dispute, *The New York Times*, June 17, p. 22C; Kotulak, R., 1975, The great promise and grave peril of genetic manipulation, *Chicago Tribune Magazine*, September 21, pp. 22-24, 26, 28, 30; Lock the labs in Cambridge? (Editorial), *The Washington Star*, July 12, 1976, p. A14; McCrary, L., 1977, N. J. asked for moratorium on genetic experimentation, *Philadelphia Inquirer*, September 13; McDougall, K. J., 1976, Genetic engineering: Hazard or blessing?, *Intellect* **104**:528-530; McWhethy, J., 1976, Science's newest magic, a blessing or a curse, *U.S. News and World*

*Report* **81** (July 12): 34-35; Rivers, C., 1976, Genetic engineers: Now that they've gone too far, can they stop?, *Ms* **4** (June):49-51, 112, 114, 116, 118; Rosenfeld, A., 1976, Should we tamper with heredity?, *Saturday Review* **2** (July 26):44-45; Rules issued to ban too dangerous DNA research, *Post*, Denver, Colo., June 23, 1976.

48. Schmeck, H. A., Jr., 1976, Guidelines issued to curb genetic research hazards, *The New York Times*, June 24; Schumacher, E., 1976, City blocks DNA research, *The Washington Post*, July 9, p. A3; Shurhin, J. N., 1977, City told about prospects for gene splicing, *Philadelphia Inquirer*, September 22; Toufexis, A., 1976, Genetic engineering storm brews anew, *Medical Tribune*, August 4, pp. 3, 20; Wright, S., 1976, Doubts over genetic engineering controls, *New Scientist*, December 2, pp. 520-521. See also articles cited in refs. 50, 71, 92.

49. Charter, Recombinant DNA Molecule Program Advisory Committee, see ref. 92, pp. 101-102.

50. *Recombinant DNA Research*, Vol. 1. *Documents Relating to "NIH Guidelines for Research Involving Recombinant DNA Molecules" February 1975-June 1976*, DHEW Publication No. (NIH) 76-1138 (August 1976), pp. 1-592.

51. Because of this lack of valid scientific reasons and the present realization that most if not all of the recombinant DNA experiments based on *E. coli* K-12 host-vector systems pose no practical risks, the Nobel laureate J. Watson aptly compared this classification of experiments and the containment assignments to an attempt to decide which kinds of witches are more dangerous, purple or green ones (see J. Watson, Director's report, Annual Report, Cold Spring Harbor Laboratory, 1976, pp. 5-15).

52. Wade, N., 1975, Recombinant DNA: NIH group stirs storm by drafting laxer rules, *Science* **190**:767-769.

53. Recombinant DNA Research Guidelines, *Federal Register* **41** (July 7, 1976):27907-27943.

54. Recombinant DNA Research—Proposed Revised Guidelines, *Federal Register* **42** (September 27, 1977): 49596-49609.

55. *Meeting of the Advisory Committee to the Director, NIH*, December 15-16, 1977, NIH Building 31, Conference room 6C; "Comments on NIH Proposed Revised Guidelines for Recombinant DNA Research," 81 pp. and 19 pp. Addendum (December 1 and 9, 1977), Office of the Director, NIH; Transcript prepared by the Office of the Director, NIH (see also refs. 56 and 60).

56. Schmeck, H. M., Jr., 1977, Rules on DNA studies viewed as too strict, *The New York Times*, December 17.

57. Statement of Dr. W. Szybalski (see ref. 55).

58. Statements of Sir John Kendrew and Dr. John Tooze, executive secretary of the Liason Committee on Recombinant DNA of European Science Foundation (see ref. 55).

59. Statement of Dr. J. Watson (see refs. 55 and 60).

60. Wade, N., 1978, Gene-splicing rules: Another round of debate, *Science* **199**:30-31, 33.

61. Exchange between Dr. W. Rowe and the members of the advisory committee, particularly Mr. P. B. Hutt, Mr. D. Helms, and Dr. H. Ginsberg (see refs. 55 and 60).

62. E.g., statement by Dr. J. King of Science for People (see ref. 55).

63. Gorbach, S. L., 1978, Interim summary of the biology of *E. coli*, Workshop on studies for Assessment of Potential Risks Associated with Recombinant DNA Experimentation, Falmouth, Mass. June 19-21; *Nucleic Acids Recombinant* Scientific Memoranda, March 15-July 15, 1977 NAR-89, pp. 5-7; see also ref. 13, Appendix M-1, and *Proceedings from a Workshop held at Falmouth, Mass. June 20-21, 1977, J. Infect. Dis.* **137**:613-714.

64. R. Freter (see ref. 13, Appendix 0-1, and ref. 63).

65. N. Murray; W. Szybalski (see refs. 13, 24, 25, 53).

66. Petrocheilou, V., and Richmond, M. H., 1977, Absence of plasmid or *E. coli* K-12 infec tion among laboratory personnel engaged in R-plasmid research, *Gene* **2**:323-327.

67. Holliday, R., 1977, Should genetic engineers be contained?, *New Scientist* **73**:399-401.

68. Certified EK2 host-vector systems, in ref. 13, Appendix H-10; Skalka, A., 1978, Current

status of coliphage λ EK2 vectors, *Gene* **3**:29-35.

69. Chang, S., and Cohen, S. N., 1977, *In vivo* site-specific genetic recombination promoted by the *Eco*RI restriction endonuclease, *Proc. Natl. Acad. Sci. USA* **74**:4811-4815.

70. Hutt, P. B., 1976, Letter to D. S. Fredrickson, Director of NIH, February 20, in ref. 71, p. 474-484.

71. *Recombinant DNA Research*, Vol. 1, Documents relating to NIH Guidelines for research involving recombinant DNA molecules, February 1975—June 1976, DHEW Publication No. (NIH) 76-1138 (August 1976), pp. 1-592.

72. Recombinant DNA Safety Regulation Act, S.1217. Reported by E. Kennedy in U.S. Senate, July 22, 1977, 95th Congress.

73. Recombinant DNA Safety Regulation Act—Report together with Supplemental Views. Mr. Kennedy, Committee on Human Resources, 95th Congress, Senate, Report No. 95-359 (July 22, 1977).

74. Recombinant DNA Act, H.R.7897. Introduced by P. Rogers in the House of Representatives, June 20. 1977, 95th Congress.

75. These legislative proposals superseded the array of earlier proposals, namely H.R. 131, 3191, 3591, 3592 and 5020 of Ottinger (January 19-March 14, 1977), H.R. 4232 of Solarz (March 1, 1977), H.R. 4759, 4849 and 6158 of Rogers (March 9-April 6, 1977), S.621 of Bumpers (February 4, 1977), and S.945 of Metzenbaum (March 8, 1977).

76. Approval of Research in the Field of Recombinant DNA. Resolution 33, 1977-78 (May 5, 1977), p. 14. Submitted by the Dane County (Wisconsin) Supervisors Anderson, Anders Walter, DeWitt, McCormick, Moyer, Kabler, Salmon, Bauman, Ginwold, Stoeger, Cooper, Mattes, Tobin, Prideaux, Morton, Bird, Goth, Redford, Nowakowski, Symon, and Dugan (referred to judiciary) (see also ref. 97).

77. A. E. Vellucci's letter, *in: Letter to Members,* National Academy of Sciences, Vol. 7, No. 4 (May, 1977). Text of the letter:

Mr. Philip Handler                                                                      May 16, 1977
President, National Academy of Science
2101 Constitution Avenue, N.W.
Washington, D.C.  20418

Dear Mr. Handler:

As Mayor of the City of Cambridge, I would like to respectfully make a request of you.

In today's edition of the *Boston Herald American*, a Hearst Publication, there are two reports which concern me greatly. In Dover, MA, a "strange, orange-eyed creature" was sighted and in Hollis, New Hampshire, a man and his two sons were confronted by a "hairy, nine foot creature."

I would respectfully ask that your prestigious institution investigate these findings. I would hope as well that you might check to see whether or not these "strange creatures," (should they in fact exist) are in any way connected to *recombinant DNA experiments* taking place in the New England area.

Thanking you in advance for your cooperation in this matter, I remain

Very truly yours,

Alfred E. Vellucci
Mayor
City of Cambridge, Massachusetts

78. Gilbert, W., 1977, Recombinant DNA research: Government regulations, *Science* **197**:208.

79. J. Abelson *et al.* (142 original signatories and about 1000 co-signers). Statement on recombinant DNA research signed by the participants in a Gordon Conference on Biological Regulatory Mechanisms held July 4-8, 1977, sent to all members of the U.S. Congress (July 13, 1977).

80. R. B. Arlinghouse *et al.* (79 signatures) Letter to Congress (June 29, 1977).

81. Handler, P., 1977, President's report, *Letter to Members*, National Academy of Sciences, Vol. 7, No. 4 (May), pp. 6-7.

82 Cohen, C., 1977, When may research be stopped?, *N. Engl. J. Med.* **296**:1203-1210.

83. Don't squander precious time on genes, 1977, *Nature* **270**:461; DNA research: Not so dangerous after all, *Time*, August 15, 1977, p. 56; Dubos, R., 1977, Genetic engineering, *The New York Times*, April 21; Feeling the draft, 1977, *Nature* **267**:658-659; Intruders in the DNA labs (Editorial), *San Francisco Chronicle*; Kilpatrick, J., 1977, Coping with the DNA research, *Wisconsin State Journal*, September 9, p. 12; Mong, B., 1977, Critic's change of mind could change recombinant DNA debate, *The Capital Times*, Madison, Wis., April 16, p. 17; No sci-fi nightmare, after all, *The New York Times*; July 24, 1977; Shurkin, J. N., Geneticists now wary of research limitations, *Philadelphia Inquirer*; Sullivan, W., 1977, Legislating the laboratories, *The New York Times*; Wade, N., 1977, Gene splicing: Senate bill draws changes of Lysenkoism, *Science* **197**:348-349; Wineke, W. R., 1977, DNA "converts" see few hazards, *Wisconsin State Journal*, August 1, Sec. 1, p. 4.

84. Sex and single cell. Much ado about cloning, *TakeOver*, Madison, Wis., July 20, 1977, p. 3. This is a satirical article with the following characteristic introduction: "The comic story of DNA recombination is not yet over, but we are at least into the third reel, the part where the aroused villagers are about to take up torches and smash into Dr. Frankenstein's lab, . . . putting an end (they fondly think) to his creation, which might have turned out a pretty *sympathetic* monster after all. Cartoons will follow the main feature. We will have *travesties of government regulations*, the burlesque of some or another politician assuring us he is saving the environment by an Act hallowed by Congress or the alderthings, and. . . ."

85. Supplemental views of Senator G. Nelson, see ref. 73, pp. 57-63.

86. Amendment No. 754 of Senator G. Nelson to S.1217, *Congressional Record-Senate*, August 2, 1977, pp. S.13312-S.13319.

87. Senator A. Stevenson, Recombinant DNA legislation, *Congressional Record-Senate*, September 22, 1977, Vol. 123, No. 148, pp. S.15410-S.15413.

88. Senator Kennedy announces new DNA bill and study commission, 1977, *ASM News* **43** (November):602-603.

89. Recombinant DNA Safety Regulation Act of 1977 (legislative draft, Senator Kennedy); see also Addendum, pp. 129-132.

90. The National Science Policy Commission Act (S.2267) introduced by Senator H. Schmitt (R-N.M.), *Congressional Record, Senate* **123** (November 1, 1977) No. 178.

91. Watkins, R. W., 1977, DNA legislation dead for this session, *and* Schmitt introduces science policy bill, *ASM News* **43**:643; Grimwade, S., 1977, DNA bill delay, *Nature* **269**:463; Culliton, B. J., 1978, Recombinant DNA bills derailed: Congress still trying to pass a law, *Science* **199**:274-277; Abelson, P. H., 1978, Recombinant DNA legislation, *Science* **199**:135.

92. Subcommittee on Science, Research and Technology of the Committee on Science and Technology, U.S. House of Representatives, 94th Congress, 1976, Genetic Engineering, Human Genetics and Cell Biology—Evolution of Technological Issues—DNA Recombinant Molecule Research (Supplemental Report II), U.S. Government Printing Office, Washington, D.C., 80-497, pp. 1-259; Subcommittee on Science, Research and Technology of the Committee on Science and Technology, U.S. House of Representatives, 95th Congress, Science Policy Implications of DNA Recombinant Molecule Research, No. 24, 93-481, (1977) pp. 1-1293; and Serial X, 21-754 (1978), pp. 1-78, U.S. Government Printing Office, Washington.

93. Stetten, D., 1975, Freedom of enquiry, *Genetics* **81**:415-425.
94. Regulation of Recombinant DNA Research, 1978, Hearing before the Subcommittee on Science, Technology and Space of the Committee on Commerce, Science and Transportation, U.S. Senate, 95th Congress, November 2, 8, and 10, 1977, Serial No. 95-52. U.S. Government Printing Office, Washington, pp. 1-432.
95. Stevenson airs issues on recombinant DNA-Halvorson testifies at hearings, 1977, *ASM News* **43**:637-640.
96. Handler, P. (see refs. 94, pp. 4-34, and 95).
97. Smithies, O. (see ref. 94, pp. 246-251).
98. Hopson, J. L., 1977, Recombinant lab for DNA and my 95 days in it, *Smithsonian* **8** (June):54-63.
99. Rage over rising regulations, *Time*, January 2, 1978, pp. 48-50.
100. Wade, N., 1977, *The Ultimate Experiment: Man-Made Evolution*, Walker, New York; Brenner, S., 1977, Molecular politics for novices, *Nature* **270**:124-125; Rogers, M., 1977, *Biohazard*, Knopf, New York; Harris, R. J. C., 1977, Genetic engineering journalese, *Nature* **270**:122-123; Goodfield, J., 1977, *Playing God*, Random House, New York; Skalka, P., 1977, The awful power to alter life, *Panorama-Chicago Daily News*, October 8-9, p. 14; May, R. M., 1977, The recombinant DNA debate, *Science* **198**:1144-1146; Goodell, R., 1977, *Washington Post*, September 11, p. E1, *Manchester Guardian Weekly*, October 2, p. 18; Medawar, P. B., 1977, Fear and DNA, *New York Review of Books* **24** (October 27):15-20; Howard, T., and Rifkin, J., 1977, *Who Should Play God?*, Delacorte, New York; Szybalski, W., 1977, UW specialist believes DNA research is key to huge benefits for all mankind, *The Capital Times*, Madison Wis., December 12, p. 22.
101. Schmeck, H. N., Jr., 1976, U.S. Agency bids lab halt work on genes, *The New York Times*, December 16; Wade, N., 1978, Harvard gene splicer told to halt, *Science* **199**:31; Cohn, V., 1977, Amid latest gene research flap, easing of rules is eyed, *The Washington Post*, December 16.
102. See ref. 94, pp. 209-243.
103. The following letter analyzes this incident (see also ref. 94, pp. 385-387):

Senators Adlai E. Stevenson and Harrison Schmitt                        January 4, 1978
Subcommittee on Science, Technology and Space
United States Senate
Washington, D. C. 20510

Dear Senators Stevenson and Schmitt:

I read carefully the transcript of the hearings of your Subcommittee on Science, Technology and Space of November 8, 1977 (No. 18 DD/fml CR5418 pp. 332-395), when Dr. William Rutter and Dr. Herbert Boyer were testifying and were cross-examined. I was very saddened and disappointed by reading this document, because I now realize that the N.I.H. Guidelines, of which I was one of the "authors," is not only a useless document that regulates nonexistent hypothetical risks, but also is a harmful document since it led to a misunderstanding between you and two dedicated scientists. Let me comment on the incident, as I see it from the logical and scientific point of view:

    1. (i) Diabetes is a serious life-threatening illness causing human suffering, (ii) there is a projected world shortage of insulin, so only rich nations and persons could afford it for treatment of diabetes, and (iii) the present insulin, being of animal origin, often gives undesirable allergic reactions.

    2. The work of Rutter's, Boyer's and Goodman's teams offers hope of producing a cheap and abundant supply of human insulin, much better and safer than the present porcine insulin.

3. The work as carried out by them and using *E. coli* K-12 host-vector systems presents no practical danger whatsoever, independent of whether using EK1 or EK2 host-vector systems and independent of whether using any physical containment (PO, P1, P2, P3 or P4). In this respect the N.I.H. Guidelines are completely wrong, and all kinds of EK1 or EK2 based novel recombinant DNA experiments should not be included in the Guidelines (see enclosed testimony of W. Szybalski at the Meeting of the Advisory Committee to the Director, N.I.H., December 15-16, 1977; and the letter of W. Szybalski to Dr. Fredrickson, of December 28, 1977).

4. If one assumes (erroneously) that the cloning of insulin genes presents some risk, the decision to use plasmid pBR322 as the cloning vehicle was a scientifically much wiser decision than employing the then certified plasmids pSC101 and pCR1, since pBR322 is much safer. By January 1977, the pMB9 and two pBR plasmids were approved by the proper expert subcommittees, and the only problem was a delay in formal certification caused by the N.I.H. bureaucracy, with pSC101 and pCR1 certified on December 6, 1976, pMB9 on April 18, 1977 and pBR 331 and pBR 322 not certified until July 7, 1977.

5. In view of facts 1-4, the only action for the honest and concerned scientist and citizen was to proceed with full speed to develop human insulin, using the pBR322 plasmid system. How could a scientist, who knows that he might be able to save many human lives and prevent human misery, delay his research just to avoid some unjustified criticism? I would not have much respect for a scientist who so worries about himself that he is not willing to help suffering humanity, especially when he knows that he could do it.

6. Drs. Rutter and Boyer deserve full praise for going ahead with insulin research, and the only criticism I have is that they unnecessarily delayed this research by changing from the pBR322 to pMB9 plasmid, which was (*i*) wasteful, (*ii*) scientifically unjustified, and (*iii*) only politically motivated.

7. I would expect you, Senators Stevenson and Schmitt, (*i*) to commend Drs. Rutter, Goodman and Boyer for trying to rapidly develop human insulin for the suffering and poor throughout the world, (*ii*) to give them all encouragement to pursue this work with full speed, and (*iii*) to admonish them slightly for sacrificing their scientific judgment when changing for no good scientific or safety reasons from pBR322 to pMB9. At the same time (*iv*) you should admonish N.I.H. for bureaucratic delays in certifying the safer pBR322 plasmid and (*v*) request that the EK1 and EK2 based recombinant DNA experiments should at once be excluded from under the Guidelines, until some authoritative study by epidemiologists and medical bacteriologists shows that there is need to regulate this very beneficial but from the practical point of view totally harmless research.

8. This incident is a good example how harmful would be any legislation leading to regulation of the recombinant DNA technique.

(a) There is no good scientific or logical reason for regulating this research.

(b) If one assumes some risks, regulations are counterproductive, since safer methods that often could be developed and tested within weeks, could not then be used for many months, because of bureaucratic delays. The present incident is just an example of it.

(c) The regulations are very unfair to suffering humanity, because of the imposed prohibitions and delays in the name of hypothetical risks, and because of their unjustified cost to the taxpayers.

(d) No legislation is justified unless strongly indicated by an authoritative risk/benefit assessment performed by those epidemiologists and medical microbiologists who are thoroughly familiar with the recombinant DNA technique. I would be glad to help you in organizing studies leading to such assessment.

(e) The United States is rapidly losing its leadership in this very important branch of science, mainly to European countries, including the U.S.S.R.

9. This incident brings up another important moral problem. What should an honest and dedicated scientist do in case he has convincing evidence that a noncertified method or

vector is safer and better (e.g., use of pBR322 which was approved by the Recombinant DNA advisory Committee but not certified) and the regulations on that subject are not up-to-date (e.g., only a less safe plasmid is certified). Should he follow scientific reason and his conscience, or just satisfy the out-of-date bureaucratic regulations? This problem will present itself all the time, since new scientific developments in this field occur and become widely known in a matter of weeks, whereas the lag in regulations is of many months or years duration. Would you kindly advise me on this serious problem?

With the warmest personal regards and best wishes for the New Year.

Sincerely yours,

Waclaw Szybalski
Professor of Oncology
McArdle Laboratory for Cancer Research
University of Wisconsin
Madison, WI 53706

104. The insurance rates for the university might also skyrocket (see Genetic research risks bother insurance firms, *Wisconsin State Journal*, November 27, 1977, Sect. 6, p. 5).
105. Zimmerman, B., 1977, Recombinant DNA regulatory legislation. A discussion of issues and analysis of legislative alternatives, Subcommittee on Health and the Environment of the Committee on Interstate and Foreign Commerce, U.S. House of Representatives, pp. 1-30.
106. Jacob, P., 1884, Translation from *Les Annales Politiques et Litteraires*, Vol. 2, cited from ref. 19.
107. Minutes of the Board of Directors Meeting, Sierra Club, January 8-9, 1977, pp. 24-29.
107a. Recombinant DNA Act, 1978, Report by the Committee on Science and Technology, (Report No. 95-1005, Part 2), Serial No. 29-006. U.S. Government Printing Office, Washington, pp. 1-32.
108. Wade, N., 1978, Congress sets to grapple again with gene splicing, *Science* **199**:1319-1322; Round another helix in the legislative helter-skelter, *Science* **200**:744.
109. U.S.-EMBO Workshop to Assess Risks for Recombinant DNA Experiments Involving the Genomes of Animal, Plant and Insect Viruses, *Federal Register* **43** (March 31, 1978):13748-13755.
110. Stetten, D., 1978, Valedictory by the chairman of the NIH Recombinant DNA Molecule Program Advisory Committee, *Gene* **3**:265-268.
111. Recombinant DNA Research—Proposed Revised Guidelines, *Federal Register* **43** (July 28, 1978):33042-33178.

# 8

# The Place of Biomedical Science in National Health Policy

## THEODORE COOPER and JANE FULLARTON

Biomedical science has played a pivotal role in the development of national health and health science policy. Biomedical research is the only major health activity which has not been challenged as an appropriate federal role in health during the past 30 years. During this period of our history, the magnitude of this federal investment has changed our academic medical centers and research institutions by providing unprecedented opportunities for the growth of research programs, the training of researchers, and the expansion and upgrading of medical school faculties as well as of the scientific quality of medical education. In the process, the pattern and scope of federal research policy and funding created a high level of expectations and an interdependence between the federal government and these institutions which recent policy and funding changes have threatened.

The past 10-12 years have brought major changes in the nature of the federal role in health. The generation of new knowledge about health is now only one federal health activity competing for increasingly scarce health resources. The past decade has seen the demand for and development of major federally supported health financing programs, direct support of health manpower development, programs of health services demonstration and delivery, expanded product safety and environmental health programs, as well as regulatory quality assurance and health planning programs. These 10 years have also seen strong challenges to biomedical research to justify its relevance to our overall health objectives as well as its share of federal health resources.

The overall federal objective in health is improving the health status of the American people. Both the health of the American people and the health care system of the nation are good and getting better. Life expectancy is increasing; the mortality rate is declining; and more people—notably the poor—are receiving more and better health care than ever

THEODORE COOPER and JANE FULLARTON  •  Office of the Assistant Secretary for Health, Department of Health, Education and Welfare, Washington, D.C. 20201.

before.[1] In contributing to this progress, the federal government has played three important roles: paying for care, regulating what is paid for, and developing the knowledge and technology of health science to permit greater effectiveness and efficiency in health care itself and the way it is organized and delivered. These three roles are intrinsically interrelated. In particular, everything we do in the name of better health is inherently knowledge-dependent. Thus knowledge development has become one of the major cross-cutting themes of our Forward Plan for Health in recent years.

The federal government supports over 65% of the health-related research in this country—over $2.5 billion—nearly 80% of which is allocated for research on the cause, prevention, diagnosis, and treatment of illness. The National Institutes of Health alone administer nearly 65% of these federal funds, and supported nearly 40% of all the nation's medical research and development in fiscal year 1975. The federal government is also a major supporter of health services research, with an annual investment nearing $50 million. While overall funds for health research are growing, health research investment is declining as a percentage of total health costs, now down to 3-4%.

The evident magnitude of the federal role in biomedical, behavioral, and health services research—with the consequent impact of federal policy and policy changes, as well as the impact of levels and consistency of funding for such research and related programs—explains the origin of widely expressed concern and controversy about health research. Even small changes in Federal research policy can have major, and unpredictable, effects on a "system" which is so dependent on federal resources. Major policy shifts, such as those of the Administration and the Congress on research training and general support for higher education, when combined with intense competition for scarce health resources increasingly funneled to Medicare and Medicaid benefit entitlements, and general trends in the economy such as 350% increases in fuel costs, have created a climate of uncertainty and a sense of instability among the institutions which are the nation's major performers of health research. Much of the discussion of the need for stability derives from this aura of uncertain expectancy which now pervades the world of research. Knowledge development is a creative enterprise, in which subtle changes in the milieu can have profound (if not easily documented) effects. Clearly we have left behind the halcyon days of unquestioning support and security for research support. Nevertheless, the federal government is as dependent on academic research institutions for the conduct of research as the institutions are dependent on the federal government for support; assuring reasonable stability serves the interest of both parties to this symbiosis, as well as the interests of the American people in having the results of that research applied to improving their health.

One of the important lines of argument about national research policy has been about the appropriate level of investment in research. This issue has been one of the most difficult as well as perennial issues in research policy, involving many attempts to delineate the stages along the continuum from the most fundamental to the most applied research and development. During the period of the most intense Congressional involvement in research policy (1960-1968), there was repeated proposal and consideration of investing a proportion of the GNP in research and development generally, or providing an annual percentage growth rate. Eight years of intensive review by the Executive Branch, by six Congressional committees, by the National Academy of Sciences-National Research Council, and by the scientific and science policy academic community added many pounds to the literature and some clarification of the semantic ambiguities of this issue, but certainly did not resolve it. The one significant result of the application of all this brain power and experience to this question over time was the general realization that there is no objective basis for determing whether the overall investment in research should be an annual 15% rate of increase (Harvey Brooks) or a percentage of the gross national product or, for health, some percentage of national health expenditures. The chairman of President Ford's Cancer Panel, Benno Schmidt, recently observed that any technology-dependent enterprise would prudently invest a minimum of 5% for knowledge development.

The relative investment in research compared to other activities, or in health research compared to other health activities, is a first-order question of social and political priorities, as cogently articulated by Alvin Weinberg in his article on "trans-science." The analytic task in relation to decisions on overall research allocations or the balance between the more fundamental and the more applied research is to clarify what various emphases and changes in policy or funding might portent for the "health" of the research enterprise and the nation.

There are many reasons why such a formula approach might be desirable (general predictability, and thus increased stability and diminished anxiety in the scientific community), but it has never been accepted as a tenet of national policy. One of the most significant reasons that a percentage-investment approach to the allocation of resources for biomedical and behavioral research has not been persuasive as a tenet of national policy is that such research is predominantly publicly supported. A percentage-investment decision may well be appropriate to corporate boardroom decision processes, but it does not allow for the intensity or extent of participation necessary and appropriate to our public decision-making processes about large public expenditures. The outcome, year to year, is certain to foster some instability—some unpredicted fluctuations in research support—a price attached to the public dollar. It is essential to do the public's business in public, to allow the many appropriate participants in national policy making to have their say, even if the process is thereby somewhat cumbersome and awkward. The public interest is determined operationally as the outcome of these public processes.

A second area of perennial concern about the allocation of resources to health research is the pressure for "applied" or "targeted" programs for particular diseases or conditions, with attendant growth of contract-supported, "directed" research. Here again, the percentage-investment approach has been proposed to protect fundamental research. While fundamental research certainly needs to be adequately supported, the public's concerns are also of importance in publicly supported programs. From a public policy perspective, the pressure for application to particular disease problems would be well thought of as a source of healthy tension in biomedical and behavioral research policy deliberations—and may the best case win. Rather than continue heavy criticism of the increasing investment in "targeted" research, it would be helpful for the scientific community to enlighten these issues with the articulation of a better rationale for the support of fundamental research as the final long-term hope for the solution of many present health problems. Major public support of research entails responsibilities, including greatly improved education of policy-makers and of the public about the processes of progress against disease. Many policy-makers and members of the public believe that a directed program of research on a disease problem may be the best or the quickest way to accomplish their intended purpose of "conquering" a disease. Effective "targeting" of resources to particular disease processes requires an adequate fundamental science base to be effective, but articulate exposition of the often serendipitous process of scientific advance is absolutely essential to greater public understanding of this process. Among the useful vehicles for such educational efforts are careful and readable descriptions of important scientific breakthroughs, including the tedium of some periods of research. (Here, Watson's *The Double Helix* always comes to mind, but also needed are books as readable as *The Andromeda Strain* or *Fever*). Also useful are "Tracers"-type studies, as well as such efforts as Dr. Fudenberg's included in this volume, and the Report of the Research Subcommittee of the Study on Surgical Services for the United States, which estimated important contributions of surgical research to health care and the impact of such advances on morbidity and mortality, related these advances to the funding of surgical research, and estimated the cost-benefit ratio of investment in surgical research. Increased public understanding of the health research process is the task to which our energies should be directed if our goal is more informed national research policy.

The discussion of the allocation of resources to health research would be incomplete if it did not consider the allocation of resources to health services research. Historically, direct statement of federal interest to influence the organization and delivery of health services is a very recent phenomenon, with the exception of Hill-Burton and the Maternal and Child Health programs. Only in the last ten years has the Federal Government testified publicly in favor of changing patterns of health care. And even in this past decade, most of our national initiatives (including Medicare, Medicaid, RMP, etc.) were implemented with legislated "no interference" clauses (i.e., no interference with the ordinary practice of medicine, fee-for-service payment, or the doctor-patient relationship). Suspicion was expressed openly in hearings in 1967 about the possible hidden, and purportedly revolutionary, objectives behind specific health services research legislation.

Historically and philosophically, there has been and remains in the United States a considerable distrust of the "soft" social sciences on which much health services research depends. There has been a backlash against the "premature" application of social science theories and research results to social policy and programs stemming from the social programs of the 1960s; a paradoxical backlash has also developed because early investment in health services research has not produced definitive answers quickly enough.

There is also an important analytic difficulty in discussing the "appropriate" allocation of resources to health services research, namely, the number of externalities which influence the world of health services research. Biomedical and behavioral research make profound contributions to health services research by changing the substance, and often the form, of what is delivered as health services. While it sounds trite to say that our health service industry is multidimensional, it is this complexity which makes it difficult to assess our present investment in health services research. Much of what we know about health services research was learned by doing, and has been retrospectively analyzed. Clearly, our only investment in health services research is not our front-end, prospectively planned and funded research. Nevertheless, it has now become clear that we are not investing enough directly in health services research, especially in relation to the $100-plus-billion industry to be studied. We are increasingly dependent for policy-related information on a health services research enterprise in which we have grossly underinvested, and the consequences of not knowing what we can know from research are becoming greater every day.

There have been frequent discussions of the need to conceptualize the role of knowledge development in the broad continuum of health activities. The characterization of the continuum of health activities is not a trivial matter. The basis for much of the criticism directed at biomedical and behavioral research is concern with the seemingly slow application or even irrelevance of research to very pressing problems of health service delivery. Therefore, the interrelation of biomedical behavioral research with the delivery system requires fuller explication. Persistent questions of "How do you know what you bought?" by investing in research must be addressed, including further efforts to describe and interpret the "process of progress" in science.

Also very important to this analysis is an attempt to present an appropriate perspective on the relation of research programs to changes in morbidity and mortality statistics for the disease areas. For example, recent criticisms of cancer research have been based on data showing increasing morbidity and mortality from cancer; the implications of the decrease in morbidity and mortality from heart disease also require thoughtful analysis, including the relative contribution of research to this trend.

Clinical trials have also legitimately become an important focus in delineating the role of research, because of their relevance to the practice, organization, and quality of clinical medicine, and also because of their cost and financing. There is an apparent lack of general agreement about the nature and role of clinical trials in biomedical and behavioral research programs, their relation to the research process, their impact and benefit, technical and ethical problems involved in initiating, conducting, and financing clinical trials, considerations involved in deciding what questions to address through the conduct of a clinical trial, and the interface of this activity with the health care system.

In attempting to delineate the role of knowledge development in health, several points must be borne in mind. "Improving health" is an enormously broad mission, and the knowledge development component of that mission extends widely throughout that mission—extending not only throughout the Department of Health, Education and Welfare but to other federal agencies and to a wide variety of public and voluntary organizations. Delineations of roles and boundaries cannot be made in a vacuum, nor can they be cast in concrete, since changes in a complex array of forces and institutions can and will occur over time. A strategy for delineation of the boundaries needs to reflect the interaction among those who formulate plans, policies, and objectives at the national level; those who are influenced by these actions and must implement the work in support of the policy and objectives of the national effort; and the American public.

Priority-setting for publicly financed health research must amalgamate a wide variety of factors and influences. Three major elements interact in the priority-setting process: the magnitude of the health problem, the public's perception of the problem, and scientific opportunity (e.g., compare cancer to heart disease).

Beyond priority-setting for health research is the overall priority context for health for the nation and the world. This broader perspective may establish priorities for health research which would not necessarily emerge from assessing the magnitude of the problem, the public's perception, or scientific opportunity, but may be indicated by emerging research knowledge. The impact on health of the environment and personal behavior and life-style are important examples of broad health influences on the context of research priorities. It has become essential to learn the ways in which health is affected by environmental influences such as occupational hazards and by life-style influences such as nutrition, exercise, smoking, stress, and patterns of early life. These are high-priority areas for scientific research, although they are difficult issues requiring careful longitudinal study to determine risk factors and causation, and to learn which are preventable. In one sense, the whole orientation of research is toward etiology—toward the elucidation of first causes; yet these areas of life-style and environment have not been popular areas for scientific investigation, considered either too mammoth to be studied or not high-class, elegant research. Determination of first causes is essential to primary prevention, which is our long-term hope for the elimination of many of the conditions that consume our burgeoning health care expenditures today.

The rapid escalation of health care costs has also had an effect on health research priorities, as it has on all health activities. The projected growth of Medicare and Medicaid expenditures for the coming year exceeds the entire budget of the Public Health Service. Health care cost escalation is one of the major forces driving all health policy in this nation. Research has been affected in at least two ways: by increasing scarcity of federal health dollars for any other health activities beyond Medicare and Medicaid, and by intensified demand for "high technology" (in Lewis Thomas's term) in research results—that is, definitive interventions or primary intervention.

There is a third area of impact of health care costs on research which has some disturbing implications for the nation's commitment to the support of research. A line of argument is gaining currency which implies that costly, technology-oriented care is being emphasized by health professionals and is a significant factor in driving up the cost of care, and further, that the underlying reason why our health system has emphasized these high-cost, halfway technologies instead of prevention and cure is that biomedical researchers have worked on "whatever esoteric" research ideas appealed to them rather than addressing national health priorities. This line of argument is being put forward in significant economic analyses.[2] What these analyses overlook is that while the cost of treating, for example, heart attacks rose from $1450 in 1964 to $3280 in 1971 (some of which can be accounted for by inflation, and some by increasing sophistication of care), nevertheless, morbidity and mortality from heart diseases are improving and primarily account for a continuing decrease in our national overall mortality rates.

Thirty years of national investment in biomedical and behavioral research has been enormously productive and has revolutionized clinical care. It is true that it has not yet been possible to prevent many of our most frequent and costly illnesses, but that is not because such "high technology" is not a goal of research; rather, it is that research progress has not yet permitted the kind of definitive interventions that antibiotics brought for many infectious diseases. It has not proved possible merely to *will* primary prevention into being. It has been possible to apply what we know thus far about many disease processes in treatments which arrest or retard deterioration; these interventions are clearly "halfway technologies" where we would all prefer "high technology." Nevertheless, 30 years and billions of dollars of public funds have been invested in this progress against disease, and the public believes it has a right to the benefits of its investment whether such benefits are "halfway" or not. The challenge facing us at the moment is to increase the breadth and quality of understanding of these issues in public debate. The failure to do so may result in public policy decisions inimical to the long-term health interests of the nation, and most particularly to its capacity to conduct research.

Another related influence on research has been public concern over what it sees as declining humanity in the way medical care is delivered, particularly as such care has become increasingly specialized. Geographic maldistribution has also become a legitimate public concern. Traditional mechanisms of federal support have not addressed maldistribution, and federal research dollars have tended to make specialty maldistributions more acute. It is now clear that we must address maldistribution by every possible appropriate means, and the leverage of financial support for professional health education is one of the most powerful tools we have. Thus both the Executive Branch and the Congress have proposed legislation which would dramatically affect academic health institutions. There is no question that the federal government must continue to support these institutions which provide trained health manpower and also conduct the bulk of federally financed research. National health priority considerations now require that academic health institutions add to their already broad missions assistance to the nation's geographic and primary care problems in exchange for the massive federal assistance they receive.

Biomedical, behavioral, and health services research cannot exist in a vacuum. The value of scientific research as a human intellectual endeavor is a separate issue from its justification as a worthy investment for public funds. In health, everything is necessarily related to everything else, and health research must respond to new directions in national health priorities. Mutual recognition of the existing interdependence of the federal government and academic research institutions is essential to the achievement of mutual goals in health knowledge development. The long history of the collaboration between the federal government and its academic and research institutions in pursuit of national health objectives provides ample basis for optimism about the future of that evolving partnership.

## REFERENCES

1. *Health Status: United States, 1975;* USDHEW, PHS, HRA, NCHS/NCHSR, 1976.
2. Scitovsky, A., Changes in the costs of treatment of selected illnesses 1951-1964-1971, Health Policy Program, UCSF School of Medicine.

# 9

# Beyond the Warring Elements: A Search for Balance in Health Funding

## DANIEL C. MALDONADO

From a federal budget view, health policy formulation resembles a factional struggle of competing, often warring, health and biomedical interests. Cancer, heart, lung, eye, and other categories of human disease and antomy vie for attention and support. The struggle for the Federal dollar becomes even more acute because of growing concerns over deficits and demands for lowered expectations.

Health observers have been critical of this Hobbesian state of personal and institutional self-interest. Long-time health analyst James Shannon decries academia's lack of interest in "the total (health) problem" as "most distressing."[1] He concludes: "Each scientific and educational group was concerned only with that part of the budget that immediately affected it, with little concern being expressed for a more realistic analysis of the total problem."[2] As a solution, Shannon calls for a policy of balance among research, education, and service. Under Shannon's scheme, however, research would be first among its peers—"research being essential for both sound education and an improvement of service."[3] Shannon's balance of interests favors a purely academic environment, free of "attempts to socialize the educational process and make it 'more responsive' to the vagaries of a conventional trend of society toward consumerism."[4]

A broader social view has been developed by Vijaya and Daniel Melnick and Hugh Fudenberg who, commenting on the biologist's role in national science policy, observe: "Unfortunately, though, few biologists approach government decisions about biomedical policy from the broad perspective of the public welfare."[5] The writers define this commitment to the public welfare as including an "active concern for regulations that protect public safety and health care delivery." They issue a call to the biologists, to the scientists: Become involved in all measures beneficial to

DANIEL C. MALDONADO • Assistant Director (Legislative and Governmental Affairs) ACTION, Washington, D.C. 20252. This article describes trends and directions evolving out of the FY 1977 appropriations process, and was written while the author was Administrative Assistant to Congressman Edward Roybal, House Committee on Appropriations.

this country's health, whether it be research or delivery of services. This altruism has a payoff, "by increasing their area of responsibility . . . research biologists will increase the size of the constituency that can be called on to support their work."[6]

Similarly, Barry Commoner in his book *Science and Survival* describes his own commitment to the public good. Commoner's commitment flows from the "damaging effects" science and technology have had on human welfare. He calls for a public (open) assessment of the potential harms of innovations, their economic and social costs, and expected benefits.[7] He writes:

> I believe that scientists have a responsibility in relation to the technological uses which are made of scientific development. In my opinion, the proper duty of the scientist to the social consequence of his work cannot be fulfilled by aloofness or by an approach which arrogates to scientists alone the social and moral judgments which are the right of every citizen. I propose that scientists are bound by a new duty. . . . We have the duty to inform. . . . We have no right to withhold information from our fellow citizens. . . . [8]

Despite varying emphasis, these writers advocate a broader policy perspective on the part of their fellow scientists. Shannon, Melnick, and Fudenberg argue for a comprehensive approach to health—one designed to reverse current parochialism. Shannon explains that this three-legged (research, educational, service) scheme will only succeed if viewed as a "total national effort and not simply a federal contribution to each function."[9]

Melnick and Fudenberg, in urging a public welfare concern, define the "constituency" of biological science as the "entire public."[10]

## THE APPROPRIATING ART

These expressions and exhortations have special relevance to the annual appropriation process in Congress, where competing interests and associations lobby for funds. The process itself is a hodgepodge of budget hearings and evaluations, staff funding recommendations, behind-the-scene negotiations, lobbying, committee warnings and instructions, monetary and mathematical games.

Health budget review and development fall under the jurisdiction of the subcommittees on Labor-HEW (of the House and Senate committees on appropriations). The subcommittee on Labor-HEW has authority[11] to (1) recommend the appropriations or funding level in support of program or research activities (or their termination); (2) through the report vehicle, earmark funds for specific programs or projects, set program directions, instruct, warn, and exhort; (3) accept or reject proposed impoundments (rescissions and deferrals); (4) approve or disapprove transfer of unexpended balances; and (5) conduct studies and examinations of agency/department operations and organization.

The appropriations subcommittees have traditionally played a prominent role in health policy by "earmarking" funds for specific activities, and "requesting" or "expecting" that a certain "emphasis" or direction be taken. [12] In summary, they set program direction, emphasis, and budget levels for health.

In health research, the subcommittees have been instrumental in the development and expansion of the NIH. Since 1947, the NIH budget has soared from a $8.3 million operation[13] to a $2.41 billion effort under the 1977 Labor-HEW Appropriations Act. [14] The act provided a 9.5%, or $208 million increase over the 1976 NIH level. With the purse-string authority, the Labor-HEW subcommittees have frequently doled out these funds by designating very specific categories of research. For example, the House and Senate subcommittee report to the 1977 Labor-HEW legislation details a plan of action for the National Institute of Arthritis, Metabolism, and Digestive Diseases (NIAMDD). First, the House report cautions that while "fundamental research" on the chemical or metabolic basis of diabetes is needed, the subcommittee "is certainly not convinced that all progress must wait on a complete understanding" of the disease. The House report expresses an impatience that "the only proper way to attack the problems of diabetes (or many other diseases) is to wait patiently for a revelation of their true causes."[15] It calls for "imaginative leadership," and "better care and control" as immediate goals. [16] The House report also singles out cystic fibrosis research by NIAMDD as "deserv[ing] priority attention" and "directs" a progress report in 1977 not only on research but on patient care as well. [17]

The Senate report, augmenting House priorities, earmarks increases for research in diabetes (especially centers), arthritis (again, centers), gastroenterology, digestive diseases (in general), nutritional disorders, psoriasis (including the formation of a task force), kidney disease (with focus on developing specialized centers for research), dermatology, and cystic fibrosis (a "highly-priority area"). The Senate adds that research training should "stress" work in diabetes and arthritis. [18]

The House and Senate reports covering NIAMDD and other research institutes illustrate the deep involvement of, and guiding role played by, the appropriations subcommittees in the research area. It also suggests, as evidenced by the increases provided for the initiation of arthritis and diabetes centers, the potential influence of blue ribbon commissions or panels whose findings capture the interest and support of subcommittee members or staff.

Some like Shannon and the President's biomedical research panel express concern over the scope and detail of this congressional guidance. They believe that the recent trend toward specialized health research legislation can be detrimental. The biomedical panel argues that appropriating funds for "specific congressionally determined program activities" can undermine the ability of NIH and ADAMHA directors to "exercise important programmatic judgments" or "respond quickly to important unanticipated opportunities or needs."[19]

The argument suffers from two basic flaws. First of all, NIH like other federal health agencies can seek reprogramming approval from the Labor-HEW subcommittees with minimal delays. Second, and more importantly, Congress serves a tax-paying constituency which is concerned about health care and delivery of services at reasonable cost. It is especially through the appropriating process that Congress details that concern in tangible, identifiable terms.

But while the House and Senate reports express Congressional will, they are not fixed and irrevocable. Agencies can make changes through timely dialogue and discussion with subcommittee members or staff.


## FUTURE DIRECTIONS

There is a growing movement in the appropriations subcommittees on Labor-HEW toward a coordinated effort within and among service, research, and training components. It has become increasingly clear that despite the illusion projected by HEW's "Forward Plan for Health" for 1978-82,[20] health programs remain disjointed and competitive, especially during no-growth years.

Not surprisingly, the Coalition for Health Funding, an amalgam of health research, service, professional, and charitable groups, also faces problems of coordination and a unified plan of action in presenting recommendations to the Labor-HEW subcommittees.[21] While its goal is "the development of a rational, comprehensive system of health care delivery, available to all Americans at reasonable cost,"[22] the coalition's life depends on its capacity to satisfy the funding wishes of each of its 52 associations.

Nevertheless, at the request of a subcommittee member, a recent effort was made to develop a priority list for a possible package amendment, but this was only possible after the bill had been reported out by the House appropriations committee.

The analysis of the subcommittee reports shows an intensified effort at improving planning and cooperation in health activities. They reveal a desire to use HEW's resources to solve the health and service problems facing rural and urban low-income communities. The reports call for:

1. "A new momentum in educational and research nutrition initiatives," involving NIH, the Center for Disease Control, and Agriculture. This effort includes developing a plan for effective nutritional monitoring in the United States. And CDC is responsible for "work[ing] very closely" with such community service programs as maternal and child health, early periodic screening, diagnosis, and treatment (EPSDT), and women, infant, and children supplemental food.[23] A progress report is to be made within nine months.

2. An expanded effort by NIH, the Assistant Secretary for Health, and other PHS agencies to communicate usable research results to the health care community, and report back before next year's hearings.[24]

3. A prevention, education, and treatment emphasis within NIH programs, including cancer, hypertension, arteriosclerosis, genetic diseases including sickle cell and Cooley's anemia, rehabilitation of heart attack victims, arthritis and diabetes, and sudden-infant-death syndrome.[25] The cancer centers, for instance, have a prevention and treatment responsibility and are designed to be focal points for community cancer activities. (The General Accounting Office, however, concludes in a March 1976 report that this goal has yet to be achieved.[26])

4. A child health plan of action in both rural and urban areas: (a) HEW must ensure a coordinated effort by the community and migrant health centers, maternal and child health, family planning, EPSDT, comprehensive health grants to state in "providing adequate treatment" and "comprehensive services" for children.[27] (b) The Assistant Secretary for Health and CDC must "vigorously encourage an integrated lead screening program and submit a report by February 1977.[28] (c) HEW must provide "greater coordination" among health services and preventive health programs to improve the immunization levels of the urban and rural poor.[29] A report is to be submitted before next year's hearings. (d) The Assistant Secretary for Health is instructed to combine the "capacity and resources" of the community health service programs to address the high risk problem associated with teen-age pregnancy.[30]

5. A commitment by the Alcohol, Drug Abuse and Mental Health Administration to solve the problem of maldistribution of mental health personnel, including staffing difficulties facing mental health and substance abuse facilities.[31] The House hearings reveal subcommittee impatience over the absence of a "precise plan" to solve the maldistribution problem. There is growing subcommittee interest in promoting a service obligation for recipients under the clinical training program.[32]

6. Closer working ties between HEW's health research and service components. For example, child health problems, such as crippling conditions, nutritional deficiency, and child abuse and neglect, would benefit from a coordinated effort, since each of these issues requires a research, training, and service connection.[33] Child mental health research is poorly coordinated with community health services, EPSDT, child development, and child welfare programs. And migrant health services would greatly benefit from a cooperative relationship with the National Institute of Environmental Health Sciences and the National Institute of Occupational Safety and Health, where no dialogue now exists. The House report states clearly that the migrant service program should focus on the "environmental factors affecting the health of migrants."[34]

7. Expansion of the rural health initiative, which combines the resources of the community health service programs into a "single integrated local . . . system."[35] The Senate report encourages the extension of this approach into urban areas as well, and coincides with earlier views expressed by Congressman Edward R. Roybal in the House report. He writes: "HEW must make every effort to develop total health response in assisting urban and rural communities. It is recommended that the Department work to develop cooperative health action plans and service networks in underserved areas. These efforts should include provisions for referral and total family and personal care, and adequately respond to manpower maldistribution."[36]

Several studies[37] have suggested the beneficial results of integrated services, outreach efforts, and family and community involvement in health. A three-year NIMH-financed study of a New Haven neighborhood discloses that mental health services for black and Spanish-speaking children can be significantly improved when joined with pediatric care and community input. A September 1976 report to HEW on rat control efforts in California concludes: "Awareness and participation of citizens is vital to insuring that environmental conditions associated with rat propagation continue to be corrected. . . . "[38]

A 1975 health report of East Los Angeles (a large Chicano community), conducted by Drs. Robert Schlegel and David Sanchez, further
documents the health damage caused by local disorganization, bureaucratic infighting, and poor community relations. Commenting on the responsiveness of the Los Angeles County-USC Medical Center, they observe: "There is an innate tendency for conservative faculties to retreat
into the confines of the hospital, rather than to (1) reach out into the
community to render services; (2) provide opportunities for education to
populations lacking incentives and knowledge to seek out careers in the
health professions; or (3) develop better ways to serve culturally diverse
people, neighborhoods, and communities."[39]

8. Recognition of "cultural barriers" and other impediments to
health care delivery.[40] Several studies have shown[41] (a) the detrimental
effect of language, class, and cultural barriers which separate the physician or therapist from the language-minority patient and discourage
treatment and follow-up; (b) the influence of racial or cultural biases and
prejudices in diagnosis, treatment, and delivery of mental health services;
(c) the humiliations and frustration experienced by Spanish-speaking
elderly when applying for medical assistance at English-only offices. The
fact that many do not return strongly suggests that the lack of bilingual
services has a discriminatory impact. Several mental health researchers
insist that bilingual-bicultural staff with close community ties "enhance
psychological and social intervention with"[42] language-minority patients.

9. Expansion of biomedical and research opportunities for minorities
through the minority access to research careers (MARC) and minority
biomedical support program (MBS).[43] The MBS program, administered
by the Division of Research Resources, is designed to increase minorities
in biomedical research and gained a $2 million boost under the Labor-
HEW Appropriations Act. The 1977 level for MBS is now $9.7 million.

These developments suggest a stronger emphasis on cooperative
relationships in research and service. Further, they show support for
community focus in basic and clinical research, as in the cancer control
and center program. Cancer centers (similarly, arthritis and diabetes centers) serve as wellsprings of research, training for treatment of cancer
victims, community involvement, and continuing education for physicians and health professionals. As stressed by the House report, community activities form an integral part of the program, "involving networks
of cooperating physicians and community hospitals, linked to major med-

ical centers, for the dissemination of the latest information and techniques in diagnosis, treatment and rehabilitation."[44]

The appropriations subcommittees have come to view research in deeper community terms (and less as isolated laboratory/academic events). That community is all-encompassing; it involves not only the research community and academia, but also physicians and patients, professional and charitable societies, local hospitals, and consumer groups. As evidenced by recent appropriation action, NIH's own mission is evolving and taking on a greater public or community welfare focus.

## ROLE OF THE HEALTH ACTIVIST

What role can or should the biomedical scientist, the physician, nurse, administrator, or community leader play in the legislative process?

The approach favored by Shannon in his article "Federal Support of Biomedical Sciences" calls for the involvement of scientists in the "allocation" process. (Shannon's use of this term appears to cover both congressional and agency funding decisions.) He argues that because of limited funds, only "mature professional input" can help determine the proper balance between research and the development of resources. Judgments about distribution priorities, he explains, require the "competence of sophisticated biomedical scientists" in assessing need and opportunity. He blames current distortions and instability in research funding on the "progressive separation of scientific competence from the decision-making process." As a solution, he urges that scientists (1) shed their parochial interests (concern only for one's own research and support level); (2) be concerned with determining the proper mix of health research, training, and service and advancing the stability of academic medical and health institutions; and (3) be involved in the allocation or distribution process. Shannon adopts an even more radical position when he suggests not only scientific input but "control of the allocation process."[45]

Shannon's point on the separation of the scientist from policy decisions is intended to be more than a statement of fact. It is a warning and exhortation that scientists expand their horizons and be involved in the legislative process. It is an excellent starting point, the first step to becoming what could be called a health activist. However, Shannon's dialectic offers too narrow a vision. First, it disregards the health policy role that (nonscientist) professionals play in legislative/appropriations committees. These professionals are required to handle larger pieces of the health puzzle, balance competing interests, and recommend priority and funding levels. Their job, of course, would be greatly enhanced by the input of scientists concerned with achieving a balance and cooperative effort in health. Second, Shannon's scheme strongly suggests an anticonsumer bias—what he describes as the "vagaries" caused by "consumerism." This position runs counter to recent legislative/appropriations efforts to place research and development in a public and community health context.

Transcending Shannon's approach, Melnick and Fudenberg push the scientist (and others involved in health and biomedical science) to a higher level of commitment: "the broad perspective of the public welfare." They believe that the scientist must broaden his/her view into the public realm: " . . . when the records of hearings on the cancer program (or a host of other health research or delivery issues) are examined, it is difficult to find a single instance in which a research biologist made a plea for increased delivery of health care. This is *not* to say that many biologists do not recognize the need; they just do not define this as their area of interest. And yet these issues have immediate relevance to basic research."[46]

I believe that it is vitally important that we as professionals, scientists, educators, or consumers concerned with health and biomedical development maintain an ideal of service to urban and rural communities. Poverty, poor housing, unemployment, and hazardous and unsanitary working conditions continue to be specters of poor health, chronic illness, and mental health problems. Recent studies have shown the relationship between social class and chronic illness,[47] unemployment, and personal and family stress.[48] (The farm worker and his family illustrate this social and economic victimization in terms of life expectancy, illness, disability, and death from infant to adult life.[49])

Several scientists and physicians have made organized efforts toward "public action and responsibility." Their success depends on (1) responsiveness of their health agenda; (2) ability to develop research, service, and manpower priorities; (3) willingness to work closely with community health organizations; (4) ability to exert influence within one's own professional association; (5) ability to show cost savings and long term benefits of research in terms of the human condition (useful measurements include mortality, morbidity, disability, chronic illness, lost earnings, hospitalization, and institutionalization)[50]; (6) talent and resources to develop easily accessible and readable backup materials for health budget hearings, markup, and debate; and (7) ability to assess the impact of health proposals on research, service, and manpower needs.

At a recent conference on "biosciences communications and health care delivery" sponsored by the Sloan-Kettering Institute,[51] several participants expressed concern over the aloofness or detachment of many physicians and health scientists to community health problems. To dramatize their point they posed three questions at the closing plenary session:

First, what practical significance will the conference have in promoting an active communication and dialogue between the biomedical and health professions, and the underserved communities and working class of this country.

Second, what steps can be taken to alleviate the existence of cultural, race, language, and class barriers to health, which continue to be obstacles to communication and health care delivery?

Third, what responsibilities do we bear in rectifying the lack of active communication and dialogue betweeen the biomedical and health professions (whether in an academic, corporate, or practitioner setting), and our underserved communities and working class?

The questions call for self-reflection; they require an inner examination of attitudes, perceptions, prejudices, and level of commitment. The questions emanate from a social perspective which views the biomedical and health professions as holding a public trust. The very nature of the biomedical and health fields raises critical questions relating to human experimentation, informed consent, life and death choices, eradication of disease, environmental health, and family and community life. All of these factors reinforce the concept of public trust and accountability in the biomedical and health professions. That trust involves a willingness to work in the public arena to improve the quality of life—in the working place, in the community, and in the home. This is the essence of a health activist.

## REFERENCES AND NOTES

1. Shannon, J. A., 1976, Federal support of biomedical sciences: Development and academic impact, *J. Med. Educ.* **51**(7, July, part 2):53.
2. Ibid, p. 53.
3. Ibid., p. 68.
4. Ibid., p. 42-43.
5. Melnick, V. L., Melnick, D., and Fudenberg, H. H., 1956, Participation of biologists in the formulation of national science policy, *Fed. Proc.*, **35**:1957.

6. Ibid., p. 1958.
7. Commoner, B., 1963, *Science and Survival,* pp. 122-123, Viking Press, New York.
8. Ibid., p. 129.
9. Shannon, pp. 68-69.
10. Melnick *et al.,* p. 1957.
11. Brown, W. H., 1975, *Rules of the House of Representatives,* pp. 349-351, 393, 396-399, U.S. Government Printing Office, Washington, D.C.
12. Read Fenno, R. F., Jr., 1966, *The Power of the Purse: Appropriations Politics in Congress,* Little, Brown, Boston.
13. Shannon, Table 2, Federal obligations for biomedical research and development, p. 85.
14. See Conference Report on H.R. 14232 in *Congressional Record,* August 10, 1976, H8614.
15. U.S. House of Representatives, *Departments of Labor, and Health, Education and Welfare, and Related Agencies Appropriation Bill, 1977.* 94th Congress, 2nd Session, Report no. 94-1219, p. 31.
16. Ibid., pp. 31, 32.
17. Ibid., p. 32.
18. U.S. Senate, *Departments of Labor and Health, Education and Welfare and Related Agencies Appropriation Bill, 1977.* 94th Congress, 2nd Session, Report no. 94-997, pp. 49-52.
19. Report of President's Biomedical Panel, p. 27; see also Appendix D, chapter on Congressional Initiatives in Biomedical and Behavioral Research, pp. 33-39.
20. See DHEW's *Forward Plan for Health, F.Y. 1978-82,* August 1976.
21. Coalition for Health Funding, *Appropriation Recommendations for Federal Health Programs F.Y. 1977,* Washington, D.C., March 1976.
22. Ibid., p. vii.
23. Senate report, p. 27-28, 37.
24. House report, pp. 23-24; and Senate report p. 40.
25. House report, pp. 22-47; and Senate report pp. 39-69.
26. U.S. General Accounting Office, *Comprehensive Cancer Centers: Their Locations and Role in Demonstration,* March 17, 1976.
27. Senate Report, pp. 29-30.
28. House report, p. 21.
29. Ibid., pp. 21-22.
30. Ibid., p. 16.
31. Ibid., pp. 47-49.
32. House of Representatives, Appropriations Subcommittee on Labor-HEW, Hearings on the Department of Labor and Health, Education and Welfare Appropriations for 1977, part 3—Health Activities, 94th Congress, 2nd session, pp. 395-398, 413-414.
33. Labor-HEW hearings, part 3, pp. 426-427; part 4—NIH, pp. 718-719; also, Senate report, pp. 27-28, 37.
34. House report, p. 16.
35. Senate report, p. 30.
36. House report, pp. 95-96.
37. See Novack, A. H., Bromet, E., *et al.,* 1975, Children's mental health services in an inner city neighborhood, *Am. J. Public Health,* **65**(2):133-138; Diehr, P., *et al.,* 1975, Access to medical care, *J. Health Soc. Behav.,* **September:**326-340; Shepard, K. F., 1975, Family focus, *Am. J. Public Health* **65**(1):63-65; Levin, S., *et al.,* 1976, The parent-therapist program, *Hospital and Community Psychiatry* **27**(6, June):407-410.
38. Mortenson, E. W., and Rotramel, G. L., A regional approach to rodent control in the San Francisco Bay Area, attached to letter of September 7, 1976, from Richard F. Peters, Vector and Waste Management Section, California Department of Health, p. 7.
39. Schlegel, R., and Sanchez, D. J., Jr., 1975, Site visit—Los Angeles, Report to Congressman Edward R. Roybal, May 21, p. 12.

40. House report, pp. 15, 95.
41. Padilla, A. M., *et al.*, 1975, Community mental health servies for the Spanish-speaking/surnamed population, *Am. Psychol.* **30**(9):892-905; Abad, V., *et al.*, 1974, Model for delivery of mental health services to Spanish speaking minorities, *Am. J. Orthopsychiatry* **44**(4):584-595; East Los Angeles Health Task Force, *Feasibility Study to Assess the Health Needs of the Spanish Speaking*, 1976; Letter of July 21, 1976, from Asian American Mental Health Research Center to Richard Shapiro, NIMH, Minority Mental Health Center; Letter of August 10, 1976, from National Center for American Indian and Alaskan Native Mental Health Research and Development to Shapiro, NIMH; Jackson, A. M., 1976, Mental health center delivery systems and the black client, *Journal of Afro-American Issues* **Winter:**28-34; Davenport, Y. B., 1975, Depressive illness: Problems of diagnosis in children and blacks, *Integrated Education* **September-October:**19-23; Cole, J. and Pilisuk, M., 1976, Differences in the provisions of mental health services by race, *Am. J. Orthopsychiatry* **46**(3): 510-525.
42. Abad *et al.*, p. 592; also Elsie Sanchez, Chairperson, *The Chicano Plan for Mental Health*, Government Printing Office, March 15, 1975.
43. House report, p. 44; and Senate report, pp. 57, 65.
44. House report, p. 26.
45. Shannon, pp. 64-72.
46. Melnick *et al.*, p. 1958.
47. Conover, P. W., 1973, Social class and chronic illness, *International Journal of Health Services*, **3**(3):357-368.
48. Brenner, M. H., 1973, *Mental Illness and the Economy*, Harvard University Press, Cambridge; Levin, H., 1975, *Work: The staff of life*, presented at APA Convention, Chicago, Ill., September; Warren, R., 1975, *Stress, primary support systems and the blue collar woman*, released March 28; NIMH note on Crisis Behavior and Mental Health, released to Congressman Edward R. Roybal; Labor-HEW hearings, part 3, pp. 422-425.
49. See Congressman Roybal's remarks in *Congressional Record*, June 24, 1976, H6606.
50. Melnick *et al.*, pp. 1958-1960.
51. Aspen Biosciences Communications Seminars, at the Given Institute, Aspen, Colorado, October 6-8, 1976.

# 10

# The Formulation of Health Policy

## ROBERT J. SCHLEGEL

Recently, a group of 100 scholars and public officials met in Aspen to discuss the state of communication between health professionals and the public.[1] The scope and complexity of policy issues considered was great, illustrating once again the difficulty in moving the nation toward a new public policy synthesis, or in marshalling a concerted national effort to improve health and health care in the United States.[2]

I believe that public policy formulation and the development of necessary programs might be served by a five-step planning process in use on a smaller scale at one of the nation's new and developing medical centers.[3] That center has been charged with developing better programs of health care, education, and research for an underserved population; however, the health policy process in use there is applicable to any population, regardless of its size or nature.

## PUBLIC POLICY PROCESS

The initial step in the process is to ascertain measured health needs and expectations of the people constituting the defined population to be served. Answers are obtained to a variety of questions. For example: What are the major causes of excess death or sickness? What factors are responsible for the premature loss of physical and mental vigor? What expectations are held by the people for health services? What resources are currently available to meet those needs and expectations? To answer these questions a variety of continuing personal interactions with community and neighboring groups are carried out by health professionals, who also do more traditional demographic studies and epidemiological surveys. In addition to monitoring of the biological denominators of disease, cultural attitudes are studied as health factors. Economic and political limitations on new health programs are specified.

ROBERT J. SCHLEGEL • Department of Pediatrics, Charles R. Drew Postgraduate Medical School, and Los Angeles County Martin Luther King, Jr., General Hospital, Los Angeles, California 90059.

Based on analysis of data collected in the initial step, an appropriate service system is planned and, insofar as possible, implemented. Elements of the service system are based on the determinants of health and the projected use of health care identified in the initial planning element. Those specified, realistic needs and expectations are translated into the objectives of service (skills, attitudes, knowledge) necessary for the health practitioner and educator.

The third step follows from the second. Health education programs for the public and for health professions derive their learning experiences and curriculum content from existing tasks being carried out in the service system. It is, of course, also necessary to make forecasts of future changes in health needs and derivative services.

The fourth step is the planning and conduct of research and evaluation. Biomedical science not targeted at isolated diseases fulfills a larger social role in professional and public education and in career development opportunities. The cost and effectiveness of services and education are measured in an organized service research program.

The fifth step is an ongoing review of the use of health resources and the acquisition of additional people and program units needed for services, education, research, and management. Justifications for fiscal outlays are based on human as well as accounting priorities. Management is tailored to fit the functional units of the entire system. Accountability of performance by both caregivers and care recipients is defined according to explicit objectives in steps 1 through 3 above.

Each step in this process must be considered in policy decisions at the local institutional level, or at the national level. Decisions emanating from concerns about one part of the process inevitably have an impact on all other parts. Too often policy-makers respond in an ad hoc fashion to limited perceptions of public interest advocates, professional organizations, educators, scientists, or public administrators.

The sequence of thought and action is as important as the comprehensive nature of the process. It assures an orientation that suits the public interest and compels logical inferences regarding services, education, research, and administration. By tracing these internal causal connections, many contrived crises are resolved and inappropriate responses to strident appeals or to moral dilemmas more apparent than real are forestalled.

## PRACTICAL APPLICATIONS

The view has been repeatedly expressed during recent years that the health care system is spinning out of control. It costs too much[4] and accomplishes too little.[5] The evidence is compelling that agencies, institutions, and professions involved in the health fields must be organized in a more systematic way and that stronger public leadership is necessary to accomplish that goal.

The policy process outlined here is one way to think about improving health and the health care system. It would guide decision making at all levels of organization, resolve current conundrums, and foster a broader personal perspective on the part of all parties concerned with health and health care.

*Community Needs and Expectations.* There is an emerging consensus that health, longevity, personal development, and the absence of disease in the populations of advanced technocracies such as ours depend more on personal behavior than on professional health care services.[6] The attitudes, self-perception, habits, and thought determining that behavior are products in part of social and economic denominators.[7] These factors are beyond the traditional grasp of the health care professions. Those professions do, however, bear a social responsibility to identify causal relationships and possible solutions to existing health problems at the community level. They also carry leadership responsibilities for health promotion and public education. In addition, health care does make a difference in poor and minority populations.[8] These populations account for the excessive mortality and morbidity rates found among Americans, in contrast with the citizens of other industrialized countries.[9] They have some responsibility for finding ways to control the increasing cost of health care, a cost that continues to rise at the expense of other human resource programs.

One might expect that schools of public health and departments of community medicine would lead their academic colleagues in the health professions into community activities. Many valuable efforts can be imagined. For example, health professionals might enrich the teaching of personal hygiene in public schools. Similarly, scientists might contribute greatly through organized programs sponsoring lectures and demonstrations. The public health experts themselves would have much to contribute in educating and informing our young people about health and the use of health services. Unfortunately, there are disappointingly few efforts of this kind, and those are transitory, sporadic, monastic, and often valueless. The public health leadership has been isolated in sanctuaries, preoccupied with abstract scholarship. In recent years, the field has been increasingly dominated by managerial and public administration interests.

One of the central purposes of clinical science is to resolve ethical problems. For example, it is no longer necessary to place urinary catheters in small children to ascertain vital metabolic information. A metabolic bed has been invented for this purpose by a physician. The stimulus for invention was to avoid psychological and physical trauma.

Advocacy for health and health care can be conducted with these limitations in benefits and trade-offs with other social enterprises in mind. Nevertheless, that informed advocacy is based on the knowledge and organized thought that proceeds through a policy planning system such as that described here. Informed advocacy should advance specific solutions to the inequitable distribution of health resources, the failure to educate enough primary care physicians, undue risks or abridgement of human rights by technology, and the inefficient use of national health resources. It is essential that health professionals, biomedical scientists, and indeed all citizens share in the organized search for solutions to these current problems.

*Health Service System.* The more comprehensive and logical approach to health care suggested here is based on evidence of the need for, worth of, and comparative efficiency demonstrated by its various coordinated components. For example, health care of the urban poor today is caught in the conflict between property taxpayers and municipal governments. State governments, also dependent on a regressive tax structure, can no longer support increases in the cost of health care for the poor.[10] While an ever-increasing share of the federal dollar goes to health care, criticism mounts that commensurate benefits are not forthcoming.[11] Private health care costs continue to mount and the assertion is made that decent private health care is beyond the means of the average American.[12]

The policy approach advocated here offers solutions superior to those resulting from merely pumping more dollars into the current system. In the past, attempts were made to increase manpower in underserved areas by increasing overall health manpower.[13] More recently, the process has been refined by programs to increase primary health care,[14] to redistribute numbers by medical specialty, to better distribute physicians by geographic region, and to encourage medical schools to develop outreach programs for underserved populations. Even these attempts, however, are too limited in scope. They fail to redistribute the economic largess that accrues to those populations having local health care institutions and adequate health manpower (the health fields are, in the aggregate, the nation's third largest employer). They provide traditional modes of service that fail to breach cultural barriers to service. They do not provide the health leadership and public information required to influence the health habits of the population, and they do not provide professional career opportunities, guidance, or professional role-modeling for the young.[15]

The policy process described here would result in increased self-reliance on the part of all American communities. Major health institutions would be developed in the communities they are supposed to serve. Institutional leadership would be representative of the users of service with respect to race, ethnic group, language, and other cultural variables. Programs of care would be the product of joint community and professional effort. The health institution would become a local cultural, social, and economic resource, as well as a provider of technical services.

In this approach the health institution also redistributes private providers of health care. For example, the King/Drew Medical Center in Los Angeles County, although only a few years old, has increased private practitioners of medicine in one of the nation's most underserved urban areas; 90 physicians per 100,000 population[3] compared with the national average of 154.[13] More than 70% of the graduates of its postdoctoral medical training programs remain in the local health region. Here they can capitalize on the learning resources of the nearby medical center, following their initial introduction to the people of the region, to their health needs, and to appropriate services responses.

*Health Education.* The overriding challenge to schools training health professionals is to provide increased manpower for primary health care.[16] The need for improved leadership in community health promotion and education for the general population is less frequently acknowledged, although it is the subject of recent federal legislation.[17] However, the curricula and training experiences in health education centers are a jealously guarded preserve of their faculties, who as a group are not as deeply committed to primary care or community education as to clinical science and to teaching hospital services. The tasks of learning and hours of instruction are set by adversarial interactions between the faculties of departments or divisions, including nonmedical scientists representing basic science departments. In recent years, students have played a more important role as members of educational policy and curriculum committees. Nevertheless, the system is subject to cultural lag, resulting from the traditional orientation and education of committee members. Hence, the increasing public demand for primary health care and the interest in developing programs that foster personal self-reliance in matters pertaining to health have met with less than enthusiastic participation on the part of many of the nation's influential educational centers.

The conservative force exerted by the educational system is in some instances useful. It serves as a constant check on rash and ill-considered ventures. For example, the term *primary health care* is used to express virtually every inchoate aspiration of the altruistic spirit of man.[18] The need for health promotion and health education among our citizens is real enough, but there is little in the way of a validated technology for carrying out desired programs that respond to that need.

Again, a comprehensive policy-planning process transcends the product of willful desire on the one hand and inertia on the other. If the services rendered respond to real health needs, have been validated through services research, and are well managed, they are obviously worth teaching. The process assures (to the extent that its components have been measured) a balance between the subjects taught that will reflect something more than the balance of power in the faculty or the personal idiosyncrasies of teachers.

In the real-world education suggested here, a more accurate apportioning is also struck between the service areas covered by training programs for health practitioners. The service system guides the quotas for primary, secondary, and tertiary care professionals. While unlikely to be highly accurate, this method would be a considerable improvement on present crude attempts to provide incentives for the training of consultant teachers which are likely to cause shortages in some vital areas of clinical service, scientific teaching, and the advancement of medical knowledge.

An increased emphasis on primary care education does seem likely, and university faculties will have to find places to practice primary care in order to teach it. They will also have to develop career fields for primary care teachers in a more effective way than current criteria for faculty appointment and promotion allow. Despite enthusiasm for it, primary care is by no means easy to teach or to practice.

At the Drew School, primary care is taken to mean a mode of practicing medicine that provides the first resource for services, and that establishes relations concerned with the whole person. Since it is the first recourse, it must be accessible, bridging current cultural, social, and economic gaps in our ill-defined complex of health care agents and institutions. It also must provide services for all conditions, even if the task is largely one of appropriate referral or emergency care. These conditions require of practitioners an unusual dedication, since availability is implied to ensure the necessary continuity of care and the assurance of personal interest in the patients' welfare. Kessner has pointed out the areas of special knowledge, not currently taught effectively, that are required to manage commonplace conditions such as middle ear infection, iron deficiency anemia, and loss of vision. [19,20]

*Health Research and Evaluation.* Man's subservience to technology has been discussed by humanists for many centuries.[21] Since World War II, however, there has been a mounting crescendo of commentary,[22-24] and both biomedical science and health care technology have been included as targets of criticism.[25] Two major issues have been (a) the social control over science fields[26] and (b) the conduct of research to suit human needs[27] rather than the inspiration of momentary wonderment[28] or the perception of the technically possible.[29]

Since the policy process outlined here proceeds from social need and involves all citizens in the genesis and control of health program activities, it might be thought to result in a protagonistic position favoring targeted bioscience research and stringent public regulation. Nothing could be further from the truth. One aim is to improve the social involvement of scientists and health professionals, resulting in a sharing of the intellectual riches of the scientific tradition and of the biological basis of medicine. Another is to provide the foundations for sound advocacy, based on the projected benefits as well as the estimated hazards of science and technology. Science and technology are a source of legitimate concern to the public, and an adequate public forum is as essential to the nurture of research as it is to the proper safeguarding of man and the whole environment.

Social science methodology has only lately been applied in the health fields, and there is a critical need for small-scale cost-benefit comparisons between different approaches to service, in order to ensure better investment in both publicly and privately supported health care ventures. Unfortunately, however, funding for the manpower and training needed in the area of services research is overly scarce, and as a result there has been an overindulgence in large-scale, uncontrolled social experiments with unknown effects on the recipient of care. These ventures might prove in the long run to be as questionable in ethical terms as were certain bioscientific investigations recently shown to have been conducted with inadequate safeguards for human subjects.

The tides have washed many times over arguments about the worth of civilization,[30] of the arts and sciences,[31] and of science and technology.[32] Just now, the context for debate is influenced by a prevalent feeling of alienation from the technological world. Is the modern science-culture a fading star? Man has thrown over previous technologies thought to be outworn.[33] Has science become irrelevant for the individual?

This debate has spread into the arena of most intimate concern for the individual man and woman, the biosciences and scientific medicine. Studies based on historical data[34] and on services research[11] indicate the preponderant role played by environmental factors, and the relatively minor part assigned to scientific medical care, in reducing the burden of illness. Further, it is asserted that bioscience has had little to do with the increasing life expectancy in advanced technical societies of the Western world.[35] This is believed to have resulted from change not purposefully directed toward the solution of health problems. The advent of scientific medicine during the 19th century is thought to have had no impact on the reduction of disease then and little now, and to offer even less promise for the relief of handicapping conditions in the future.

These attacks on the worth of bioscience and medical technology have been coupled with a mounting crescendo of criticism concerning the hazards associated with laboratory discovery and the misuse of new technologies.[36] It is asserted that "biocrats," an elite dissociated from the general public, respond to imperatives of behavior that endanger the public safety and fail to respond to human needs.

This critique has been largely parochial, occurring in industrialized nations of the West and conducted by the privileged class of college-educated political and social leaders. It neglects both the observed need for relief of misery and human degradation in third world countries and the observed avidity with which leaders in those technological backwaters seize on the opportunities provided by science and technology to solve their problems and to advance their peoples. Further, it neglects the observed role of scientific medicine in reducing mortality among disadvantaged and minority populations in the industrialized nations themselves.

Hence, it is worthwhile to examine briefly some of the remarkable conclusions drawn by recent critics of bioscience and scientific medicine. First, few would deny that the burden of illness was lifted by the science and technology that allowed improved nutrition through the advancement of agriculture, or improved sanitation through the construction of modern sewage disposal systems. Further, it is clear that personal hygiene has improved, and the knowledge that infection is caused by microbial agents must be acknowledged as having played a role in reducing illness since, for example, our ancestors suffered from preventable plagues, infestations, and body sores despite the availability of abundant stores of clean water.

As for more current developments, modern chemotherapeutics and vaccines may indeed be mixed blessings.[36] However, smallpox, the scourge of the majority of mankind, has been eradicated in our time. Even in the West, pneumonia, a terrible menace to all when many of us began the practice of medicine, has now been eradicated in virtually every age group save the very old. When available, medical care of pregnant women and their newborn infants improves the chance of survival and the future health of both mothers and children.

Further, in the future the public must turn more and more to the biosciences for information about personal health habits and the hazards of new technologies. Scientific medicine has elucidated miner's lung, the hazards of industrial exposure to arsenic, asbestos, and polyvinyl pyrolidine, and the hazards of cigarette smoking, lack of exercise, and diets rich in calories and cholesterol. More recently, bioscientists have called a moratorium on their own research involving the development of new life forms through genetic experiments.

The collection of knowledge is the first step in improving health. It is true that the major killers of today are social and behavioral. However, once made explicit through demonstration, these causes also respond to public concern. Is a shortened life-span based in part on lack of physical exercise? Jogging and individual sports (e.g., tennis) become increasingly popular and organized. Life insurance companies provide incentives for exercise. Industrial plants install gymnasia. Is diet a major factor? Health foods and popular literature on diet are increasingly in demand (although some are based on fad or fancy). Americans learn more about nutrition, escape blind ethnic habits, and give themselves and their children better diets.

This is the true social responsibility of the bioscientist: to inform the public, the helping professions, teachers, scholars, and public officials. It is unrealistic to assume that the poor of this world will relinquish the hopes of technology. For that matter, it is unthinkable that the industrialized nations of the West would return to some paleolithic condition of life, characterized as they are by vast populations requiring advanced technologies for their daily subsistence. Seen in this light, it is unnecessary to excuse science by conjuring up the myth of progress or by fostering targeted research. Instead, it follows that science must be made to restrain technology (as well as the hostile forces of nature), provide us with health and leisure for the good life, and foster both moral honesty and the venturesome spirit of man.

Many years ago, Alfred North Whitehead defined the functions of reason to be threefold: survival, the comfortable life, and the pursuit of goodness.[37] Man seems fated to live by his wits.[38] Revelations that modern scientists are narrow-minded[39,40] and self-centered,[41] that the primacy of publishing first motivates many[42] and that their ambitions lead to deceit or dishonesty[43] are all the more troublesome because of our need for the humanizing influence of science.[44]

The tasks of public policy for science are to capture its discoveries and to preserve and protect its integrity. We have not begun to capitalize on the basic wellsprings of scientific wonder to inform ourselves and to educate our children. The power of demonstration has been little used to validate mandated programs of regulation, service, or public safety. Instead, we have attacked the personally disinterested search for truth by demanding immediate technical applications. The public policy outlined here would encourage the full participation of scientists in everyday life, but as a special group, uniquely equipped to contribute to the public welfare.

*Resources and Management.* Responses to the myriad structural defects in health systems have been unsystematic, expensive, and often insufficiently justified. They have been carried out in an atmosphere created by rhetorical as well as actual crisis. For example, the fiscal plight of contemporary urban health care is all too painfully real.[45] On the other hand, hazards due to food preservatives appear, in some instances, to have been alleged with more strident vehemence than a considered review of the evidence would warrant.[46] As a result, piecemeal reforms have not always proved durable or effective.[47]

It does seem clear that deficiencies are qualitative and not always susceptible to a guns *and* butter approach. Studies on the metabolism of the national health dollar have shown higher per capita spending in some disadvantaged areas than in affluent communities already adequately supplied with health manpower and other resources.[48] Obviously, the recipients of care have not received benefits commensurate with spending. Closer scrutiny reveals an inefficient use of expensive elements of the health care system rather than less costly and often superior services.[49]

Many studies have demonstrated that the poor have been habituated to use expensive hospital emergency rooms for primary care[50] because of the lack of primary care services in their communities. Due to lack of facilities for primary care, disproportionate numbers are hospitalized unnecessarily. Of course, the care rendered is low in quality and fails to fulfill necessary prerequisites of primary care discussed here. It is also more expensive than primary care. For example, in Los Angeles County, the charge for an initial outpatient visit at one public hospital is $100, considerably higher than the charge for a thorough initial physical checkup in the average private physician's office in one of the affluent sections of the city. The daily rate for hospitalized patients is $200.

Recognizing these cost-benefit factors, the County Department of Health Services launched an ambitious plan several years ago to develop a series of primary care ambulatory centers, deemphasizing the hospital's role in services for ambulatory patients. Unfortunately, this commitment has been suspended due to the current fiscal shortfall. Hospitals, on the other hand, have continued to enjoy the highest priority for funding because of their role in serving the critically ill. Primary care centers and their staffs receive the brunt of the cutbacks because preventive services and the care of apparently minor illnesses (primary care) enjoy a lower funding priority.

The situation in Los Angeles County is part of a national problem affecting all public hospitals.[51] While generally considered to be one aspect of the urban crisis, it is more accurately part of a public institution crisis. For example, in the state of California all public hospitals are in trouble. More than half have been closed during the past three years, including those in rural areas. Many reasons are cited: unwieldy and expensive civil service systems, cost inflation in the health care industry, hospital overbuilding, among others. Indeed, the problems are so complex as to defy solution, unless elected officeholders and appointed public officials make use of a more rational policy process that arranges services according to human needs. Resource allocations, including personnel, can be defined quantitatively and qualitatively, once the services responses have been adequately justified and, of course, established to be cost-efficient and effective.

While the most immediate impact of dismantling the public health system is on the poor, the general population also is affected. The long-range costs of dropping programs of disease prevention and early treatment with regard to increases in chronic disease care, intensive care of serious disease complications, and loss of social productivity of the handicapped cannot be accurately calculated, but would appear to be high. There are also more diffuse consequences on personal attitudes, career opportunities, and employment that contribute to social discord and the apathetic anarchy of the 1970s.

In this regard, it should be remembered that elimination of metropolitan health systems is accompanied by cutbacks in other public programs affecting health (e.g., school health). The resultant increase in crime, the spread of contagion to the general population, drug addiction, and the other symptoms of social disorganization are even further from the current capabilities of measurement systems. It is certain, however, that there will be untoward consequences for all Americans.

The private health sector is beset by comparable cost inflation and inappropriate priorities in the allocation of resources for service.[52] Unfortunately, in both private and public facilities, the first step in developing services, research, and education has been the acquisition of resources. Institutions have developed according to the availability of dollars for the construction of beds and development of research projects and the availability of classrooms and funded personnel. This has resulted in a backward planning process that is wasteful and fails to respond to rational planning priorities based on the needs of people, of manpower quotas, or of the orderly acquisition of new knowledge.

Unfortunately, governments at all levels have encouraged this disorder. For example, federal Hill-Burton funds for the construction of hospital facilities have resulted in expensive overbedding in most communities. Manpower training dollars have contributed to specialty maldistribution by encouraging the development of elaborate training facilities for surgical subspecialties in university hospitals. Targeted contracts and grants for cancer research have drained personnel and interest away from basic science and into the further proliferation of new technologies.

The central policy issue is frequently posed as an antagonism between organized ("rational") programming on the one hand and "categorical" responses to isolated health problems on the other. Administrators in the great public agencies seek large-scale coordinated programs (e.g., national health insurance). Politicians prefer more direct, smaller-scale efforts, each designed to meet an immediate need of constituents.

There is no way to resolve this issue without a generally agreed-upon public policy process. National health insurance (in whatever form) is again a good example. It will be expensive, and the money will inevitably be taken from programs providing resources to underserved areas, the poor and minorities. By itself, it will not resolve the complexity of our current health policy. On the other hand, anyone who has worked on Capitol Hill can attest to the increasing fanaticism of single-issue advocates who cause waste through expensive and unnecessary federal regulations[53] or to the many poorly verified legislative responses to vested interest scientists, educators, and health professionals.[54] Single-issue fanatics will tell an elected public official that no matter how well he has done his job, they will oppose him with votes and money if he doesn't vote their way on one issue (e.g., therapeutic abortion). Their stance, although at fundamental odds with a democratic system of government, can be effective. The special-interest groups can point to the economic impact of a new hospital in the district, with equal effect.

Yet, it is the task of leadership to resolve complexity. Cost escalation, waste, inequities, and poor standards in both private and public health care sectors can be traced to the disorganized nature of advocacy, services, education, and research. Resolution depends on a unifying effort and the achievement of a new synthesis. Public administrators will have to involve themselves with organized advocacy, the heterogeneous service needs of all Americans, the development of competency-based educational programs, and the humanistic basis for the pursuit of technical knowledge before they can lead the nation toward a simpler and better health care system.

Documentary evidence betrays the unfamiliarity of our most important public administrators with specific categorical needs of the people, as well as the corruption of our most important documents of public managerial information. Take, for example, the forward health plan of the federal Department of Health, Education and Welfare.[54] While the necessary obeisance is made to health promotion and disease prevention, there are no operational suggestions as to how these top priorities (specified in the plan) are to be carried out. Consider the President's Budget for Fiscal Year (FY) 1976.[55] Fiscal outlays projected by the federal Office of Management and Budget are compared with mythical projected outlays from the President's FY 1975 budget rather than those resulting from congressional interaction with the executive branch.[56] This was done to cover up budget cuts by the President.[57] These are hardly evidences of the moral standards or technical information expected of our managerial and public leadership (or increasingly exacted by them of others in the health professions).

It has been correctly stated that in a democracy the people rule, and that they rule well in proportion to their education.[58] Our people should be given an opportunity to learn about health, health care, health care education, scientific research, health economics, and health administration by the health professions created to serve the public interest. Each of the professions in turn must participate together with the others in a rational and organized public policy process such as the one advocated here.

## CONCLUSIONS

Improved communication in the health fields depends on the clarification of thought. Most decisions are not at present based on evidence and logical inference. A process of logical analysis regarding health should proceed through an orderly consideration of human needs, services based on those needs, manpower training based on services, and a systematic advancement of knowledge, before resources are acquired or managerial systems are developed.

Logical planning is unusual at the local institutional level. Master planning committees develop buildings prior to deciding exactly what should happen in them. Policy-makers find themselves with empty hospital beds that they must scramble to fill. Third-party payers of health services, both public and private, provide incentives to keep both medical care expenses and hospital bed occupancy high, because hospitals are otherwise unable to balance their budgets.

Science is insulated from education. The recent emphasis on primary care has often led to castigation of the scientific basis of clinical thought and practice. The result, as any department chairman can tell you, is that there are insufficient numbers of high-quality specialists and scholars being trained to adequately staff our teaching hospitals.

Education has been so long divorced from the needed skills of practice that we systematically mistrain our physicians, nurses, and other health care providers. Only recently have attempts been made to develop explicit educational objectives and formal, performance-based learning experiences in schools of medicine. Relating such objectives and experiences to the daily tasks and needed competencies of practitioners is a still more distant future goal.

Organized medicine often finds itself advocating programs of service for which there is no validating evidence of worth. For example, when the American Academy of Pediatrics sought to prevent underfunding of the nation's Maternal and Child Program in 1975, it was defending one of our better administered and most effective federal health ventures; however, data indicating that the services cut mortality or morbidity or improved the health and well-being of American children were embarrassingly scanty.

It is surprising that professions which glory in being "scientific" and a nation whose political principles are derived from British empiricism have developed such an upside-down way of doing things. The former characteristic implies an intellectual method based on direct observations of real-life facts, proceeding through postulates and theories to establish truths.[59] The latter principles presuppose that an informed public makes the decisions that govern it.[60] Neither is compatible with the processes of thought and the governance of a central professional or managerial elite. I suggest that we should reclaim our democratic and scientific heritage in the health policy field.

## REFERENCES AND NOTES

1. Aspen Biosciences Communications Seminars, 1976.
2. Richmond, J. B., 1969, *Currents in American Medicine,* Harvard University Press, Cambridge.
3. Schlegel, R. J., 1976, Phase II Robert Wood Johnson Primary Health Care Planning Project, Charles R. Drew Postgraduate School, Director M. Alfred Haynes.
4. Controls on Health Care, Institute of Medicine, National Academy of Sciences, Washington, D.C., 1975.
5. Dubos, R., 1959, *Mirage of Health,* Doubleday, Garden City, New York.
6. Fuchs, V. R., 1974, *Who Shall Live?,* Basic Books, New York.
7. Lalonde, M., 1974, A new perspective on the health of Canadians, Ministry of National Health and Welfare, Ottawa, Canada.
8. Kessner, D. M., Singer, J., Kalk, C. E., and Schlesinger, E. W., 1973, Infant death: An analysis by maternal risk and health care, Institute of Medicine, National Academy of Sciences, Washington, D.C.
9. Eisenberg, B. S., and Aherne, P., 1974, *Socioeconomic Issues of Health,* American Medical Association, Chicago.
10. Okun, A. M., 1975, *Equality and Efficiency,* Brookings, Washington, D.C.
11. Cochrane, A. L., 1972, *Effectiveness and Efficiency,* Burgess and Son, Berks, London.
12. Ehrenreich, B., and Ehrenreich, J., 1972, *The American Health Empire,* Vantage, New York.
13. The Supply of Health Manpower, DHEW Publication No. (HRA) 75-38.
14. Alpert, J., and Charney, E., The Education of Physicians for Primary Health Care, DHEW Publication (HRA) 74-3113.

15. Carlson, R. J., 1976, *The Frontiers of Science and Medicine*, Regnery, Chicago.
16. Andreopoulos, S., 1974, *Primary Care*, Wiley, New York.
17. Roy, W. R., 1976, An agenda for physicians and legislators, *N. Engl. J. Med.* **295**:589.
18. Parker, A. W., 1972, *The Team Approach to Primary Health Care*, University of California Press, Berkeley.
19. Kessner, D. M., Kalk Snow, C., and Singer, J., 1974, Assessment of medical care for children, Institute of Medicine, National Academy of Sciences, Washington, D.C.
20. Kessner, D. M., 1973, A strategy for evaluating health services, Institute of Medicine, National Academy of Sciences, Washington, D.C.
21. Mumford, L., 1963, *Technics and Civilization*, Harcourt, Brace and World, New York.
22. Toynbee, A., 1976, *Mankind and Mother Earth*, Oxford University Press, London.
23. Carson, R., 1962, *Silent Spring*, Houghton Mifflin, New York.
24. Commoner, B., 1971, *The Closing Circle*, Knopf, New York.
25. Dubos, R., 1965, *Man Adapting*, Yale University Press, New Haven.
26. Hiatt, H., 1976, The use of basic research, *New York Times*, September 8.
27. Melnick, V. L., Melnick, D., and Fundenberg, H. H., 1976, Participation of biologists in the formulation of national science policy, *Fed. Proc.* **35**:1957.
28. Pieper, J., 1952, *Leisure*, Pantheon, New York.
29. Polanyi, M., 1966, *The Tacit Dimension*, Doubleday, New York.
30. Toynbee, A. J., 1947, *A Study of History* (Abridgement of Volumes I-VI by D. C. Somerwell), Oxford University Press, New York.
31. Rousseau, M., 1952, *On the Origin of Inequality*, Great Books of the Western World, Encyclopedia Britannica, Chicago.
32. Moore, W. E., 1972, *Technology and Social Change*, Quadrangle Books, Chicago.
33. Huizinga, J., 1924, *The Waning of the Middle Ages*, Edward Arnold, London.
34. McKeown, T., and Lowe, C. R., 1974, *An Introduction to Social Medicine*, 2nd ed., Blackwell, Oxford.
35. Leach, G., 1970, *The Biocrats*, McGraw-Hill, Philadelphia.
36. Moser, R., 1965, *Diseases of Medical Progress*, Mosby, Philadelphia.
37. Whitehead, A. R., 1929, *The Function of Reason*, Beacon Press, Boston.
38. Bronowski, J., 1966, *The Identity of Man*, American Museum Science Books, Garden City, New York.
39. Russell, B., 1931, *The Scientific Outlook*, Free Press, Glencoe, Ill.
40. Watson, J. D., 1968, *The Double Helix*, Atheneum, New York.
41. Snow, C. P., 1962, *Science and Government*, Harvard University Press, Cambridge.
42. Merton, R. K., 1973, *The Sociology of Science*, University of Chicago Press, Chicago.
43. Hixson, J., 1976, *The Patchwork Mouse*, Doubleday, Garden City, New York.
44. Bronowski, J., 1976, *Science and Human Values*, Harper & Row, New York.
45. Bird, D., 1976, Controversy rages on whether municipalities should run own hospitals, *New York Times*, October 14.
46. Turner, J. S., 1970, *The Chemical Feast*, Grossman, New York.
47. Davis, K., 1973, *Rising Hospital Costs: Possible Causes and Cures*, Brookings, Washington, D.C.
48. Community Funds Flow Study, East Los Angeles Health Systems, Inc., 1972.
49. Davis, K., and Russell, L. B., 1972, *The Substitution of Hospital Outpatient Care for Inpatient Care*, Brookings, Washington, D.C.
50. Hestor, A. W., and Berki, S. E., 1972, The nation's health: Some issues, *Ann. Am. Acad. Polit. Soc. Sci.* **399**:1.
51. Blake, E., and Bodenheimer, T., 1974, Hospitals for sale, *Ramparts* **12**:28.
52. Davis, K., 1974, *Economic Theories of Behaviour in Private Nonprofit Hospitals*, Brookings, Washington, D.C.

53. McKie, J. W., 1974, *The Ends and Means of Regulation*, Brookings, Washington, D.C.
54. Miles, R., Jr., 1974, *The Department of Health, Education and Welfare*, Prolger, New York.
55. Special Analysis, Budget of the United States Government, Fiscal Year 1976.
56. First Concurrent Resolution on the Budget, Fiscal Year 1976, Senate Report No. 94-97.
57. Blechman, B. M., Gramlich, E. M., and Hartman, R. W., 1975, *Setting National Priorities. The 1976 Budget*, Brookings, Washington, D.C.
58. Hutchins, R. M., 1943, *Education for Freedom*, Louisiana State University Press, Baton Rouge.
59. McKeon, R., 1952, *Freedom and History*, Noonday Press, New York.
60. Dewey, J., 1933, *How We Think*, Heath, New York.

# 11

# Specialization as Scientific Advancement and Overspecialization as Social Distortion

## DONALD W. SELDIN

Specialization has been construed to be central to the problem of the allocation of medical manpower in the United States. I would like to begin by challenging this supposition which is implicit in the health manpower legislation now under discussion.

To my mind anyway, we owe nearly everything to medical specialization. It is the singular expression of the manner in which biomedical science has evolved. Before the Second World War, most physicians were largely spectators on the medical scene—concerned, kindly, decent—but nevertheless spectators. Medicine was dominated by a priestly function: the provision of sympathetic care by a physician in a paternalistic relationship with a patient based on understanding and trust. No one can fail to be inspired by the nobility inherent in such a relationship. But medical knowledge and skills were primitive, and played little role in anchoring the bonds of the relationship to the capacity of the physician to mitigate sickness.

It was essentially the development of biomedical sciences, in particular the application of the generalizing sciences, physics and chemistry, to biology, that fostered the emergence of a powerful scientific framework for the management of disease. Such a development provided medicine with the scientific base that distinguishes the physician from all other healers. This vital ingredient may be defined as the application of the theoretical knowledge incorporated in medical science to the relief of pain, the prevention of disability, and the saving of life in individual patients.

Since the Second World War, the scientific base of medicine has expanded enormously. Some diseases, previously occupying the forefront of medicine, have been virtually eliminated. By way of illustration, certain

Reprinted from *Clin. Res.* **24**:245-248, 1976, with permission.

DONALD W. SELDIN • Department of Internal Medicine, University of Texas Southwestern Medical School, Dallas, Texas 75221.

types of pneumococcal pneumonia and poliomyelitis come quickly to mind. In other instances the personal and social burdens of disease have been enormously reduced: the substitution of antibiotics for sanatoria in the treatment of tuberculosis constitutes a monumental triumph for medicine even though the disease is still with us. These instances illustrate the successful reduction of a disease process to its causal root and its subsequent elimination. In the terminology of Lewis Thomas, the cure or prevention of a disease by removing the cause is a high technology—enormously effective and comparatively simple. Indeed, where the causal grounds of a disease can be understood and eliminated, the disease often disappears or becomes readily manageable. For this reason many of the great triumphs of medicine—particularly in infectious disease—are now unnoticed because the diseases have virtually disappeared.

We focus on what remains. But despite past triumphs, what remains is a legacy of increasing responsibility for the physician. In part, successful prevention and treatment of many infectious diseases have been responsible for increased life expectancy. In consequence an older population, vulnerable to a different set of disorders—poorly understood and inadequately treated—assumes the center of the arena. The therapeutic armamentarium applied to these disorders is often weak or incomplete. The cry is then raised that the inadequate medical care is the consequence of a failure to apply basic knowledge to clinical problems. It is more accurate to acknowledge that the theoretical knowledge required for the understanding of the major diseases is painfully fragmentary. The conquest of cancer is a laudable social goal, but its realization on the basis of present theoretical knowledge would be akin to charging pre-Newtonian physics with the responsibility of designing and fabricating an atomic reactor.

Lacking full causal explanations for the principal remaining diseases, medicine has nevertheless not been paralyzed. Partial understanding of a disease process permits the development, again in the terminology of Thomas, of halfway technologies—measures designed to alleviate the consequences of disease rather than eliminate the cause. Dialysis and transplantation for kidney disease, pacemakers for heart disease, respirators for pulmonary disease, and phenothiazines for psychoses are representative of the extensive surgical, medical, and pharmacologic technology developed to reduce suffering and postpone death.

Short of eliminating its cause, there is a further and more subtle way medicine intervenes to treat sickness. Until comparatively recently illness was conceived as a collection of discrete disease entities. It is now increasingly possible to analyze sickness as derangement of regulatory function. Correction of the derangement may restore normal function irrespective of the particular cause of the disease even when the disease process is inactive. The administration of potassium salts, for example, may be life-saving, though causes such as vomiting or diarrhea may have disappeared or cannot be identified. In this way the physician mitigates or even cures disorders on the basis of understanding the mechanism of a derangement even when no cause is identifiable. This explosive advance of the explanatory power of medical science pervades every branch of medicine.

Admittedly responsible in part for the forbidding perception of modern medicine as impersonal, disembodied, mechanical, it is nevertheless this growth of medical science and its ancillary technology that has been the driving force for the greatly expanded competence of the physician in diagnosis and treatment. In cardiology it is the insight gleaned from the newer theories of circulatory performance coupled to the data provided by the technology of cardiovascular evaluation—electrocardiogram, phonocardiogram, echocardiogram, cardiac catheterization, roentgenographic visualization, and the like—that has served to sharpen existing diagnostic categories, uncovered hitherto unsuspected disturbances, and permitted objective assessment of therapeutic interventions. Like any other rapidly advancing discipline, medicine may be plagued with mistakes and misuses. However, the surest way to reduce or eliminate inept performance is to incorporate the most enlightened knowledge into medical practice. Inevitably, this means specialization. Nephrologists, cardiologists, neurosurgeons, and similar specialists are required so that the complex conceptual and technologic machinery of medicine may be applied to patients for the alleviation of sickness. Viewed from the framework of medical science, therefore, specialization is the inexorable consequence of expanding medical theory and technology.

Outside the boundaries of medical science specialization is seen from a different vantage point. In the social domain, which is the matrix of medical practice, the overriding national need is perceived to be the allocation, at reasonable cost, of physicians with competence in primary care to sparsely populated rural areas and impoverished urban slums. Some observers regard specialization as the greatest barrier to the attainment of this admittedly laudable social goal. The heavy concentration of specialists in attractive medical and social environments has had the effect of draining medical manpower and misallocating physicians to locations and disciplines already oversupplied. Moreover, the complex technology associated with specialization results in inordinate cost inflation, whether borne directly by the patient or passed off to a third party. Finally, it is contended that the highly refined specialist is so dependent upon his expensive diagnostic and therapeutic machinery and so restricted in his area of competence that he is fundamentally unsuited for the task of ministering primary care.

The principal device proposed to correct this maldistribution of medical manpower is a revision of the medical curriculum. Basic sciences are reduced or eliminated; clinical demonstrations generously decorate basic lectures and seminars; students are assigned for clinical clerkships to the offices of physicians often only marginally connected with the medical faculty; coercive social devices are imposed with the aim of distributing students to rural areas or deprived communities. In a real sense there has been a capture of the medical curriculum, not as an expression of a fresh educational philosophy but rather to correct a pressing social problem.

It is my belief that this attempt to resolve the problem of allocation of physicians by tampering and tinkering with the medical school is tragically misguided. Such an invasion of the academic curriculum may well destroy the structure of the medical school as an institution to provide students with an education that is based soundly on the biomedical sciences, while leaving wholly untouched the social forces driving toward increasing misallocation of discipline and location.

Specialization, like the division of labor, is the inevitable outgrowth of advancing knowledge. The emergence of specialized disciplines simply gives concrete expression to the requirement to limit one's focus when a domain of knowledge becomes intellectually complex. Specialized knowledge may be incorporated into medical practice in two ways. Physicians—internists or other generalists—may comfortably command a central core of medicine; their knowledge is broad. A second group of physicians, by contrast, devotes itself to a narrow discipline in which its expertise is presumably highly penetrating. Both activities are the natural outcome of the growth of biomedical science, and consequently are the institutional devices through which biomedical theory is applied to diagnosis and treatment of patients.

We are now confronted with the problem of *overspecialization*. This is not a simple consequence of the influence of biomedical science or the type of medical education. Overspecialization is a social problem. It arises because the social incentives for certain types of specialty practice are greater than for alternative modes of practice. Its cure lies in the domain of social rewards and penalties, not education.

Consider how the medical student and house officer perceive the exhortations exalting the need for physicians competent in primary care. On the one hand the critical importance and moral dignity inherent in the role of family physician are emphasized; on the other, social emoluments in the form of financial rewards, leisure, and prestige are disproportionately awarded to the specialist. In some hospitals an all-night vigil for the treatment of diabetic acidosis or hepatic coma is rewarded with a standard $8 fee for professional care. In contrast, a ten-minute endoscopy in the same institution earns $100. All sorts of *procedures*, however routine, however marginally important, are abundantly rewarded. The financial returns are generous, the surroundings attractive and stimulating, the commitment of time often brief. Even the requirement for profound understanding of the deranged physiology involved may be modest. On the other hand, the painful mastery of medicine and extended commitment of time and effort required for the management of many chronic diseases is often unaccompanied by those social reinforcements—money, educational opportunities, well-supported medical facilities—that would counterbalance the formidable disadvantages in medical and social environment.

Our message is schizophrenic. We emphasize to students and house staff the crying need for primary care, at the same time that we signal them surreptitiously, by way of financial incentives and other attractions, that enormously greater rewards lie in the direction we are telling them to forego.

If we are overspecialized, why should the rewards be so generous to the specialists whom we do not want? Why do we continually reinforce what we wish to discourage? In one department of medicine, 18% of the income is derived from endoscopic procedures; if electrocardiography and cardiac catheterization are added, 60% of the total income is derived from three technical maneuvers. No wonder endoscopy is all the rage and every community hospital requires a modern catheterization unit. The last new note in medicine is identified by what we reward, not by what we piously proclaim. Our practices, not our precepts, are triumphant.

Physicians are probably no worse than anybody else but certainly no better. Students and house officers partake of ordinary human frailty. Let us not flagellate the educational system for the misallocation of medical resources it can neither prevent nor correct.

I take a different view of the role of the academic medical center from that advocated by proponents of primary care who would restructure the medical curriculum. Their formulations contain several assumptions that deserve to be made explicit. One is the notion that what has not been taught cannot be learned, that one learns only from formal communication in a structured teaching syllabus. According to this view, education is a contrived and formal affair, a matter of courses and lectures.

The second tacit assumption is the postulate that there is a special domain of knowledge—a specific and unique area of learning—that is subsumed under the name of primary care, a domain that is not covered by our present educational structure.

I am not aware of any body of knowledge unique to primary care. To be sure, the medical issues that dominate primary care occupy the central core of medicine and often are of a mundane rather than highly technical nature. But the framework of biomedical science required to manage such problems with medical competence is already incorporated in the standard clinical disciplines of internal medicine, pediatrics, obstetrics and gynecology, and psychiatry. What is distinctive about primary care is the social setting—the family unit, the interaction of patient and physician in the environment of the community over long periods of time, and the complex relationships imposed by the requirement for *care* as well as medical science.

No one challenges the importance of these activities. Everyone recognizes the intricate fusion in medical practice of medical science, social arrangements, and sympathetic concern. No one doubts that effective primary care requires well-trained nurses, good records, efficient office management, and the like. But these necessary skills are presumably acquired as part of active practice. They do not constitute a formal domain of knowledge. Given a sound educational background, we learn primary care while doing it.

Other countries have struggled with similar problems. In Sweden, for example, it is a critical social necessity to attract physicians into the north to furnish medical care for the workers in iron mines and steel mills. The arctic cold is apparently a major deterrent, even to Swedes. Were a similar problem to arise in the United States, I suppose the automatic response would be a frenzied alteration of the medical school curriculum to prepare and encourage physicians for northerly migration. In socialist Sweden the issue is not regarded as educational. Rather, social and economic incentives are employed to the extent required to counterbalance the unattractive environment.

In England, whatever the issues plaguing the National Health Service, the provision of primary care physicians is no problem. By offering them a greater remuneration than specialists, they are now dealing with the problem of an oversupply, a problem quickly rectified by diminishing appropriately their financial rewards.

In my opinion it is a serious confusion to pose as educational problems the misallocation of physicians with respect to both specialization and geographic location and the mounting costs of medical care. To be sure the medical school furnishes the foundation of biomedical science that is the indispensable basis of intelligent medical practice. How and where the physician utilizes this background is determined in the aggregate principally by social forces.

At present the major allocating device in this country is the fee-for-service system, a system that is not allocating medical resources in accord with social needs. The failure is not hard to understand. The abundance of funds for medical care ensures that financial resources are available in areas oversupplied with physicians no less than in underserved areas. Since the former are likely to be accompanied by attractive medical, cultural, and social assets as well, physicians will be drawn to areas where they are least needed. If third-party payments afford a sumptuous reward for procedures requiring a complex technology, we are in effect encouraging the purchase of expensive equipment and the payment of high medical fees. This would be justified if the procedures were desperately needed and in short supply. However, the purchase of expensive technical equipment is often generously supported and its utilization highly rewarded, even though the medical value is minor and the procedures conveniently available.

Clearly, the market mechanism is not allocating resources and personnel in accordance with social needs, and this misallocation is powerfully reinforced by both private and public programs of medical benefits and insurance. If we are committed to redress the misallocation of medical personnel, financial and social incentives must be used to alter market forces so as to provide rewards in accord with our social goals. By intelligently deploying the enormous leverage of social incentives and disincentives, using our resources to reinforce our social goals, we should be able to correct the problem of overspecialization and at the same time benefit from the power of specialization to mitigate human suffering.

The medical school has as its necessary responsibility the education of the physician and the development of the conceptual and technical tools required for him to function. This is its primary obligation, to the immediate community as well as to the community at large. To discharge this function may be only a small contribution to the arena of medicine, but it is a contribution that only the medical school can make, and if made well it is not an insignificant achievement.

# 12

# The Education of Black Health Professionals

## LOUIS W. SULLIVAN

Of the 357,000 practicing physicians in the country today, only 6840, or 2.2%, are black, although the nation's 25 million blacks represent 12% of the total population. Nationally, there is one white physician for every 528 white persons, whereas the ratio of black physicians to the black population is 1 to 4100. Furthermore, at the present rate of entry of minority students into medical school, the optimal physician ratio will not be reached for another 20 years or more.[1]

Clearly, U.S. medical schools are not adequately addressing the need for more minority physicians. In 1971-72 the nation's 108 medical schools enrolled 43,650 students, of whom 2055 were black Americans. In 1975-76 there were 114 medical schools in the United States, with 55,818 students, of whom 3456 were black Americans: In other words, six new medical schools and 12,168 new places in medical schools, representing a 27.8% increase in places, as compared with an increase in black medical students to only 6.3% of the total first-year enrollment during this interval.

These statistics speak for themselves. During the past ten years, at the height of the minority recruitment effort, the number of students admitted to medical schools has almost doubled. However, black and other minority students occupied less than 10% of these places. While American minority groups constitute close to one-fifth of the nation's total population, only one in every 15 first-year medical school seats is held by a black, Mexican-American, mainland Puerto Rican, or native American.[2]

The situation is critical. Whatever optimism one can muster when reviewing the history of black physicians must center on the exceptional achievements of those determined men and women who have succeeded

Reprinted from *PHYLON* **38**:181-193, 1977, with permission.

LOUIS W. SULLIVAN • School of Medicine at Morehouse College, Atlanta, Georgia 30304.

in the medical profession despite the enormous barriers to their full and equal participation in this important area of American life.

## HISTORICAL PERSPECTIVE

It is important to remember that from the earliest days of their presence in this country, blacks were counted among the successful medical practitioners. The first African physician in the colonies, Lucas Santomee Peters, was voted a special grant for his service in 1667 by the New York colony where he practiced.[3]

In contrast to Dr. Peters, who had been formally educated in Holland, there was the South Carolina slave named Caesar, who, though self-taught, was a well-known and successful medical practitioner. In fact, Caesar's remedy for snakebite was so effective and in such demand that it was published in 1792 in the first black medical publication in America, *Massachusetts Magazine*.[4]

At the time of the American Revolution, the majority of medical practitioners, both African slaves and white colonists, were either self-taught or apprentice-trained. The slaves brought with them from Africa their own "materia medica," an understanding of how to make mineral, plant, and herb concoctions which were effective medicines. Some of the women slaves who practiced midwifery performed Caesarean section deliveries, a procedure they had learned in Africa.[5]

Some slaves were able to gain their freedom through their skill in medicine. One of the most famous former slaves to become a physician was James Derham, who, as a boy, was sold to a doctor. After learning to mix drugs and work with patients, Derham was sold to another doctor. The latter was so impressed with Derham's medical skill that he allowed him to purchase his freedom and helped Derham set up practice. By 1789 Dr. Derham was earning $3000 a year in his own thriving medical practice.[6]

There were also instances of apprentice-trained practitioners who eventually attended medical school. Such was the case of Dr. Martin Delany, who attended Harvard University Medical School. Since there were no black medical schools until 1868, all black physicians who received formal professional training either attended white schools, where they were not readily accepted, or studied abroad. Dr. Delany had applied to and been rejected by four medical schools in this country before he was finally accepted at Harvard in 1850.[7]

Dr. James McCune Smith, who came from a "free Negro family," was admitted to the University of Glasgow where he received his M.D. degree in 1837. He later returned to practice medicine in New York City.

Another 19th-century black physician who, because of racial discrimination, was forced to get his medical training in a foreign country, was Dr. Alexander T. Augusta. He received his M.D. in 1856 at Trinity Medical College in Toronto, Canada. Dr. Augusta, who was in charge of the Freedmen's Hospital in Washington, D.C., became the first black to head a hospital in the U.S.[8]

The early struggle of blacks to gain admission to white medical schools deserves special notice. Those blacks who sought formal training in medicine were usually taken under the preceptorship of an established professional physician and were sometimes permitted to attend lectures at a medical college, but were not awarded M.D. degrees.

The education of David K. McDonough, a former slave, illustrates this method of medical training. McDonough's owner sent him to Lafayette College in Pennsylvania, where he received a B.A. degree and graduated third in his class. After graduation, McDonough was sent to New York City, where he received training under a preceptor, Dr. John K. Rodgers, an eminent surgeon and professor of surgery at Columbia's College of Physicians and Surgeons. McDonough was allowed to attend lectures at the college and upon completion of his training obtained a license and was appointed to the New York Eye and Ear Infirmary.[9]

It was not until 1847 that Dr. David J. Peck became the first black American to graduate from a northern medical school, Rush Medical College in Chicago.[10]

By 1860 there were nine northern medical schools which had admitted one or more blacks: Bowdoin in Maine, the Medical School of the University of New York, Caselton Medical School in Vermont, Berkshire Medical School in Pittsfield, Massachusetts, Rush in Chicago, Eclectic Medical School of Philadelphia, Homeopathic College of Cleveland, American Medical College, and the Medical School of Harvard University.[11]

The fact that these schools had admitted blacks for medical training did not mean that this was by any means accepted practice in the 19th century. The training of blacks in the field of medicine was discouraged in most cases unless the would-be doctor intended to practice in Liberia or some other country.[12]

Following the Civil War, the masses of freedmen in Washington,

D.C., found themselves in wretched conditions, faced with the need for emergency health, education, job-placement, and welfare services.

Responding to these needs, Howard University was founded in 1866, and two years later its medical school was opened. The first medical students, seven black and one white, attended classes from 3:30 P.M. to 10:00 P.M. so they could work during the day as federal government employees. Howard's early students represented a wide geographic area—13 states, Washington, D.C., six foreign countries, and the West Indies.[13]

In 1876 Meharry Medical College was opened in Nashville. Its students, mostly from the South, had only rudimentary preparatory education.[14]

Until 1882 Howard and Meharry were the only black medical schools in this country. During the last part of the 19th century six additional black medical schools were founded in response to the social changes that took place following Reconstruction.[15] They were: (1) Leonard Medical School of Shaw University in Raleigh, North Carolina, founded in 1882 and supported by the Baptist Mission Society for Negroes. The North Carolina state legislature contributed the site for a medical building, hospital, dispensary, and dormitory, and the faculty consisted of the leading white physicians of Raleigh. The school graduated a total of some 500 physicians. (2) The Medical Department of the University of West Tennessee in Memphis, founded in 1900 by Dr. Miles V. Lynk, an apprentice-trained physician who was also a graduate of Meharry, and publisher of the *Medical and Surgical Observer*, the first Negro medical journal in the United States. The school graduated 266 physicians. (3) The Louisville National Medical College, founded in 1888; (4) Flint Medical College of New Orleans, founded in 1889; (5) Knoxville Medical College, founded in 1895; (6) Chattanooga Medical School, which existed from 1902 to 1904.

In 1908, the Carnegie Foundation for the Advancement of Teaching commissioned Abraham Flexner to conduct a study of medical education. His report, entitled *Medical Education in the United States and Canada*, was published in 1910 and set the standard for American medical education and medical colleges for the next 50 years.

Flexner's report, which contained a section evaluating the seven black medical schools in existence at the time, was particularly significant in the history of black medical education. Based on personal observation, Flexner recommended that all black medical schools be closed except

Howard and Meharry, because, in his words, they were ineffectual, wasted money, and produced undisciplined men who lacked real training but who carried the M.D. degree. Furthermore, Flexner's comments demonstrate his assumptions that black physicians and nurses would serve only their own race and he urged that medical training for blacks emphasize hygiene rather than surgery.[16] Since the publication of the Flexner report, Howard and Meharry, which both received grade-A accreditations, have provided the country with the bulk of its black physicians.

A complete medical education encompasses more than mere attendance at a medical college. It includes internship and residency, opportunities for specialization, and opportunities for continuing education through interaction with other members of the profession. Blacks have encountered de jure and de facto discrimination in connection with each of these aspects of medical education.

By 1890 a majority of the former Confederate states and border states had succeeded in repealing the civil rights laws enacted during Reconstruction, putting an abrupt end to any opportunity black Southerners might have had to participate fully in all aspects of sound medical education, beginning, of course, with admission to medical school.[17] Here and there, exceptional black students were given the opportunity of entering some of the older medical schools in the East, such as Harvard, Yale, and Pennsylvania, and the newer ones in the Midwest, such as Indiana, Northwestern, and Michigan.[18] However, discriminatory admission policies, which completely excluded black students from white medical schools in the South and provided only token admission in the North, seriously limited the number of black physicians.

The situation did not begin to change until after World War II, when the civil rights movement included an intense campaign to establish the principle of equal rights in the education and training of black doctors and nurses. Particular emphasis was placed on cracking the tough segregationist opposition in the South.

At the beginning of that period, one-third of all the medical schools in the country—26 out of 78 approved medical schools—were in southern and border states. All 26 of these institutions were closed to black students. In its fight to eliminate racially discriminatory policies, the National Association for the Advancement of Colored People instituted a series of legal proceedings which resulted in a number of favorable Supreme Court decisions.[19]

In 1948 the University of Arkansas admitted Edith Mae Irby. Before that, Meharry was the only medical school in the South that blacks could attend.[20] One year later, St. Louis University and the University of Texas admitted black medical students for the first time. Gradually, during the 1950s the doors of medical schools in southern and border states began opening to black students. In 1951 five medical colleges—Washington University, University of Louisville, Medical College of Virginia, University of Maryland, and the University of North Carolina—began admitting black students.[21] By 1960 six more were added to the list. Thus, within a decade, more than half of all southern medical schools—14 out of 26—were admitting black students, although on a token basis.[22]

By the summer of 1963 sufficient advances had been made to open the doors of almost every medical college in the country to black applicants. By then as many as 19 Southern medical schools had admitted black students. Later, by the fall of 1963, two more in the South, Duke and Emory, and one in the border state of Maryland, Johns Hopkins, had followed suit. By the summer of 1966 four additional schools, Baylor, Louisiana State, Vanderbilt, and the Medical College of Alabama, had reversed their white-only admission policies. This brought to 26 the number of southern medical schools that had dropped their racial bars since 1948.[23]

Modern medical training does not stop with graduation from medical school. It includes a one-year internship plus residency training, both of which must be accomplished in an accredited hospital. The internship also became a prerequisite for a license to practice. This was an acute problem for black physicians because there were few accredited hospitals that would accept black trainees. Regardless of how well qualified the black applicants for internship were, there was always the likelihood of their being rejected because of race.[24]

In the late 1930s only 3 large white hospitals accepted black interns—Cook County in Chicago and Harlem and Bellevue in New York. Of the black hospitals, only 12 were approved for 68 internships, and Freedmen's Hospital in Washington, D.C., had as many as 24 interns. Since there were more than 100 black graduates each year from medical schools around the country, this meant a deficit of 30 or more internships annually. The situation gradually improved during the 1930s as the available supply of black internships jumped from 68 to 168.[25]

Some progress was also made during these years in regard to residencies for black physicians. Whereas in the 1920s there were no such posts available, during the 1930s they began to open up in accredited black hospitals. By 1939 seven black hospitals reported a total of 31 residencies for black physicians in eight specialties. Five years later, 25 additional residencies were approved, in addition to those established at Harlem Hospital. The residency was a reflection of the growing trend toward specialization. [26]

The period from 1945 to 1960 also saw black medical school graduates pushing ahead in the important area of postgraduate education. More internships and residencies were opened to them than at any time in the past as an ever-growing number of predominantly white hospitals dropped their racial bars. In 1947, of the 119 graduates of Howard and Meharry, only 49 served internships in 8 white hospitals. In 1956, of their 129 graduates, 77 had internships in 46 white hospitals. Thus, in less than a decade, the number of predominantly white institutions which accepted Howard and Meharry graduates increased almost 500%. Moreover, in 1956 three out of every five graduates of Howard and Meharry served their internships in white hospitals. Whereas in the early 1930s black medical school graduates might have been unable to secure internships, in 1956 there were more such approved posts than there were medical graduates. The same favorable situation prevailed in respect to residencies. In 1956 the number of residencies available to black physicians was sufficient to accommodate all those who sought them, and, as in the case of internships, most of the residencies were in predominantly white hospitals. [27]

By the late 1950s, as a result of the hospital-building program under the Hill-Burton Act, there were 5000 more approved internships than there were students graduating from the medical schools of the country. During the first half of the 1960s, black medical graduates were no longer finding it difficult to secure internships at approved hospitals. In 1965, 134 Howard and Meharry graduates were appointed as interns to 68 hospitals throughout the country. Significantly, few of these hospitals were in the South. By the mid-1960s, there was also an ample supply of residencies for black physicians. This was most important, because by then, approximately 85% of all interns went on to become residents, in keeping with the growing trend toward specialization. [28]

After the completion of formal training, which includes internship and residency, it is important for a physician to further develop his skills through continuing education. There is general agreement among physicians, medical educators, and others who have studied this question that good medical care requires that physicians have access to the important changes and developments in medical knowledge. Probably the most important single element in the continued education of physicians is affiliation with a hospital. The nature of the affiliations and the type of hospitals with which a physician is affiliated is probably the best index of his ability to keep abreast of good medical practice.[29]

In the late 19th and early 20th centuries, the South's hospital accommodations for black patients either were nonexistent or consisted of poorly equipped "colored" wards. As a rule, black physicians did not have the right to attend patients or perform operations in these hospitals. Black physicians responded to these deplorable conditions by taking the lead in building hospitals which would offer care to black patients and provide opportunities for training black physicians. These hospitals were generally sponsored by black schools, churches, and individuals. Freedmen's Hospital, which was connected with Howard University Medical School, was the only one of these early black hospitals that received support from the federal government.[30]

In addition to affiliation with a hospital, membership in professional societies is an important aspect of continued medical education. This was yet another area in which black physicians were denied equal opportunity. It was not unitl 1964 that the American Medical Association voted to accept black members in its local component societies. The struggle for admittance to the AMA began in 1869, when three eminent black physicians applied for membership to the Medical Society of the District of Columbia, an AMA affiliate, and were rejected.

After several unsuccessful attempts to join, a group of black and white physicians, including Howard medical faculty, formed the National Medical Society of the District of Columbia in 1870. This group tried to gain recognition by the AMA at three national conventions, 1870, 1872, and 1874, but was turned down each time. Finally, a group of white physicians who belonged to the AMA affiliate organization in Washington, D.C., announced its disapproval of the organization's racial policy and joined with black physicians in organizing a biracial group in 1884 called the Medico-Chirurgical Society of the District of Columbia. However, as its white members died and were not replaced by other white members, it eventually became an all-black organization.[31]

Several separate medical societies were formed in response to the AMA policy of excluding black physicians: the National Medical Society of the District of Columbia in 1870, the Medico-Chirurgical Society of the

District of Columbia in 1884, the Lone Star State Medical Association of Texas in 1886, and the Old North State Medical Society of North Carolina in 1887.

These efforts finally culminated in the formation in 1895 of the National Medical Association in Atlanta, Georgia. Its credo was stated in 1908 by Dr. C. V. Roman, and remains the same today: "Conceived in no spirit of racial exclusiveness, fostering no ethnic antagonism, but born of the exigencies of American environment, the National Medical Association has for its object the banding together for mutual cooperation and helpfulness, the men and women of African descent who are legally and honorably engaged in the cognate professions of medicine, surgery, pharmacy, and dentistry."

Gradually most local medical societies dropped their policy to specifically exclude black physicians from membership; however, they were rarely admitted. For example, the constitution of the Fulton County Medical Society (Atlanta, Georgia) provided that membership be open to "any reputable and legally qualified physician of Fulton or an adjoining county who has been graduated from a class-A medical college."[32] The listing of various types of membership in the medical society also included a "scientific membership," which was described as follows: "Negro physicians, if meeting qualifications, as set forth in chapter 1, may become scientific members of this society upon application and shall be awarded the privilege of participation in all scientific sessions. Such member shall not be required to pay dues."[33]

According to a study conducted in 1956 by Detrich Reitzes, none of the 36 black physicians in Atlanta was a member of the Fulton County Medical Society, the local affiliate of the AMA.

We must not underestimate the burdens with which these black physicians had to cope and the exceptional human force required to gain admittance to a closed society. They were a rare breed of men and women and an inspiration to those who follow. That is not to say that the way is now easy. True, legal segregation is behind us, but the vestige of a separate and unequal system and all it implies for future generations is very much with us today.

## CONTEMPORARY VIEW

Since the 1950s and early 1960s, the problems of black medical education have shifted from concerns about discriminatory admissions policies and the unavailability of continuing educational opportunities to concerns about effective preparatory education for medical training, motivation of black students to study medicine, and financial aid. Dr. Franklin C. McLean said in the mid-1950s:

> The problems of Negro medical students have shifted dramatically and consistently in recent years. Whereas at one time the basic problems were the discriminatory admission policies of most medical schools and the limited physical facilities of the Negro medical schools to train an adequate number of Negro students, the problems at the present time are the preparation of young Negroes for medical school, the motivation of qualified Negroes to select medicine as a career, and the provision of financial aid to pay for the required extended medical education.[34]

Black students who look forward to a career in medicine have been confronted by an educational system which gave them an inadequate scholastic preparation from the beginning. In the South, the "separate-but-equal" schools which black children attended were poorly financed and inadequately staffed. Those who managed to graduate were ill prepared to continue their studies. In the larger cities and towns of the North, where de facto segregation prevailed, schools in the black ghettos, though generally better equipped and staffed than in the South, were run-down, overcrowded, and inferior to those in most white areas. Dropouts were a serious problem, as too few blacks went to high school and still fewer to college. Only the exceptional students were able to matriculate into medical school, graduate, take an internship, and pass state board licensing examinations.

Because of discrimination in the American educational system and the type of preparatory education received by black students today, there are proportionally fewer black students who meet medical school entrance requirements, including MCAT standards, than white students.

Other factors tending to turn black students away from careers in medicine are the time, money, and effort needed to prepare for a profession long rooted in racial discrimination. Today the typical medical student is 26 years old before he or she completes a formal education. Upon graduation, the student continues training for an additional year as an intern in an accredited hospital. Usually the intership is followed by three more years of residency to qualify as a medical specialist. Not until the age of 30 does the average doctor begin earning a living, a serious deterrent to those whose parents are barely able to survive on what they earn.

Relegated to an inferior economic position in our society, the vast majority of black parents are simply unable to send their sons and daughters through high school, college, medical school, and the period of postgraduate medical training. Even black families in middle-income brackets have difficulty with the economic burden of keeping their children in school for so many years.

And exactly what is the financial burden? Medical education is the most expensive and longest course of study of any professional training. In the late 1960s it was estimated that the cost of completing eight years of college and medical school was $35,000. Today, the average tuition for medical school is $5000 to $6000 per year, with an equal amount needed for living expenses. Thus, $40-50,000 is needed for four years of medical school. Tuition costs are rising at an alarming rate and may be as high as $10,000 per year at some medical schools by the fall of 1978.

A survey of black professionals has indicated that a greater proportion of medical students get financial assistance from their families than any other group.[35] This is true in spite of the fact that approximately 70% of today's black medical students come from families with gross annual incomes less than $10,000.

The implications for black students are serious. It means that most black medical students, unlike most white students, experience overwhelming financial tensions in addition to the normal pressures associated with medical training. Most black students are dependent on outside financial support in the form of scholarships, grants, government loans, and so on. As the availability of financial assistance has decreased in the past few years, there has been a corresponding decrease in enrollment of black students in medical school.

The efforts of organizations and individuals over the years to provide financial aid to black medical students have been extremely helpful. For example, as the cost of a medical education spiraled during the inflationary years following the Second World War, black students, especially those whose families were in low-income brackets, were aided by a group of physicians in Chicago who in 1946 founded Provident Medical Associates, Inc. The body grew in size and influence, and by 1952 it changed its name to National Medical Fellowships, Inc. By 1959 the organization had awarded a total of $745,230 in grants to 246 individuals.[36]

## THE ROLE OF THE SCHOOL OF MEDICINE AT MOREHOUSE COLLEGE

Discrimination and poverty have had a disastrous effect on the training opportunities for black medical students. For years, most blacks could not even consider a career in medicine because of the attitudes and policies of predominantly white medical schools that barred their entry by both overt and covert means. Today a career in medicine for black Americans is also difficult to pursue, for a variety of different but related reasons. The high cost of a medical education has discouraged many bright, able young students from considering medicine as a possible career option. Inadequate academic preparation (which is not a problem peculiar to blacks but one peculiar to poor people) is another barrier to pursuing a medical career.

Because there are so few black physicians in the United States and the black population is particularly underserved in the critical area of health care, we believe there is a special role for the medical school we are building at Morehouse. While the School of Medicine at Morehouse College will emphasize the training of black students for careers as physicians, it will have a mixture of students from various backgrounds. We will have individuals who are white, have Spanish surnames, are American Indians, and are from other ethnic backgrounds, for we acknowledge the common interests and needs that have always been shared among the underprivileged of all races.

Our focus will be to train students who are responsive to the health care deficiencies that the poor—a large percentage of whom are black—are afflicted with, namely, malnutrition, inadequate health care, a scarcity of physicians, and certain specific medical problems such as hypertension and diseases related to poverty.

We shall address those particular cultural and ethnic needs of the poor and minorities, while at the same time building an institution of academic excellence whose graduates will be as capable and competent as the graduates from any other school and, we hope, more compassionate. Our institution will have a particular sensitivity to problems of the poor from a minority perspective. We feel that nonblack students will also want to see these problems from our special perspective.

Since our primary mission will be to train more physicians in the primary care specialties, including family practitioners, internists, and pediatricians, we intend to demonstrate that a career in primary care can be just as stimulating, just as challenging, just as important as any other specialty. Indeed, our vision of a primary care physician is one who has to be a very talented and multifaceted individual. He or she has to keep abreast of a broad range of changes and become a citizen advocate on health matters.

Because we are dedicated to primary care for underserved areas, we will put a special emphasis on recruitment of students from rural and urban families; experience tells us that a majority of physicians do return to their communities or very similar communities after they have completed medical training.

Our recruitment effort will include the colleges of the Atlanta University Center. We will make special efforts to recruit women. We expect to have, as a minimum, between 25 and 35% women in the new medical school, or at least as high a percentage in the school as are in the applicant pool.

The specific problems our recruitment efforts must address include an expanded counseling effort for poor and minority high school students to broaden their career horizons. While money is always a problem, there are a number of sources of support we are seeking, including scholarships, government-insured loans, work study.

Secondly, we must inform students that it is not necessary to be a genius to be a good physician. Indeed, if students have reasonable intelligence, maturity, and motivation, they can become successful physicians. At present, our outreach activities include (a) relating the activities of the medical school not only to Morehouse but also to the other colleges in the Atlanta University Center, and providing faculty for counseling about preparation for medical school; and (b) working with the Atlanta Board of Education in preparing a science curriculum for the new Benjamin E. Mays High School—a pilot program which we hope will influence other high schools and medical schools throughout the United States. Further, because the quality of health care for the majority of black Americans is very poor and is generally crisis care, we plan to work with local community groups in the area of general health maintenance and health education.

The health care field will soon be number one in terms of employment opportunities in this country. More than $140 billion is spent every year for health programs, and this amount will increase. We are optimistic about the role that black health professionals can fulfill in the years ahead.

We are also pleased with the role that will be played by the School of Medicine at Morehouse College in preparing physicians to meet the challenges of the future. The new medical program will provide benefits to all of the schools of the Atlanta University Center. Looking beyond Atlanta University, we can provide a focus of leadership in medical education throughout the country. We are confident that in future years the School of Medicine at Morehouse College will have a significant impact on medical education and health care in the United States and around the world.

## ACKNOWLEDGMENT

Dr. Sullivan's work is supported part by a contract with the Southern Regional Education Board.

## BIBLIOGRAPHY

Abarbanel, Karis. "Is a Relapse Ahead for Minority Medical Education?" *Foundation News* **November/December** (1976).

Cobb, William Montague. *The First Negro Medical Society: A History of the Medico-Chirurgical Society of the District of Columbia, 1884-1939.* Associated Publishers, Washington, D.C. 1939. Ann Arbor: University Microfilms (microfilm-xerograph), 1971.

*Medical Care and the Plight of the Negro.* National Association for the Advancement of Colored People, New York, 1947. Ann Arbor: University Microfilms (microfilm-xerograph), 1971.

Cobb, William Montague. "The Black Physician in America." *The New Physician* **19**(1970).

Curtis, James L. *Blacks, Medical Schools, and Society.* Ann Arbor: University of Michigan Press, 1971.

Hutchins, Edwin B., Reitman, Judith B.; and Klaub, Dorothy. "Minorities, Manpower, and Medicine." *Journal of Medical Education,* **42**(1967).

Johnson, Leonard W., Jr. "History of the Education of Negro Physicians." *Journal of Medical Education* **42**(1967).

Kenney, John A. *The Negro in Medicine.* 1912. Ann Arbor: University Microfilms (microfilm-xerograph), 1971.

Lamb, Daniel Smith. *Howard University Medical Department, Washington, D.C.* 1900. Freeport, N.Y.: Books for Libraries Press, 1971.

Morais, Herbert M. *The History of the Negro in Medicine.* New York: New York Publishers Company, Inc., 1968.

Reitzes, Dietrich, C. *Negroes and Medicine.* Cambridge, Mass.: Harvard University Press, 1958. Published for the Commonwealth Fund.

Roman, Charles Victor. *Meharry Medical College: A History.* Nashville: Sunday School Publishing Board of the National Baptist Convention, Inc., 1934.

Seham, Max. *Blacks and American Medical Care.* Minneapolis: University of Minnesota Press, 1973.

Toppin, Edgar, A. *A Biographical History of Blacks in America Since 1528.* New York: David McKay Company, Inc., 1971.

## REFERENCES AND NOTES

1. Abarbanel, K., 1976, Is a relapse ahead for minority medical education?, *Foundation News* **November/December:**13.
2. Ibid., pp. 15, 16.
3. Curtis, J. L., 1971, *Blacks, Medical Schools, and Society,* p. 5, University of Michigan Press, Ann Arbor.

4. Morais, H. M. 1968, *The History of the Negro in Medicine,* p. 12, Publishers Company, New York.
5. Ibid.
6. Toppin, E. A., 1971, *A Biographical History of Blacks in America Since 1528,* p. 278, David McKay Company, New York.
7. Morais, p. 28.
8. Ibid., p. 37.
9. Ibid., p. 13.
10. Ibid.
11. Curtis, p. 10.
12. Johnson, L. W., Jr., 1967, History of the education of negro physicians, *J. Med. Educ.,* **42**:440.
13. Morais, p. 40.
14. Ibid., p. 48.
15. Ibid., p. 59.
16. Ibid., pp. 226, 227.
17. Ibid., p. 59.
18. Ibid., p. 60.
19. Ibid., p. 137.
20. Ibid., p. 138.
21. Ibid.
22. Ibid.
23. Ibid., p. 174.
24. Ibid., p. 94.
25. Ibid., pp. 94-95.
26. Ibid., p. 95.
27. Ibid., p. 174.
28. Ibid.
29. Reitzes, D. C., 1958, *Negroes and Medicine,* p. 275, Harvard University Press, Cambridge. (Published for the Commonwealth Fund.)
30. Morais, p. 82.
31. Ibid., pp. 52-58.
32. Reitzes, p. 273.
33. Ibid., pp. 273-274.
34. Ibid., p. xxi.
35. Ibid., p. xxiv.
36. Morais, pp. 138-139.

# 13

# Women in Health Care Decision Making

## NINA B. WOODSIDE

The status of women in health care decision making is a complex subject since women serve not only at the provider level but also as consumers and procurers of health services. These several roles have been shifting in recent times in this country as well as in the rest of the world.

Decision-making positions are those which hold sufficient status for the development and implementation of policy. Such positions are found in all levels of government, among health professional organizations and societies, in the academic community, and in all facets of the health care delivery system. Women, in any of their roles, are noticeably absent from decision-making bodies and positions.[1]

## STATUS OF WOMEN IN EDUCATION

The trend toward the improvement of the legal position of women has accelerated markedly in recent years around the world and the principle of equal rights for men and women is now recognized with regard to such things as education of women and their employment outside the home, though the role of homemaker still is assigned primarily to the woman.[2,3] Today, this still traditional role unnecessarily becomes of major consequence when considering ways to increase the opportunities not only for women to enter gainful employment but also for them to participate at decision-making levels.

In general in the educational and academic world, women continue to be disadvantaged at all levels compared to men, although progress is being made in this country by recognition of the special needs of women (and men) for such things as reduced or otherwise flexible schedules, child care alternatives, role models, and the like. Nevertheless, a proportionately smaller percentage of qualified women than men attend college and the majority of all well-qualified students who do not go to college are

Reprinted from *Philadelphia Medicine*, October 1975, with permission.

NINA B. WOODSIDE • Northern Virginia Mental Health Institute, Falls Church, Virginia 22042.

women. Also, women have fewer opportunities for financial support, are restricted in geographic mobility especially if married, and today have a shrinking job market to face upon completion of studies.[4] With regard to status in the academic system, studies of trends in academic rank and tenure have shown that even after allowance for a sizable number of other variables much of the differential in rank is still attributable to sex per se, even though substantial progress has been made since federal regulations against discrimination of sex have been in effect.[5]

## WOMEN IN THE HEALTH FIELD

As of 1973, 91% of all active physicians are in direct patient care, while 88.5% of active women physicians are in direct patient care.

Interestingly, a slightly higher proportion of active women physicians than men physicians is found in either medical teaching or administration as the primary activity as opposed to direct patient care. Three percent of women physicians are in medical teaching compared to 1.7% of all physicians in medical teaching, and 4% of women physicians are in administration compared to 3.3% of all physicians in administration. Likewise, 3% of women physicians are in research activities compared to 2.3% of all physicians being in research.[6]

In the beginning of academic year 1972-73, women physicians constituted 8% of the physician full-time faculty and 3.6% of the physician part-time faculty, which represents a twofold increase over the last 20 years. However, the largest number of women faculty members, counting both physician and nonphysician, in U.S. medical schools is in the medical libraries. When only physician faculty positions are considered, the highest percentage of women is in pediatrics departments.[7]

With regard to the decision-making positions in the health care delivery system, Navarro points out that sex and class are clearly intertwined for most women in the health sector, that their status is related to the analysis of the class composition of the health sector, and that the so-called problems of women are really the problems of men and society. There are parallels between the relative roles of men and women in the family and their relative roles in the socioeconomic and health sectors of American life. There is, in fact, very low representation of both women and the lower and middle working classes, which constitute the majority of the United States population, in decision-making levels of American health institutions, including governmental health agencies. In the total U.S. labor force about 40% of the workers are women compared to about 75% in the health labor force. However, fewer than 10% of the members of boards of trustees of foundations and private and state medical teaching institutions are women. Further, fewer than 12% of the boards of voluntary hospitals are women.[8]

In the United States there are several professional routes for entering health administration activities.[9] It is interesting that in recent years female graduates in public health programs at the undergraduate level have shown a marked decline as of 1972 while increasing at the graduate level. The opposite is true in the hospital and health administration programs, with a marked decline in women at graduate level and a marked increase in women at bachelor's degree level.[10] Similar data are needed on the newer so-called medical care administration educational programs and an analysis of the causes for these trends is necessary.

It is important at this point to reflect on the goal. The assumption is made that women should be more equitably represented in decision-making positions, as should minorities and other disadvantaged groups. Equal representation, however, is not for the purpose of equal access to the miseries and woes of decision-makers but rather for equal access to the exercise of the rights and responsibilities which come with women's role in the provision as well as the procurement and consumption of health services and medical care. Although there are many parallels in the protests and progress by women with those by minorities, women have the further disadvantage of being everywhere, that is, all-pervasive in society, which denies them the group distance that minorities have. Therefore they get heard or seen even less readily.

## STATUS OF WOMEN IN HEALTH CARE DECISION MAKING

Women's slow progress in achieving status as decision-makers in health care is primarily linked to influential factors in both professional life and personal life.

The primary professional factors are well known. Among these is the reluctance, which most physicians share, to infringe upon opportunities for patient contact or contact with other clinicians by increasing administrative activities. For women, this is aggravated by such things as the psychological and sociological barriers faced because they do not have access to the informal channels of communication among their male peers, by the real hardships of being the token or solo women in a decision-making body, and by their relative lack of credentialing compared to men. The differences in the achievement of specialty board certification status between men and women are significant as the participation of women in medicine is increasing dramatically. Overall, 54% of the male physicians in a recent study by the AMA are board certified compared with only 40% of the women. In no specialty group does the proportion of women physicians who are board certified exceed that of men.[11]

Women are in particular need of access to stimulating colleagues, to challenging interaction with other professionals, to adequate socialization into the field of medicine as well as resocialization after a period of inactivity, for equal access to a sponsorship or protégé system for recognition and achievement, and for other such automatic opportunities which do not necessarily depend solely on individual initiative.[12]

Other factors of note include unprofessional statements by detractors in both public and professional media, such as the one made by a prominent physician on the Democratic National Committee several years ago to the effect that women are unfit to hold high office because their decision-making process is influenced by the menstrual cycle[13] and those of observers of group functioning who feel that women have a subculture of their own which causes them to be dependent, flirtatious, and politely competitive, which in turn is said to hamper decision making in teams consisting largely of or led by women.[14]

And, not least of all, women are adversely affected by the simple and unintentional lack of awareness among good men in health and medical institutions, voluntary agencies, and policy-making boards and committees about the role of women in decision making and how to enhance it.

Some primary factors in the personal life of women which influence achievement of status in decision making include confused self-identity and fear of success. Changes in the traditional and limited roles of women require a change in the role of men and in the traditional division of work between the sexes. Horner[15] observed that motivation to avoid success is an internal psychological representation of the dominant societal stereotype which views competence, independence, competition, and intellectual achievement as qualities basically inconsistent with femininity even though positively related to masculinity and mental health. The expectancy that success in achievement-related situations will be followed by negative consequences arouses fear of success in otherwise achievement-motivated women which then inhibits their performance and levels of aspiration.

These and other factors in professional and personal life create many problems for women, resulting in relative exclusion of women from decision- and policy-making positions and their resultant powerlessness in the health sector.[16]

Women physicians, often co-opted by the traditional (male) medical establishment, unconsciously adopt the attitudes of their male colleagues and frequently are accused, especially by other women health workers, of becoming "one of the boys." They may unwittingly neglect to use the power that their prestige would give them to increase the options for all women in health care. Also, the highly skillful and successful kind of women now reaching decision-making level is often held up as a standard which other aspiring women must meet—as superwomen. Both men and women must change, in effect breaking up remnants of the "old boys club" as an inhibiting system rather than striving to join it.[17]

Where women are subjected to socialization into "traditional" male and female roles, they may be crippled in their creativity and intellectual development, but more importantly they are at risk of falling into the trap of elitism in which they as physicians are not at ease relating to women at lower ranks in the health field. Participation in problem solving must come from women and men at all levels of education and employment in the health sector. Those few women physicians and other health care workers who have achieved levels of policy and decision making must be aware of the danger of "stepping on" other women in order to get ahead and keep in power.

Another result of all of these factors is the downgrading effect, that is to say, relatively lower salary and status, which may be produced by rapidly increasing the number of women in any particular field. A current example in the United States is comprehensive health planning, which is seen by some educators as a "good" field for women as opposed to health administration. Another fear being expressed is that one way to make or keep primary care specialties lower in status is to encourage large numbers of women to go into those fields.


## SOME STRATEGIES TO IMPROVE THE STATUS OF WOMEN IN HEALTH CARE DECISION MAKING

In light of what is known about these and other problematical factors, some strategies can be identified to improve the status of women in health care decision-making positions.

## EXTRA MARKET ROLE EVALUATION

Women as health advocates for their family have extensive experience in utilizing the health care system. Women are active in uncompensated work in voluntary health agencies, in the provision of child care in their home as well as care for aged dependents or sick family members, and they are also responsible for the feeding and nutrition of their family. These services are related to but are outside of the health system, the so-called extra market services.[18] Thus women, because of their currently unique role, serve as the interface between these nonpaid but health-related responsibilities and the health care system.

These contributions to society by women today need economic analysis and their value as planning, coordinating, and decision-making activities need identification and recognition.

## POLITICAL AND PUBLIC INVOLVEMENT

Women need and are now seeking greater involvement in the political process and public life. The proportion of women holding policy-making positions in the legislative, judicial, or executive branch of government is growing but remains pitifully small in most nations including the United States. Moreover, where women have government posts they often are entrusted primarily with responsibility for women's kinds of programs, such as maternal and child health activities. These are good for starters, certainly, but women should not stop with such positions. Women health workers, including physicians, must be involved in public and political processes enabling them to speak for matters related to their profession, such as better services and research regarding the health of women, social services for the aged, improved services for prisoners, research in male and female contraception, the mental health of women, and others. It is an unfortunate and, in plain words, an offensive oversight that not a single woman is included on a recently appointed committee in the executive branch of government for the purpose of advising the president on expenditure of scarce funds for biomedical research.[19]

## CAREER OPTIONS AND CAREER ADVANCEMENT

At the 1974 Action Planning Workshop sponsored by the Center for Women in Medicine of the Medical College of Pennsylvania, a series of recommendations for research and for program development were made regarding increasing career options and promoting career advancement to acquire power for women. Research was recommended to determine who controls professional groups (for example, surgery compared with pediatrics), to determine the representation of women on decision-making committees and in professional organizations, to identify officers in various professional organizations, to identify how panels and programs for professional meetings are organized, to identify who hires, and to evaluate affirmative-action plans for each medical school. Once the data are available presumably appropriate action can be taken.

Recommendations for program development made at that workshop included the publication and dissemination of curriculum vitae of women physicians by specialty so that people with the power to hire will have names to consider, the encouragement of women to apply for positions, and the development of a pool of legal resources for women in medicine to support affirmative action, the publication of legal actions concerning women in medicine, the encouragement of professional organizations to include adequate representation of women and their contributions on panels and programs, and the establishment of liaison with groups accrediting hospitals and medical schools to determine and advocate the representation of women on staffs, faculty, and decision-making committees.[20]

## ACQUISITION OF MANAGEMENT SKILLS

Women physicians still are less apt than men to enter entrepreneurial activity such as private solo practice. They need management and decision-making skills in order to take leadership roles wherever they find themselves practicing—whether they are in medical teaching, group practice, or organized centers, or are salaried in government, hospitals or other institutions, or community agencies, or are doing research. It should not matter whether they are working full time or some flexibly scheduled part-time arrangement. The center's 1974 workshop recommended the establishment of effectiveness workshops to train women physicians and other health workers in management skills covering topics such as how to be invited to join professional meetings and decision-making committees, how to influence behavior at meetings, how to become a leader in group settings, how to influence policy-making committees, and the rules and routes to obtaining funding.[21] This effectiveness or "how-to" training can be carried out on the job through relationships between educational institutions and service agencies or organizations. It is disappointing that the just-published report of the Commission on

Education for Health Administration is almost completely silent on this subject.[22] Such training programs in self-development in management might include discussions about developing self-awareness as women, improving interaction with others in organizations, developing managerial skills, integrating professional and home life, and translating awareness into action. Women in the health field in order to improve their status and decision-making ability need to develop a career and life strategy, to learn how to manage individual stress, conflict, and change, and to know a lot about organization effectiveness in order to function effectively themselves. These kinds of training programs should be sought out and requested by women, should be promoted and developed by women's organizations, and should be supported by educational and health institutions and organizations.

## ASSERTIVENESS TRAINING

When women have acquired these skills they must put them to use. Men and women must assertively pressure for the inclusion of women in policy making on voluntary and professional boards, committees, and task forces, on panels in Federal agencies, on health-planning bodies, and on governing boards of health care institutions, as well as for the employment of women in policy- and decision-making positions at all levels. Collectively women and men in all health occupations must achieve power over their own conditions of work and practice, the content of their discipline's knowledge base, and credentialing in their field.[23]

As women move into these decision-making positions it is necessary to assure that there is always more than one woman so placed. A solo woman is at risk of becoming a deviant member of the group, isolated or low in status, and such a woman must become independent, assertive, and competent in group functioning. Group leaders, of course, also need some training in allowing for and maximizing the effectiveness of women in the group. Men have more opportunity to learn how to function in a group early in life. One way to give such opportunities to women is to begin to include them as students on decision-making committees.[24,25]

## CAREER PATH REASSESSMENT AND LIFELONG LEARNING

Less than full-time activity or even discontinuity will continue to be a fact of life for women who are working less than full time as well men in the health field. For both women and men as full-time practicioners, continuing education, reeducation, and periodic opportunities to learn material in related fields is essential.

The Commission on Education for Health Administration recommended the establishment of a national program in lifelong learning and nontraditional education and further recommended the establishment of one or more centers for advanced study in health administration. Early in their professional life women especially should become familiar with what these opportunities will mean to them and should closely coordinate them with periodic career self-assessment. Retraining and reentry opportunities as well are mandatory for women (and men) who have been inactive or who have worked in highly specialized areas of research or teaching and wish to return to clinical activity.[26] White points out that in order to maintain their career commitment women need both the same opportunities as men and special opportunities to keep up with the explosion of knowledge and to fulfill their life in these times of increasing longevity. Because of the trend toward more complex educational and occupational patterns for both men and women, the innovative programs developed to meet women's needs are being sought by men as well.[27]

## NEW CAREER PATTERNS AND INSTITUTIONAL CHANGES

New career patterns and institutional rearrangements are by no means limited to women but will offer women an advantage to improving their status. Such things as reduced-schedule graduate training, flexibly scheduled or shared-time jobs, commuting life-style, partnership or peer working arrangements with spouse, group practice, and team teaching or team service provisions, all help women overcome the barriers to full involvement in the mainstream of health care. White points out that whether or not women are able to achieve membership in the "club" can be a circular kind of dilemma, with women being reluctant to put themselves forward or protest their exclusion and men being indifferent or unaware of it. The remedy is not necessarily more assertiveness but must also encompass rearrangements in health institutions and programs so that achievement by women does not depend solely on individual initiative.[27] Navarro[28] calls in addition for the introduction of institutional democracy in the health sector as a political strategy for change, with control of the institutions by those who work in them (the majority of whom are women) and those who are served by them. He further calls for more equitable socioeconomic class representation in the health sector as well as the representation of women and other disadvantaged groups.

## NETWORKS FOR VARIOUS PURPOSES

Women are learning to support one another and encourage acceptance of leadership roles. There is a need for more systematic national communication among women in health care and for identification of those able to communicate about women in health care. Through such tools as newsletters and speaker's bureaus, a network of concerned women in leadership positions could be responsible for a women's focus at national conferences of health or professional associations and for periodic meetings of persons with particular interests in women in health careers, health care delivery, and health care decision making. Likewise, extensive national networking through talent banks, job banks, and placement services would identify and match up qualified and willing women with opportunities for service in decision-making groups and positions.

Networking can help in the attainment of an adequate self-image for women in health fields, through supportive groups and individual relationships providing role models and opportunities to share, compare, and examine feelings, experiences, and behavior. As Strauss[29] puts it, women need continuity of peers among other women, for once they get through their professional education they frequently lose touch with women colleagues they had in high school or college and find themselves relatively alone on the fringes of a man's world. Ramey[30] advocates a "biddy" system in contradistinction to the buddy system that men traditionally use for recruitment and placement. These networks of women should not exclude men, however, and further they should be representative of students, faculty, and staff, at all ranks.

## AFFIRMATIVE ACTION AND LEGAL ROUTES

Another strategy utilizes affirmative action and other legal routes. Women in the health field need contact with legal expertise in the area of equal employment opportunities and affirmative-action requirements in order to develop a plan for interventive action prior to the point of actual discrimination, to design and disseminate methodology for anonymous or nonpunitive legal action for women who are discriminated against, and to develop rosters of local resources for legal assistance. The simple procedure of how to file a complaint for fair hearing is very important knowledge for women. Women in health fields need to effectively utilize the field of law to correct inequities, and networks should therefore include women and men in law. Women must involve themselves in policy and decision making on issues relevant to the health system of which they are a part. This major concept is known as affirmative action for women and minorities in the labor force.

And finally, the most important and perhaps most difficult strategy of all must take into consideration the conditions for women in the home place as well as the work place. In the long run changes in the socialization and life of women and men at home will be the ultimate and permanent solution to the question of the status of women in decision-making positions. Programs to improve conditions must include a wide variety of readily available options for care and education of children plus the development of innovative services which make it easier and more efficient to run a household and enjoy a satisfying family life. Sokolowska[31] describes family responsibilities as threefold: first, the biological fact of maternity, which is not transferable from women; second, the social aspect of "maternity," such as the education and care of children, which are certainly transferable and sharable between women and men; third, housework and the maintenance of the home place, which also can be divided. Women are recognizing that they can share without guilt the social aspects of "maternity" and housework responsibilities and they should begin to transfer these in equitable fashion, not only to the spouse but to all other members. As new patterns are evolving for the individual development of women, the changing role of the children as well as the spouse must be fostered. Duties and responsibilities within the family have to be shared by all. Sokolowska further remarks, "We must give the family a hand and not just give the women a hand."[32]

For women, social change, control over fertility, and the gradual passing of the male-headed family structure mean a wider range of choices and greater status in decision making not only at home but at work. Our world is certainly less of a man's world today, but it is still not yet a people's world. Even in many nations where legislation requiring equal rights and responsibilities for women has been around for many years, the process has been slow. Lest we become discouraged too soon, we should not overlook the underlying importance of the time factor in the emergence of changes for the better in the status of women in health care decision-making positions. In time, as their numbers, skills, assertiveness, and socioeconomic power increase at all levels, women will achieve due status in decision making in the health care field.

## REFERENCES

1. Navarro, V., 1975, Women in health care, *N. Engl. J. Med.* **292**:398-402.
2. United Nations, UN/OPI/CESI, Note IWY/18, United Nations Work For Women, New York, December 1974.

3. United Nations, UN/OPI/CESI, Note IWY/15, The Situation and Status of Women To-day: Some Essential Facts, New York, December 1974.
4. American Association of State Colleges and Universities, Women's Stake in Low Tuition, Washington, D.C., 1974, pp. 5, 6-10.
5. Bayer, A. E., and Astin, H. S., 1975, Sex differentials in the academic reward system, *Science* **188:**796-802.
6. American Medical Association, *Profile of Medical Practice '74*, Chicago, 1974, pp. 95, 97, 99, 107, 116.
7. Center for Women in Medicine, Resource Booklet, Philadelphia, 1974, p. 63.
8. Navarro, V., Women in health care, pp. 399-401.
9. *Report of the Commission on Education for Health Administration*, Vol. 1, Health Administration Press, Ann Arbor, 1974.
10. Maryland Pennell, M., and Showell, S., 1975, Women in Health Careers, Chart Book for International Conference on Women in Health held June 16-18, APHA, Washington, D.C., pp. 90-91.
11. American Medical Association, *Profile*, pp. 39-41.
12. White, M. S., 1970, Psychological and social barriers to women in science, *Science* **170:**413-416.
13. Barnes, A. C., 1972, The opening of the second front: Dr. Berman and the ladies, *Obstet. Gynecol.* **37:**157-175.
14. Robin, S. S., 1971, Observation in a mental hospital: A sociological prespective, *Ment. Hyg.* **55:**253-259.
15. Horner, M., 1972, Toward an understanding of achievement related conflict in women, *J. Soc. Issues* **28:**157-175.
16. Maggie Matthews, D. P. H., personal communication, 1975.
17. Center for Women in Medicine, Report of a Workshop, Women in Medicine: Action Planning for the 1970s, Philadelphia, 1974, pp. 63-64.
18. Eugenia Carpenter, M. P. H., University of Michigan, personal communication, 1975.
19. President's Panel on Biomedical Research, Appointed by President Gerald Ford, April 1975.
20. Center for Women in Medicine, Report of Workshop, pp. 33-34.
21. Center for Women in Medicine, Report of Workshop, p. 28.
22. The Report of the Commission on Education for Health Administration.
23. Maggie Matthews, D. P. H., personal communication, 1975.
24. Wolman, C., and Frank, H., 1975, The solo woman in a professional peer group, *Am. J. Orthopsychiatry* **45:**164-171.
25. Center for Women in Medicine, Report of Workshop, p. 25.
26. Report of the Commission on Education for Health Administration.
27. White, M. S., 1970, Psychological and social barriers to women in science, *Science* **170:**413-416.
28. Navarro, V., 1970, Women in health care, *N. Engl. J. Med.* **292:**398-402.
29. Janet Strauss, M. P. H., Commission on Education for Health Administration, personal communication, 1975.
30. Estelle Ramey, Ph.D., Georgetown University, personal communication, 1974.
31. Sokolowska, M., Some reflections on the different attitudes of men and women toward work, *International Labour Review* volume and date not known: 35-50.
32. Sokolowska, M., 1975, All or nothing, *World Health* **January:**27-29.
33. Gallagher, E. B., 1972, The health enterprise in modern society, *Soc. Sci. Med.* **6:**619-621.
34. Sokolowska, M., 1973, *Women's Emancipation and Socialism: The Example of the People's Republic of Poland*, publisher and place not known.
35. Sokolowska, M., Some reflections on the different attitudes of men and women toward work, *International Labour Review* volume and date not known: 35-50.

# 14

# Technology Assessment and Genetics

## LeROY WALTERS

No one—not even the most brilliant scientist alive today—really knows where science is taking us. We are aboard a train which is gathering speed, racing down a track on which there are an unknown number of switches leading to unknown destinations. No single scientist is in the engine cab, and there may be demons at the switch.[1]

There can be no question that many of the benefits of modern life are the direct result of scientific research and technological development.[2] During the past decade, however, it has become increasingly apparent that technology is not an unmixed blessing. One attempt to cope with the mixed character of technological development is the technology-assessment movement.

### CONCEPT OF TECHNOLOGY ASSESSMENT

The term *technology assessment* (TA) seems to have been coined in a report of the House Subcommittee on Science, Research, and Development.[3] Due primarily to the tireless efforts of the subcommittee and its chairman, Emilio Q. Daddario, the concept of TA gradually spread into the academic world, where it was picked up in particular by engineers and physicists. During the year 1969 a scholarly literature on the subject of TA began to develop; indeed, it is possible to identify ten recent reports or books which have achieved almost canonical status within the movement.[4] Late in 1971 an International Society for Technology Assessment was formed to "contribute to the structuring, study, control and resolution of the world's technological challenges and dilemmas."[5] The society, in turn, began publishing a quarterly journal. *Technology Assessment,* in the summer of 1972.

What precisely is meant by the term TA? Joseph F. Coates, a program manager in the National Science Foundation, offers the following concise explanation: "Technology assessment may be defined as the systematic

Reprinted from *Theological Studies* **33:** 667-683, 1972, with permission.

LeROY WALTERS • Center for Bioethics, Kennedy Institute, Georgetown University, Washington, D.C. 20057.

study of the effects on society that may occur when a technology is introduced, extended, or modified, with special emphasis on the impacts that
are unintended, indirect, and delayed."[6]

Two phrases in Coates's definition merit brief elaboration. Practitioners of TA generally construe the idea of "effects on society" in rather broad
terms. Their particular concern is to take into account environmental and
other social consequences of technology and to avoid an exclusive focus
on economic profit and loss. When Coates employs the terms *unintended,
indirect,* and *delayed* to describe certain of these consequences, he alludes
to another major emphasis within the TA movement, namely, second-
order consequences. Immediate, direct, and intended effects of
technological change are generally termed first-order consequences. The
primary focus of TA is on the less obvious social impacts of technology,
that is, on second-, third-, and higher-order consequences.[7]

Writers on TA have distinguished several subtypes of assessment.
For example, an obvious distinction can be drawn between retrospective
and prospective analyses, between studies of the past and of the future.
Closely related is the distinction between problem-initiated and
technology-initiated assessments. The former type surveys currently
available technologies in quest of a solution to a specific problem; the
latter mode of assessment attempts to follow through time "the inherently proliferating set of impacts" of a particular technology.[8]

If the above definitions and classifications indicate the general con-
tours of TA, they do not yet give a clear picture of its methodology. There
is, in fact, no single universally accepted method for performing TA.
Perhaps the most thorough and systematic attempt to formulate such a
methodology is a study written by Martin V. Jones, an economist at the
MITRE Corporation.[9] In his programmatic essay Jones lists seven major
steps to be taken in performing a comprehensive technology assessment:

Step 1.  Define the assessment task: Establish the scope of the inquiry.

Step 2.  Describe relevant technologies: Outline the state of the art in
the major technology being assessed as well as in related
technologies.

Step 3.  Develop state-of-society assumptions: Identify and describe
the major nontechnological factors influencing the application
of the relevant techniques.

Step 4.  Identify impact areas: List the societal characteristics that will
be most influenced by the application of the assessed technology.

Step 5. Make preliminary impact analysis: Trace and integrate the various specific impacts of the assessed technology upon society.

Step 6. Identify possible action options: Develop and analyze various programs of obtaining maximum public benefit from the assessed technologies.

Step 7. Complete impact analysis: Analyze the degree to which each action option would alter the specific societal impacts (listed in Step 5) of the assessed technology. [10]

The method outlined by Jones will now be described in somewhat greater detail. In taking Step 1 the assessor decides whether to attempt a total-impact assessment or whether to be content with a partial assessment. Having made that choice, he proceeds to Step 2, a precise description of the technology under consideration. According to Jones, this description should answer the following questions: (1) What is the current state of the art in the assessed technology? (2) What is the current state of the art in related or supporting technologies? (3) What technical breakthroughs are needed? (4) What future developments in the state of the art are anticipated and within what time frame? (5) What are the current and prospective uses and applications of the assessed technology? [11]

Steps 3 and 4 refer to the complex reciprocal relationships between society and technology. In Step 3 the assessor of technology attempts to project general trends in the society of the future and to predict how these social phenomena might accelerate or retard the development and application of the technology in question. In Step 4 the process is reversed: One seeks to identify the general spheres of human life which are most likely to be affected by future developments in the assessed technology. These general spheres, or major impact categories, include personal and community values, the environment, demographic trends, social goals and problems, economic factors, and institutions. [12]

Steps 1-4 are preparatory to Step 5, which is the primary goal of the assessment. Here the assessor attempts to anticipate and describe specific consequences of technological development. A helpful framework for this impact analysis is provided by Jones in his methodological essay (Table I).

The final two steps in a technology assessment consider whether various types of monitoring or control mechanisms could modify the rate or direction of technological development and thus alter its social impact. Among possible action options the most important are methods of allocating research and development funds; other financial incentives,

**Table I.** Key Impact Questions[13]

| Questions | Types of answers |
| --- | --- |
| *Technology* | |
| Development | Describe the initial effect of the development: to lower cost, to improve performance, etc. |
| Application | Describe the use to which this development is put. |
| *Social* | |
| Social Impact | Identify the first level impact of the application. |
| *Impact characteristics* | |
| Affected Group | What social group will be most affected: old or young, rich or poor, workers or managers, the sick or well, etc.? |
| How Affected | For better or worse, and in what specific way? |
| Likelihood | E.g., 50-50 chance. |
| Timing | Estimate dates both for initial impact and later widespread effect. |
| Magnitude | Preferably in dollars, percentage increase, number affected, etc., rather than adjectives like "large," "small," etc. |
| Duration | Indicate whether initial impact will improve or worsen and for how long. |
| Diffusion | Breadth and depth of impact. An unfavorable impact of equal total magnitude (e.g., dollar volume) that is concentrated on a few people will cause more social distress than if it were diffused through many people. |
| Source | Indicate the source (industry, federal government, foreign source, etc.) from which the development leading up to this impact originates. |
| Controllability | Is it likely that a public program could heighten or dampen the impact generated by the technology? |

including taxes; legislation; court action; mass-media publicity; education; and the construction of new systems or facilities.[14]

In addition to the *how* of TA it is necessary to consider the *who* question: Who should participate in the complex process of assessing technology? Much of the current initiative for systematic TA comes from the Congress, some of whose members fear that the executive branch is gaining a monopoly over scientific information. Currently under debate is a bill which would establish a Congressional Office of Technology Assessment, modeled on the pattern of the General Accounting Office.[15] Other possible forums for TA include departments and administrative agencies in the executive branch, the courts, industry, international organizations, professional societies, ad hoc task forces, research institutes, and university-based interdisciplinary research teams.[16]

Perhaps equal in importance to the locus of TA is the composition of the group which makes the assessment. Self-evidently, research scientists from the relevant physical or life sciences must be involved. The presence of engineers on the assessment team frequently serves to bridge the gap between research and application. During recent years there has also been increasing sentiment in favor of including social scientists in the assessment process. In addition, some advocates of TA have ventured to suggest participation by "concerned individuals outside science: industrial executives, lawyers, clergymen, and journalists."[17]

Even if TA sounds plausible as a proposal and a theory, one must raise the practical question: Has TA been tried, and, if so, with what degree of success? The answer, in brief, is that until now very few full-scale assessments have been attempted. Pilot studies have made partial assessments of the following present or future technologies: sea farming, mechanized teaching aids, computer-communications networks, industrial enzymes, microwave diodes, and the supersonic transport.[18] Problems which have been assessed in a preliminary way include: automotive emissions, water pollution through domestic wastes, the Alaska pipeline, and a snow-enhancement project for the Colorado River Valley.[19] Only in a few cases—for example, the Jamaica Bay-Kennedy Airport Study—can one speak of a comprehensive or total-impact assessment.[20]

## ASSESSMENT OF BIOMEDICAL TECHNOLOGY

As the foregoing examples illustrate, TA has until now been concentrated on two major areas: environmental problems and developments in the physical sciences. The field of biomedical technology has been almost totally ignored.[21] In her comprehensive review of TA in the federal government Vary T. Coates noticed this gap in current TA studies and voiced concern about the possible long-term consequences of such neglect:

> Biomedical technologies, especially bioengineering and pharmacology, are producing or are likely to produce some of the most profound effects on social mores and behavior of the future. It is likely that public policy issues will soon arise from this area in great numbers, and that these policy issues will be profoundly interwoven with religious, social, economic, cultural, and ideological factors. Very little anticipatory assessment is being done and almost none by the federal agencies which are financially supporting much of the scientific research driving this technological development, or which may be called upon to exercise whatever regulatory authority society may choose to impose. Public opinion and political leadership will therefore lack a firm base of information and issue analysis to guide public discussion, and action will very likely be taken in a crisis situation, with a corresponding plethora of irrational and uninformed charges and countercharges. Or no action at all will be taken, until social change is irreversible and irremediable. Therefore the opportunity for postive social direction of a burgeoning but still rudimentary technology will be lost, and with it the opportunity to identify societal options and the opportunity to influence developments along socially and individually desirable paths.[22]

A partial explanation for the lack of TA in the biomedical field may be that there are significant differences between the physical sciences and the life sciences. For example, technologies based on research in the life sciences are usually applied to human beings by licensed medical practitioners, that is, by a unique social group with a distinctive tradition and code of ethics. Successful TA in the biomedical field is thus heavily dependent on active cooperation by the medical profession. In addition, developments in biomedical technology are supported primarily by public funds; according to one estimate, approximately two thirds of all money spent on research and development in biomedicine and health comes from the federal government. Thus, advances in biomedical technology already reflect public-policy decisions to a much greater extent than do technical advances in the field of physics and physical engineering.[23]

A third distinction between the physical and life sciences is somewhat more elusive. It could perhaps be called a difference in the intimacy of effects. The development of new products and devices has always had a profound impact upon society. However, when biomedical technology is applied directly to man, to human flesh, the stakes seem to be higher, and human concern is correspondingly greater. Hans Jonas has captured the significance of this difference in a few terse lines:

> Among the sciences that progressively contributed to the technological revolu-

tion, *biology* has so far not figured. Are we perhaps on the verge of another—conceivably the last—stage of that revolution, based on biological knowledge and wielding an engineering art which, this time, has man himself for an object? This has become a theoretical possibility with the advent of molecular biology and its understanding of genetic programming. . . . [24]

These differences between the physical and life sciences raise a fundamental question: Can a single methodology be employed to evaluate technological developments in both fields? To rephrase the issue, can the TA methodology which was outlined in Part 1 be applied to biomedical technologies?

The thesis of this essay is that the same methodology, with minor adjustments, is applicable to the biomedical field. Preliminary evidence in support of this thesis is contained in a forthcoming study made by the Committee on the Life Sciences and Social Policy of the National Research Council.[25] This study, coordinated by Dr. Leon R. Kass, investigates present and potential developments in four biomedical technologies. According to Dr. Kass, the committee considered the following set of issues in selecting the technologies and in making its assessments: (1) stage of development of the technology, (2) scale of use, (3) relation to other technologies, (4) ease of monitoring and control, (5) reversibility, (6) nature and scope of societal consequences for users of the technology and for society, and (7) questions of public policy.[26] On the whole, the committee's method of study parallels precisely the progression of thought in the TA methodology outlined above. More specifically, the seven issues discussed in the committee report are virtually identical to those raised in Steps 2, 5, and 6 of the proposed TA methodology.

There are numerous developments in biomedical technology which could be made the subject of assessments. The pioneering study of the Committee on the Life Sciences and Social Policy concentrates on four technologies: in vitro fertilization, techniques for predetermining the sex of children, "techniques to slow the biological process of aging," and "techniques for the modification and control of the nervous system and behavior."[27] Other innovations predicted by experts in biomedicine include the following: implantable artificial hearts and other mechanical organs; safe, inexpensive contraceptive agents capable of being administered on a mass scale; asexual reproduction, or cloning, of human beings; chemotherapeutic cures for various types of cancer; an artificial placenta, which would allow extrauterine development of the fetus; methods for stimulating the regeneration of the central nervous system, organs, or limbs; and techniques for the repair or alteration of specific genes.[28]

## ASSESSMENT OF GENETIC TECHNOLOGY

A significant subcategory of biomedical technology is based on the science of human genetics and allied disciplines. Indeed, it can be argued that recent developments in the general field of genetics are comparable in importance to the discovery and utilization of atomic energy a generation ago. In the words of Dr. Bentley Glass:

> The discoveries of molecular biology and genetics during the past 20 years are now generally acclaimed to be the most significant basic scientific advances of our present generation, just as the understanding of the focus of nuclear energy in the atom was that of the preceding generation. Like the application of nuclear energy to both destructive and constructive uses, the application of the spectacular finding that deoxyribonucleic acid (DNA) is the chemical basis of heredity offers man a magnificent extension of power over nature and at the same time lays on his conscience a frightening responsibility in the use of that power.[29]

Strictly defined, the term *genetic technology* includes the following present or potential developments: the detection of genetic defects in the unborn through amniocentesis; techniques for identifying, or screening, heterozygous carriers and homozygous victims of genetic disease; and gene repair through DNA therapy.[30] A somewhat broader definition of genetic technology might encompass as well the techniques of in vitro fertilization and cloning, both of which have obvious eugenic applications.[31] In the paragraphs which follow, this second, more comprehensive definition of genetic technology is employed.

Until now, no published study has attempted a comprehensive assessment of any of the five genetic technologies noted above.[32] However, numerous books and articles have discussed the possible long-term impact of genetic technology in a mode *akin to* that of TA. In my view, these studies—which might be called partial assessments—constitute important building blocks for future efforts to provide comprehensive assessments in the field of genetic technology.[33]

Two examples will serve to illustrate the close resemblance between these studies and the seven-step TA methodology outlined above. In a lecture given at the Kennedy Foundation's International Symposium on Human Rights, Retardation, and Research and subsequently published in *Journal of the American Medical Association*, Paul Ramsey discusses the issue of in vitro fertilization.[34] After defining the scope of his topic and briefly sketching the current state of the art, Ramsey notes a major nontechnological factor which in his view should inhibit the application of this particular genetic technology to human beings, namely, certain generally accepted rules or codes concerning human experimentation. In the second part of his essay Ramsey turns from this deontological argument to a more teleological mode of analysis, arguing that the general impact of in vitro fertilization in human beings would be to replace reproduction with manufacture and to pervert the traditional function of the medical profession.[35]

More specific social impacts are discussed by Professor Ramsey under the rubric of the "thin end of the wedge" argument. In an eloquent passage Ramsey argues that the application of in vitro fertilization to human beings would have serious detrimental second-order consequences:

> To be valid . . . the wedge argument need not, like my reasons drawn from medical ethics, attempt to show the inherent immorality of a given sort of action or practice. It need only show that if we do this particular action or permit or encourage a particular practice (perhaps because of undeniable immediate values, e.g., enabling a woman to have a child) we will influence others and cause ourselves to take following steps that in foreseeable succession add up to immense disvalue for the human community. So we shall have to assess in vitro fertilization as a long step toward Hatcheries, i.e., extracorporeal gestation, and [toward] the introduction of unlimited genetic changes into human germinal material while it is being cultured by the Conditioners and Predestinators of the future.[36]

Ramsey does not propose the adoption of any specific action option to forestall such possible developments, but the very publication of his essay in a leading medical journal constitutes an effort to educate a significant group of decision-makers and thus to alter or avert the potential impact of in vitro fertilization on society.

A second example of partial TA in the field of genetics is contained in a recent article by Bentley Glass entitled "Human Heredity and Ethical Problems."[37] Again in this essay one can easily discover the seven steps of Martin Jones's suggested TA methodology. After defining the scope of his study, Dr. Glass devotes a great deal of attention to describing the state of the art in genetics and molecular biology. According to Glass, the techniques of transduction, amniocentesis, and genetic screening have made possible significant advances in euphenics[38] and negative eugenics. Such methods pale, however, in comparison with Glass's list of potential developments in positive eugenics, or genetic engineering: selective breeding, in vitro fertilization, embryo transfer, gestation in an artificial placenta, laboratory cultivation of human reproductive organs, cloning, genetic surgery, and gene transfer.[39]

Glass notes that several nontechnological factors affect the development or application of the various genetic technologies. Inhibiting factors are the expense of currently available tests, ethical objections to abortion, the small number of scholars in certain critical disciplines, and society's lack of unanimity on a definition of genetic superiority. On the other hand, Glass observes, the economic cost of caring for persons afflicted with genetic disease tends to push society toward more rapid adoption of available genetic techniques.[40]

In the opinion of Glass, the general impact of employing genetic-engineering techniques would be to help mankind avoid global disaster. Without such techniques, he argues, the human race would at best suffer gradual genetic deterioration; at worst, "if in the aftermath of dreadful nuclear war, survivors are unable to provide the necessary artifices—drugs, surgery, and prosthetic devices—to maintain life in spite of their genetic burdens, mankind may perish."[41] Glass also lists several specific impacts which would probably result from the widespread application of present and future genetic technology: "a complete liberation of the sexual life from its relationship to reproduction"; "greater freedom of choice in new respects"; and recognition of the "right of every person to be born physically and mentally sound, capable of developing fully into a mature individual."[42]

Certain possible action steps are mentioned or recommended during the course of Glass's essay: these include mandatory sterilization for retinoblastoma patients, obligatory abortion of seriously defective fetuses, routine genetic testing of all newborn infants, and a licensing procedure to limit the number of children born to each couple.[43] The intent of these measures would not be to alter the societal impacts of genetic technology. Rather, if I understand Glass correctly, their purpose would be to ensure that the desired impacts did in fact occur.

In the concluding paragraph of "Human Heredity and Ethical Problems," Glass issues a ringing appeal for broad, interdisciplinary involvement in the assessment of technology:

> I have asked many questions which cannot at present be answered. I predict a future in which many cherished values of our society and many ethical standards will be questioned or superseded. It is not sufficient to have a few scientists raise such issues. . . . Only a prolonged and profound attention by many of the wisest men of our times, men of philosophy and religion, students of society and of government, and representatives of the common interests of men throughout the world, together with teachers and scientists, may achieve a wise and sober solution of the crisis of values evoked in our world by scientific discoveries and their applications.[44]

The foregoing analysis of the essays by Ramsey and Glass tends to confirm the thesis that the TA methodology is applicable, at least in principle, to the assessment of biomedical technology. The diametrically opposed conclusions of Ramsey and Glass serve to underline the relatively modest role of the TA methodology. It functions as a formal aid to systematic analysis; in no sense, however, does it predetermine the assessor's final evaluation of a particular technology.

## A THEORETICAL PERSPECTIVE ON TECHNOLOGY ASSESSMENT

This concluding section seeks to appraise TA from the standpoint of moral philosophy and Christian ethics. It begins by investigating the intellectual-historical roots of TA, then proceeds to note possible strengths and weaknesses of the TA methodology.

Without question, I think, the intellectual roots of the TA movement are to be found in the ethical tradition known as utilitarianism.[45] This heritage can be traced both generally and specifically. The general connection of the TA movement to utilitarianism has perhaps been mediated through social scientists, several of whom have been deeply involved in developing the theoretical foundations of TA.[46] For a variety of reasons, scholars in the social sciences generally tend toward a utilitarian normative theory. In the words of Braybrooke and Lindblom:

> Utilitarianism, at least in the English-speaking world, is the school toward which most social scientists are inclined, if they are inclined toward any. There are historical reasons for this inclination: Important branches of social science, among them economics and sociology, grew out of utilitarian preoccupations. There is also a natural convergence in preoccupations between utilitarianism and social science. Utilitarianism, after all, insists more strongly than any other ethical theory on forcing moral judgments to the test of facts—the facts of social science.[47]

To this general connection between TA and utilitarianism a more specific link can be added. When it focuses on the second-order consequences or social effects or impacts of technology, the TA movement clearly identifies itself as a utilitarian school of thought. At times the very words employed in assessing social consequences are reminiscent of classical utilitarianism. For example, the key impact questions listed by Martin Jones (Table I) are virtually identical to Jeremy Bentham's categories for measuring the effects of an action. According to Bentham, seven circumstances must always be taken into account: intensity, duration, certainty or uncertainty, propinquity or remoteness, fecundity, purity, and extent.[48]

The type of utilitarianism espoused by the TA movement is both comprehensive and rather sophisticated. Unlike Bentham, who tended to reduce all ethical argument to a calculus of pleasure and pain,[49] theoreticians of TA are willing to take into account a wide variety of consequences—economic, social, political, environmental, legal, and moral.[50] To phrase the same point in more general terms, the TA movement is not necessarily committed to any particular theory of nonmoral value; rather, it seems willing to accept the positive worth of a plurality of values.[51] Advocates of TA also realize full well the complexity of the task which is to be accomplished. In its final report the Panel on Technology Assessment of the National Academy of Sciences listed numerous "problems and pitfalls" of the TA enterprise, including shortcomings of modes of analysis, failures of imagination, deficiencies in the data base, and institutional constraints.[52]

One can, I think, be profoundly grateful for the positive contributions of the TA movement. In the first place, it has introduced a broadened perspective into the analysis of technological development. Most traditional assessments of technology have been focused almost exclusively on internal costs and benefits. In the words of the National Academy of Sciences panel, "With few exceptions the central question asked of a technology is what it would do (or is doing) to the economic or institutional interests of those who are deciding whether or how to exploit it."[53] In contrast, the TA movement urges that this traditional calculus be supplemented by a humane evaluation of external social consequences.

The flexibility of the TA methodology is also a point in its favor. As noted above, the employment of this method does not commit the assessor either to a particular value-theory or to a predetermined evaluation of a particular technology. The methodology acknowledges a reciprocal influence of technology and society, thus avoiding any commitment to a partisan ideological position.[54] It is also sufficiently comprehensive to allow for consideration of a variety of nontechnological factors, such as values, institutions, education, and political action.[55]

Third, the TA methodology lays the foundation for an expanded concept of moral responsibility. Its overall thrust is to hold men accountable for the remote, as well as the immediate, consequences of their decisions and actions. Spatially interpreted, this concept of responsibility could easily include members of the human community living in other nations.[56] Temporally extended, TA would serve to protect the interests of future generations.[57] To rephrase the point in theological terms, the TA methodology calls to our attention a whole new group of neighbors, toward whom concern and love can and should be directed.

Without denying these positive contributions of TA, one can, in my view, also raise certain fundamental questions about the TA methodology. First, to what extent should policy or morality be based on an assessment of possible consequences? Practitioners of TA are already keenly aware of this problem; in fact, one study of TA exclicitly warns that projections which attempt to see more than five years in to future are likely to contain gross inaccuracies.[58] The great German philosopher Kant was even more pessimistic about man's ability to predict the consequences of his acts. Arguing that omniscience would be required to ensure accurate prediction, Kant wrote off the entire enterprise of hypothetical ethical analysis and turned his attention instead to the formulation of categorical imperatives.[59] Even if one rejects Kant's extreme position, there remains the question whether ethics or policy should be based solely on a comprehensive assessment of consequences.

This problem can be formulated more precisely with the help of an illustration. Let us assume what Kant would have denied, namely, that in a given case the social consequences of a particular technology could be comprehensively and accurately assessed. One might proceed to record the results of one's analysis on a bar graph as in Figure 1. Several questions can be raised about this hypothetical result: (1) How can the various kinds of impacts be compared? Is there a common denominator? (2) Which impact, if any, takes precedence over other possible impacts? Does a negative impact within a particular category, e.g., a negative moral impact, automatically lead to a negative assessment of the technology? (3) How are the various impacts distributed among members of the society? Would a serious negative impact on a few persons be outweighed by a slight positive impact on many persons?[60]

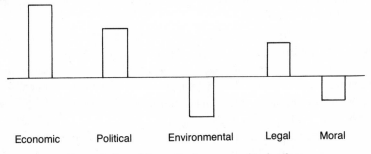

Figure 1. Overall impacts of an assessed technology.

Because of such inherent difficulties in consequential analysis, many moral philosophers and Christian ethicists have suggested that utilitarianism should be supplemented by a second ethical dimension. William Frankena and John Rawls, for example, emphasize the principle of justice or fairness.[61] For Charles Curran, the concept of human dignity serves to limit what may be done, even for the sake of good consequences.[62] Paul Ramsey has repeatedly expressed the view that the Christian ethic is primarily an ethic of means, not of ends.[63] In the theology of Karl Barth, the religious obligation to obey the command of God virtually supplants the duty to calculate consequences.[64]

A final, somewhat more theoretical question can be raised concerning TA: Does the general perspective of TA tend to overlook or obscure certain phenomena of human life? The meaning of this question can be illustrated in two ways. As we have noted, the TA methodology can be applied either to a particular technology or to a particular social problem. Would the same methodology be applicable to philosophical questions like the following: What goals should we adopt as a nation or an international community? or, What is the end of human life?[65] If the methodology could not address such questions directly, would it allow one's answers to the same questions to affect a significant way one's overall assessment of a technology or a problem?

The thrust of this final question can also be illustrated metaphorically. In his book *The Responsible Self*, H. Richard Niebuhr distinguished three images of man: man-the-maker, man-the-citizen, and man-the-answerer. The first image depicts man as a producer of ideas, actions, and things. In the second image, man's duty to obey the civil and moral law predominates. The third image focuses on "man engaged in dialogue, man acting in response to action upon him."[66] It is quite clear that the TA movement emphasizes the first of these three images, the metaphor of man-the-maker. In so doing, it inevitably tends to neglect other important aspects of human experience.

In summary, the technology-assessment methodology provides a coherent framework for analyzing the social impact of technological change. Although the method was devised primarily in response to environmental problems and developments in the physical sciences, it is in principle applicable to advances in biomedical technology. In fact, several studies of biomedical technology in general, and of genetic technology in particular, have employed analytical categories which parallel precisely the various steps of the TA methodology.

Because of its intellectual rootage in utilitarianism, the TA movement tends to focus primary attention on man-the-maker. However, the formal character and inclusive categories of the TA methodology allow for a significant degree of flexibility in the assessment process. One hopes that in the future this useful analytical tool will be systematically applied to a wide variety of technologies and particularly to the series of complex problems arising in the field of human genetics.

## REFERENCES AND NOTES

1. Lapp, R. E., 1965, *The New Priesthood: The Scientific Elite and the Uses of Power,* p. 29, Harper & Row, New York.
2. In this essay science, whether basic or applied, is defined as an information function. Technology, on the other hand, is conceived as the development and social use of scientific information. In practice it is not always possible to draw a clear line between science and technology. See U.S. Congress, House, Committee on Science and Astronautics, 1972, "Science Policy: A Working Glossary," Prepared for the Subcommittee on Science, Research, and Development by the Science Policy Research Division, Congressional Research Service, Library of Congress, U.S. Government Printing Office, Washington, D.C., p. 53.
3. U.S. Congress, House, Committee on Science and Astronautics, 1966, "Inquiries, Legislation, Policy Studies Re: Science and Technology," Second Progress Report of the Subcommittee on Science, Research, and Development, 89th Congress, second session, U.S. Government Printing Office, Washington, D.C., pp. 27-28. Mr. Philip B. Yeager, Counsel to the Subcommittee, is generally given credit for having coined the term *technology assessment.*
4. The most important works on TA are the following: (A) Four reports to the Subcommittee on Science, Research, and Development of the House Committee on Science and Astronautics: (1) Science Policy Research Division, Congressional Research Service, Library of Congress, *Technical Information for Congress* (April 25, 1969; revised, April 15, 1971); (2) National Academy of Sciences, *Technology: Processes of Assessment and Choice* (July, 1969); (3) Committee on Public Engineering Policy, National Academy of Engineering, *A Study of Technology Assessment* (July, 1969); (4) National Academy of Public Administration, *A Technology Assessment System for the Executive Branch* (July, 1970). (B) Two volumes of hearings before the same Subcommittee: (5) *Technology Assessment* [1969] and (6) *Technology Assessment-1970.* (C) Two books: (7) Bauer, R. A., 1969, *Second-Order Consequences: A Methodological Essay on the Impact of Technology,* M.I.T. Press, Cambridge, Mass; (8) Kasper, Raphael G., ed., 1972, *Technology Assessment: Understanding the Social Consequences of Technological Applications,* Praeger, New York. (D) Two other studies: (9) Jones, M. V., *et al.,* 1971, *A Technology Assessment Methodology* (7 vols.), MITRE Corporation, Washington, D.C.; (10) Coates, V. T., 1972, *Technology and Public Policy: The Process of Technology Assessment in the Federal Government* (2 vols.), Program of Policy Studies in Science and Technology, George Washington University, Washington, D.C. The best and most comprehensive bibliographical essay on TA appears in the first issue of the journal *Technology Assessment:* Knezo, G. J., 1972, Technology assessment: A bibliographic review, *Technology Assessment* 1:62-83.
5. This quotation is taken from a descriptive brochure entitled The International Society for Technology Assessment. The American office of I.S.T.A. is located in Suite 5038, 1629 K Street, NW, Washington, D.C. 20006.

6. Technology assessment: The benefits . . . the costs . . . the consequences, 1971, *Futurist* **5**:225.

7. Bauer, *Second-Order Consequences*, passim.

8. Committee on Public Engineering Policy, National Academy of Engineering, *A Study of Technology Assessment*, p. 5.

9. *A Technology Assessment Methodology* **1**: *Some Basic Propositions* (hereafter cited as *TAM* **1**).

10. Adapted from Jones, *TAM* **1**:26.

11. Adapted from Jones, ibid., pp. 29, 46.

12. Jones, ibid., p. 67.

13. Ibid., p. 82 (slightly revised). Reprinted by permission of the author.

14. Adapted from Jones, *TAM* **1**:102.

15. Shapley, D., 1972, Office of Technology Assessment: Congress smiles, scientists wince, *Science* **175**:970-73.

16. Daddario, E. Q., 1971, Technology and the democratic process, *Technology Review* **73**:19-23; Kash, D. E., and White, I. L., 1971, Technology assessment; Harnessing genius, *Chemical and Engineering News*, November 29, pp. 40-41.

17. Lear, J., 1970, Predicting the consequences of technology, *Saturday Review*, March 28, p. 44; cf. Committee on Public Engineering Policy, National Academy of Engineering, *A Study of Technology Assessment*, p. 4.

18. Jones *et al.*, *TAM*, Vols. 3, 4, and 5; Committee on Public Engineering Policy, National Academy of Engineering, *A Study of Technology Assessment*, pp. 37-75, 107-42; Bowers, R., and Frey, J., 1972, Technology assessment and microwave diodes, *Scientific American* **226** (February): 13-21; Chatham, G. N., The supersonic transport, *in:* Science Policy Research Division, Congressional Research Service, Library of Congress, *Technical Information for Congress*, 2nd ed., pp. 685-748.

19. Jones *et al.*, *TAM*, Vols. 2 and 6; J. Coates, *Technology Assessment*, p. 229.

20. Ebbin, S., 1972, The Jamaica Bay study: A case history, *Futurist* **6** (February): 27-28.

21. Of 206 citations in Genevieve J. Knezo's bibliographical essay, only three (nos. 140, 169, and 190) refer to articles which discuss biomedical technology (Technology assessment: A bibliographic review, pp. 80-82). In her study of TA and the federal government Vary T. Coates was able to discover only three examples of already completed assessments in biology or medicine; the studies dealt with cardiac replacement, abortion, and the use of drugs in the treatment of behaviorally disturbed children (*Technology and Public Policy* 1, chap. 3, pp. 17-22). A general attempt to anticipate the social impact of future developments in both biology and physics is: Gordon, Theodore J., and Ament, Robert H., 1969, *Forecasts of Some Technological Developments and Their Societal Consequences*, IFF Report R-6, Institute for the Future, Middletown, Conn.

22. *Technology and Public Policy* 1, 26-27.

23. For the distinctions and information contained in this paragraph I am indebted to a personal communication from Dr. Leon R. Kass.

24. The scientific and technological revolutions: Their history and meaning, 1971, *Philosophy Today* **15**: 99.

25. The study, which was belatedly published in 1975, is entitled *Assessing Biomedical Technologies: An Inquiry into the Nature of the Process* (A Study by the Committee on the Life Sciences and Social Policy, Division of Behavioral Sciences, National Research Council, National Academy of Sciences).

26. For the information contained in this paragraph I am indebted to a personal communication from Dr. Leon R. Kass.

27. Personal communication from Dr. Kass.

28. Gordon and Ament, *Forecasts*, pp. 24-28.

29. Human heredity and ethical problems, 1972, *Perspect. Biol. Med.* **15**:237.

30. Roblin, R., 1972, Some recent developments in genetics, *Theological Studies* **33**:403-410.
31. Of these five technologies the first two, amniocentesis and genetic screening, are currently in use. Technically speaking, in vitro fertilization in humans seems to await only the solution of certain minor difficulties. The application of cloning and DNA therapy to man, on the other hand, faces major technical obstacles; these techniques should therefore be regarded as future possibilities rather than as imminent developments.
32. The forthcoming study of the Committee on the Life Sciences and Social Policy includes an extended, systematic analysis of in vitro fertilization. See refs. 25 and 27.
33. The following are among the most important currently available studies in this field: the series of articles which appeared in the September 1972, issue of *Theological Studies;* Hilton, Bruce, *et al.*, eds., 1972, *Ethical Issues in Human Genetics*, Plenum, New York; Curran, C. E., 1970, Theology and genetics: A multifaceted dialogue, *Journal of Ecumenical Studies* 7:61-89; Edwards, R. G., and Sharpe, D. J., 1971, Social values and research in human embryology, *Nature* **231**(May 14):87-91; Glass, Human heredity (see no. 29 above); Gustafson, J. M., Roblin, R., Lappé, M., *et. al.*, 1972, Ethical and social issues in screening for genetic disease, *N. Engl. J. Med.* **286**:1129-32; Hamilton, Michael, ed., *The New Genetics and the Future of Man*, 1972, Eerdmans, Grand Rapids, Mich.; Harris, Maureen, ed., 1971, *Early Diagnosis of Human Genetic Defects: Scientific and Ethical Considerations*, Fogarty International Center Proceedings, no. 6, U.S. Government Printing Office, Washington, D.C.; Kass, L. R., 1971, Babies by means of in vitro fertilization: Unethical experiments on the unborn?, *N. Engl. J. Med.* **285**:1174-79; Kass, L. R., Making babies—the new biology and the "old" morality, *Public Interest* **Winter** (26):18-56; Ramsey, P., 1972, Shall we "reproduce?" I. The medical ethics of in vitro fertilization: II. Rejoinders and future forecast, *J.A.M.A.* **220**:1346-50; 1480-85; Ramsey, P., 1970, *Fabricated Man: The Ethics of Genetic Control*, Yale University Press, New Haven; Sorenson, J. R., 1971, *Social Aspects of Applied Human Genetics*, Social Science Frontiers, no. 3, Russell Sage Foundation, New York. For further bibliography and penetrating analysis of several of the works cited above, see the essay of Richard A. McCormick in the September 1972 issue of *Theological Studies.*
34. Shall we "reproduce"? (see ref. 33).
35. Ibid., pp. 1347-49, 1480-82.
36. Ibid., p. 1481.
37. See ref. 29.
38. Euphenics can be defined as the effort to compensate for a genetic defect by controlling the phenotype rather than the genotype; for example, diabetics use insulin as a compensatory measure.
39. Glass, Human heredity, pp. 238-43, 246-49.
40. Ibid., pp. 240, 247, 242, 251-52, 241-42.
41. Ibid., p. 246.
42. Ibid., pp. 253, 252.
43. Ibid., pp. 242, 252, 240, 250-51.
44. Ibid., p. 253.
45. For a succinct characterization of classical utilitarianism, see Rawls, J., 1971, *A Theory of Justice.*, pp. 22-27, Harvard University Press, Cambridge, Mass.
46. For example, of the seventeen members who participated in the National Academy of Sciences' study of TA, seven were social scientists (*Technology: Processes of Assessment and Choice*, pp. 151-63). Martin Jones, who developed the comprehensive TA methodology surveyed above, is an economist.
47. Braybrooke, D., and Lindblom, C. E., 1963, *A Strategy of Decision: Policy Evaluation as a Social Process*, pp. 205-6, Free Press, New York.
48. *An Introduction to the Principles of Morals and Legislation*, chap. 4, par. 4.

49. Ibid., chaps. 1 and 3.
50. National Academy of Sciences, *Technology: Processes of Assessment and Choice*, pp. 29-30.
51. For general discussions of value-theory, see Frankena, W. K., 1963, *Ethics*, pp. 63-77, Prentice-Hall, Englewood Cliffs, N.J.; and Moore, G. E., 1965, *Ethics*, pp. 96-108, Oxford University Press, New York.
52. *Technology: Processes of Assessment and Choice*, pp. 43-71; cf. pp. 29-32.
53. Ibid., p. 26 (italics removed); cf. pp. 53-54, 67.
54. See Steps 2 and 3 in Jones's methodology.
55. See Steps 3 and 6.
56. Livingstone, D., 1970, International technology assessment and the United Nations system, *American Journal of International Law* **64**:163-171; cf. Weisband, E., and Franck, T. M., A rationale for international technology assessment: Towards an ethical science, New York University Center for International Studies, Policy Papers, Vol. 4. The importance of extending TA spatially is already apparent in current discussions of the ocean-pollution problem.
57. On this topic see the following companion essays: Callahan, D., 1971, What obligations do we have to future generations?, *American Ecclesiastical Review* **164**:265-80; and Golding, M. P., Obligations to future generations, *Monist* **56**:85-99.
58. Committee on Public Engineering Policy, National Academy of Engineering, *A Study of Technology Assessment*, p. 5.
59. Kant, I., 1964, *Groundwork of the Metaphysic of Morals* (tr. H. J. Paton),pp.82-86, Harper & Row, New York.
60. Martin Jones argues: "An unfavorable impact of equal total magnitude . . . that is concentrated on a few people will cause more social distress than if it were diffused through many people" (see the explanation of the term *Diffusion* on the chart cited in ref. 13). In order to justify this argument, Jones would have to introduce some nonutilitarian, or nonconsequential, ethical principle. For a discussion of this point, see Frankena, *Ethics*, p. 32.
61. Frankena, *Ethics*, pp. 38-42; Rawls, *Theory of Justice*, pp. 3-22.
62. Theology and genetics, pp. 83-85.
63. See, e.g., *Fabricated Man*, pp. 29-30; cf. *Deeds and Rules in Christian Ethics*, 1967, pp. 108-9, Scribner's, New York.
64. *Church Dogmatics* (English tr.) 2/2, 650. Barth accepts the legitimacy of considering consequences but argues that obedience to the divine command is "not merely the highest duty but also the highest good" (ibid., p. 652).
65. The 1975 study of the Committee on the Life Sciences and Social Policy, *Assessing Biomedical Technologies* (see fn. 25) attempted to address precisely such questions.
66. *The Responsible Self: An Essay in Christian Moral Philosophy*, 1963, pp. 49-63, Harper & Row, New York.

# Index